Defending Religious Diversity in Public Schools

Defending Religious Diversity in Public Schools

A Practical Guide for Building Our Democracy and Deepening Our Education

Nathan R. Kollar

PRAEGER
An Imprint of ABC-CLIO, LLC

A B C 🟊 C L I O

Santa Barbara, California • Denver, Colorado • Oxford, England

Library of Congress Cataloging-in-Publication Data

Kollar, Nathan R.
    Defending religious diversity in public schools: a practical guide for building our democracy and deepening our education / Nathan R. Kollar.
        p. cm.
    Includes bibliographical references and index.
    ISBN 978-0-313-35997-2 (hard copy : alk. paper) — ISBN 978-0-313-35998-9 (ebook)
1. Religion in the public schools—United States. 2. Cultural pluralism—United States.
3. Religion and politics—United States. 4. United States—Religious life and customs.
5. United States—Social conditions. I. Title.
    LC111.K65   2009
    379.2′80973—dc22   2009015911

13   12   11   10   9   1   2   3   4   5

This book is also available on the World Wide Web as an eBook.

Visit www.abc-clio.com for details.

ABC-CLIO, LLC
130 Cremona Drive, P.O. Box 1911
Santa Barbara, California 93116-1911

This book is printed on acid-free paper ∞

Manufactured in the United States of America

To Rudolph, Eleanor, Rudy, and Judy who gave me life and now live it more fully.
To David, Carrie, Sharon, Todd, and Jean who give me life and share it joyfully.

CONTENTS

LIST OF TABLES

ACKNOWLEDGMENTS

This book, while written by one, was created by many. Among those whose keen eye, probing mind, and stubborn adherence to truth (theirs) made this book what it is, in alphabetical order, are Carrie, David, Jean, and Sharon. Thanks for all your time and ideas. Special thanks to Jean who listened to my mumbles, clarified my thoughts, and offered the love out of which this was born.

INTRODUCTION

In a room full of people, very few practice the same religion; they differ in belief, vary in what they say and do on holidays, condemn different sins, and may or may not go to the same house of worship. This is true in our country and needs to be recognized in our public schools. This book focuses upon these diverse religious individuals in our schools, as well as the ancient religious wisdom they represent.

Recently a teacher in a suburban Midwestern school experienced this religious diversity. Before the beginning of winter break, she asked her third graders what they would do when class ended. The conversation went something like this:

> "We decorate a big green tree, sing songs, eat a lot, watch television, and get lots of presents.
>
> Oh, that's when the New Year begins." Most everyone shook their heads.
>
> "Oh, you mean Christmas. We have a birthday cake with candles, sing happy birthday to Jesus, and blow the candles out.
>
> How can he have a birthday? He's God and eternal.
>
> No, he died on the cross.
>
> No, only his body died. He's still alive in heaven with his Father.
>
> No, he's alive walking around.
>
> No, he's alive but I eat him when I go to communion."

A few more added their theological opinions about Jesus, Christmas, and the New Year until someone stated firmly: "I don't believe in Jesus. We have Hanukkah." This stopped the conversation until the teacher, ever observant, asked some who had said nothing what they did. An additional flood poured forth proclaiming Kwanzaa, Yule, Al-Hijra/Muharram, Eid al Adha, Gantan-sai, and Three Kings as necessarily included during the winter break.

This discussion could easily have taken place in a teachers' lunchroom, at an administrative holiday party, or at a school board meeting. This classroom is a microcosm of our country where each person's religion, or lack thereof, is part of who they are. We ignore people at our own, and our country's, risk. Very few people live their religion as preached by the clergy and lived by their elders. These "experts" may call those different from them ignorant, heretics, sinners, or nonbelievers. No amount of name-calling, however, erases the fact that there are many different religions in our country, and thus in our public schools. These religions are there not only because of life cycle changes among local citizens, but also because people are moving from place to place due to life's circumstances such as jobs, education, leisure, or retirement. Any place that has television and Internet has the ideas, images, sounds, cultures, and religions of other peoples. Almost overnight our communities have changed and become interdependent. The variety in religions reflects this change. Are we prepared for a future of dealing with those who may, at times, be radically different from us?

This book admits this change and provides ways to learn from this interdependence. It explains and demonstrates how we should be attentive, respectful, and hospitable to everyone, of all religions, and of no religion. It shows how we can be comfortable in offering descriptions of other religions as well as skills for listening to those who differ religiously from one another.

Why are respect, hospitality, learning, and listening necessary? Because our nation needs them—a pluralistic democracy collapses unless we honor those who differ from us. And, because someone who intends to deal maturely with those outside her or his home needs to recognize differences, learn how to handle differences, and seek to form a community based on the shared values, needs, and concerns of everyone in the community. If we do not do this, the future of both our economy and democracy is imperiled because we stand in continual ideological warfare struggling for one ideology's dominance.

Human needs and survival imperatives seldom determine policy and human interaction when cultural and religious ways of life are threatened.[1] Research indicates that people usually react in one of four ways. For example, my four-year-old niece pulled her turtleneck sweater over her head whenever loud adults would enter the room. Some people react that way when anything different enters into their world/vision. It is a kind of running away from what threatens them. Others will continue on with what they were doing, ignoring the offensive sounds, smells, sights, and ideas that might enter the room. Still others become highly offended by those entering the room and scream at them, trying to make them leave. These, of course, are the typical reactions to threat of any kind: flight, fight, and boredom. We will look at these reactions in the following pages. But there is a fourth reaction to threat and deep difference: adaptation. What this book suggests is that our schools stop presupposing there is one uniform culture and adapt to the reality that we are many cultures, both foreign and domestic. We should adapt to this reality by learning about them, having empathy for them, being hospitable to them, and building a community with them. The reason is simple. There is no choice. We cannot cease dealing with them. We need them. When we interact with these other cultures, at home or abroad, do we want to be avoided, forcefully removed, or ignored? Do we want to spend our entire life with our turtleneck pulled up over our heads? Or yelling at all who do not look, sound, or believe as we do?

We are a pluralistic society. We need to embrace the differences present within our community. Schools are where we learn of our past, present, and future. To learn the reality of the present prepares us for a myriad of possible futures. Every religion deals with both an idealized present and future. To neglect an understanding of and an ability to live with other people's religions in the preparation for our common future leads to the threats mentioned previously.

Religion is one of those words that we use in everyday speech. Yet it means different things to different people. These differences many times, unknowingly, cause controversy. *Religion*, for many, has another, unstated, word next to it—*my*. "My religion" usually refers to the way I practice what our culture has designated as "religion."

Usually we practice a religion similar to our parents. The knowledge and practice of this religion expands in concentric circles from the unique way we practice it, to the way our parents practice it, to the way our co-religionists practice it. If the particular religion is more than local, then we are also influenced by the spokespersons for that religion at the national, and perhaps, international level. We may be taught this religion from books approved by these authoritative spokespersons. Almost inevitably this religion is one of the classic religions that have existed for thousands of years known to many as world religions. The names of these religions developed over the centuries, but in general they refer to a community with a common sense of what is wrong with our world and how to improve it. The norm for improvement is found in the community's experiences over the centuries and displayed in its books, songs, chants, and writings of famous individuals in this religious community. Each religious community has a way of ritualizing what is important to it that is displayed in manners of worship, prayer, and other public actions. Since these are norms, each community also clearly displays what one should and should not do to improve the world and ourselves. Some of these communities say these norms were revealed by a god or gods; others say the norms were revealed by the insight of one or several religious geniuses. The "my religion" of about 75 percent of Americans affirms belief in one God who inspired the writings found in one book in which the basic ethical imperatives may be found. They also believe that this God is bound to them in a special way, covenant, or testament. Most Americans also do not know what is in that book, cannot recall all the principal moral imperatives, and have significantly different ideas of who God is and what God wants. Most Americans do not realize that the Christianity they see proclaimed by the majority in their country is only a small representation of a worldwide way of life whose majority of members are black, speak Spanish, and live in a culture that does not celebrate a Santa Claus Christmas; whose Bible opens most easily to passages of leaving home, end of the world, and Jesus' identification with the poor.[2]

So we return to the classroom with its students, all with their own "my religion" motivating the way they regulate their lives, interact with others, and speak their beliefs. Yet their understanding of the motives, beliefs, and actions of others is both similar and different than their own. This book looks at typical religious motivators as well as ways to discover and understand these differences. We do this so we may learn to talk with each other in seeking knowledge and a common base for bettering our lives.

We could not communicate with one another if we did not have some similarities such as a common language and motivation to talk and listen to one another. We see both the grandeur and challenge of communication every day of our lives as we try to choose the right words and actions to talk to someone. The South African government found a clear example of miscommunication when it tried to fight obesity among some of the tribes. To do so, it designed two posters. One showed a fat woman standing next to an overloaded truck with a flat tire. "Both carry too much weight," the poster said. The other poster showed a thin woman sweeping up dirt under a table while a fat woman stood nearby, painfully, leaning, breathless, on the table for support. "Who do you want to look like?" the slogan asked. Obvious miscommunication was discovered when they heard people saying that the first poster showed a lucky woman who was so rich that she was fat and owned so many things that her truck was overloaded, and the second one portrayed a rich lady with a servant sweeping up trash. We communicate through symbols. Words and gestures are two important communication symbols. The experts who constructed the posters chose symbols whose meanings differed among the people in the community. Symbols, like the fat lady, always have different meanings to people. Religion consists of a multiplicity of symbols. To understand and be able to use the multiple meanings of symbols is important in dealing with people as well as forming an educational community.

Education should help us understand and have empathy for the symbols used by those we live and work with and help develop the means to work and live together in peace. An important skill for helping us do this is listening. If we can learn to quiet ourselves for a few moments while we listen to others, we will have perfected a skill that transports us to many worlds and builds a highway to the future. Many of our chapters will introduce or reinforce this skill of listening.

Learning about religions in a public school, however, is a very sensitive topic. It seems some individuals do not believe in freedom of religion, but want their religious perspective imposed on those third-grade students, teachers, and staff. They have not learned to listen to the religious "other" but, as classroom bullies, impose their view on everyone in the school. We treat this issue in the chapter on religious bullies. Yet we have learned that cultures carry with them historical impulses that threaten to destroy them. How many American companies had to modify the typical American managerial style as they expanded into the international market? How many times were our troops spit upon because they, unknowingly, did not recognize a culture's dietary laws or norms for mingling of the genders?

When our public schools were founded, they reflected the surrounding culture that was a certain type of Protestant Christianity. That is one reason why Catholic Christians and Lutheran Christians built their own school systems. It is only since 1963 that public schools stopped praying Protestant prayers, reading from Protestant Bibles, and quoting the Protestant Ten Commandments. This may be one of those historical impulses that will ultimately drive public schools, through charter schools, for example, to become an amalgam of religious communal schools—each school reflecting a different religion and being supported by public dollars. The gated community will give birth to its gated school, marking the end of a place where people of different religions, cultures, salaries, and sexes can mix and learn from and about each other. But until that happens, our public schools should reflect the pluralistic community we are and the pluralistic world we are becoming, no matter how sensitive the topic of religion. This book prepares us for a pluralistic country by defending and advocating for the recognition of and learning about the religious diversity in our schools.

Chapter 1 enables us to discover community members interested in our schools, religion, and education. While acknowledging, stating, and clarifying the role of law in dealing with religion in our schools, Chapter 2 takes the position that law is insufficient for solving our human problems. Rather than attorneys and judges arguing over legal issues, we need to have those concerned citizens arguing, disagreeing, and seeking common solutions to common problems. Any group of humans who sit down to discuss an issue brings with them their past and present personal histories. Chapter 3 examines religious identity—how it comes to be and how it influences us. Part of this examination is an offer of several ways of understanding religion. Only in understanding the various meanings of religion, and how all of us are influenced by them, can we be clear about what we are advocating. Only when we become sensitive to the various religions present in our midst can we come together in community. Chapter 4 challenges us to take the difficult road of community building. It refines our idea of community and, in the light of that idea, shows how diversity is a necessary element in communal growth. Educational, religious, and political communities are reviewed to see how the acknowledgment and learning about religions would support such growth. Growth, however, never occurs without some individual and communal tensions and conflicts. Chapter 5 investigates how conflicts arise in the midst of change and provides ways of dealing with conflict in a positive manner. One constant in communal conflict management is good leaders. Chapter 6 deals with how leadership functions in building an educational community. Leadership is never in a vacuum. Culture, institutional development, and mission imperatives condition the type and function of leadership. Chapter 6 also shows how these conditions influence one's advocacy of religions in the schools. Chapter 7 provides the necessary ideas, principles, and skills to teach about religion in our classrooms. But conflict never goes away. There are always those who wish to impose their will on everyone else—either in the classroom, the school, or on society at large. Chapter 8 looks at and shows ways for dealing with the religious bullies attempting to disrupt our learning and pluralistic democracy. In the last chapter, we look back to what we have discussed as a vision of hope for the future. Present in all these chapters are the basic theoretical and practical tools to defend and advocate for religions in the public schools.

The ability to continually update these theories and tools is provided in the appendix dedicated to resources. It enables you to build upon what you have here to design the unique educational institution needed in your community. *Defending Religious Diversity in Public Schools* brings together decades of educational learning and experiences of both professionals and concerned citizens striving to improve our schools. My hope is that you will continue their mission and add to their knowledge and experience.

One last point: I use the word *wholistic* or *wholism* throughout the book. Many times dictionaries provide only one spelling for this word: *holism*. There are two reasons I retain the *w*. One is that we are whole. To sustain our wholeness we must pay equal attention to every part of our being: body, mind, soul, and spirit. To reduce us to only one of these manifestations of who we are deprives us of our humanity. The second reason is that, like the letter *w* in *wholistic*, we are someone who seeks to touch, hear, see, taste, and smell. We are someone who is curious and seeks to know, understand, and connect with "the other" and "others." We are all this and more. We are whole. The *w* in *wholistic* is like our arms stretching out to every living and nonliving being—with outstretched arms with open palms to engage in the dance of life with them all. That is what it is all about and why we must grow in what is necessary to build our educational culture.

CHAPTER 1

The Stakeholders: Recognizing and Respecting Sacred Ground

Two Cautionary Tales
Humpty Dumpty sat on a wall.
Humpty Dumpty had a great fall.
All the king's horses and all the king's men
Couldn't put Humpty together again.

***

They burst out of all the school doors. Some with their spouse. Some with their children. Some alone. But angry, happy, singing, shouting, and talking, they walked hastily into the evening air.
No one quite knows how it happened.
At the same time, as the crowd came out of the school, two of the staff were taking down the American flag. As it reached ground level one of the parents ripped the flag from the pole and out of the hands of the staff. But it still remained attached to one of the ropes.
He then pulled out a knife and cut it free from the rope leaving part of it in his hands and the rest behind at the feet of the astonished staff. Holding it aloof, he shouted "This is what it's all about."
And, with his child in his arms, ran to his car. At the same time someone else angrily ripped a piece off, put it in her pocket and trampled the rest hard to the ground. Others gathered pulling, cutting, grabbing, ripping, and shouting over pieces of the flag. Their flag—as they took it with them. Good citizens somehow turned themselves into a mob of destruction and took their booty home.
The media, who were there to cover the school board meeting, quickly took advantage of the situation. They interviewed and postured the most photogenic and energized to get their quotes and pictures for the early news. The whole town woke up to a story of the American flag's desecration by a mob at the high school.

It was a Saturday morning so there were two days before school began on Monday. Sunday afternoon the District superintendent called an emergency meeting of her central staff and principals. They discussed whether they should do anything at all or leave it to the sheriff. Slowly a plan evolved to, hopefully, begin to put the community back together again. They gathered the necessary personnel and contacted each home by phone and e-mail. They asked the parents to provide their children with a short paragraph describing why people took pieces of the flag and asked whether they should sew it together. The children would be asked to explain to the class what their parents had written. If the parents had taken a part of the flag they were asked to drop it off at the school. No questions asked.

Only half the children brought a note from their parents. The media covered it for two days. Some parents objected strongly that this had nothing to do with education. Most said nothing. Three weeks after the request three quarters of the flag had been returned.

THE STAKEHOLDERS: RECOGNIZING AND RESPECTING SACRED GROUND

This chapter will look at who has a stake in making things better. Yet "better" to some is "worse" to others. These sometimes conflicting sacred visions of life's betterment are found especially in the world's religions. They can break us apart. They can help bring us together. We look first at religion's complexity and necessity. We then review education's role in recognizing and respecting our diverse sacred perspectives. Finally, we offer means of improving our common life through advocacy coalitions.

What Do the Tales Tell?

There are many unknowns here. After all, who is Humpty Dumpty? Stereotypes presented by the media over the centuries cast him as an egg. Is he really an egg? If so, is the egg really male? The tale does not say so. The people pouring out of the buildings were obviously at a school board meeting, but why were they there? What brought them together? Why were they exiting? Why were they so diverse in their reaction to what happened? Why did they attack the flag the way they did? Did someone tell them to? Did the topic of the meeting urge them to? In the light of so many unknowns, certainly the first thing the tales tell us is to be cautious in the light of our own ignorance.

At the same time these tales are read and pondered, they tell us that we must act. Humpty Dumpty is broken to pieces; the flag is desecrated; people are angry and happy; the king's men are unable to help Humpty; the supervisor's plan gets only partial response. Something has to be done.

They tell us that all the stakeholders do not share the same concerns: Humpty Dumpty, the horse trainers, the king's men, the king, the makers of the wall—they all look at his fall differently. The media, those who did nothing to the flag, those who did not attend the meeting, and those who took pieces of the flag out of sense of victory, of defeat, of anger, or of curiosity, the school board, and teacher's staff—they all reacted differently.

They tell us, too, that some are not aware that they are stakeholders and do not act. Symbols such as a flag may become so commonplace that people lose their connection to them. Education is either left behind at graduation by some or becomes a part of everyday life by others. Taxes are paid. Complaints may be made. But a sense of everyone having a stake in our country and education is many times lost.

They tell us that a common event provides an opportunity for a communal response, but many times differences get in the way of that response and dealing communally with a real problem.

Finally, they leave us with a feeling that no one can "tell" us what the tales mean. Only we know how we feel. No writer can capture everything we feel. Each tale speaks to us as a unique, whole person—a uniqueness that becomes more evident as we discuss these tales with others.

RELIGION: LOOKING AT ITS COMPLEXITY AND IMPORTANCE

Religion is often portrayed simply as God's word spoken, written, experienced, and acted upon. Religion, today, is also portrayed as dogmatic, authoritative, demanding, and bound in a restrictive manner to the past. Yet, as the children in our Introduction suggest with their discussion of holidays, it is not so simple; and, the wish to understand it, live it, and pass it on to the next generation is not so simple either.

Take, for example, the fact that at least 78 percent of Americans profess adherence to Christianity.[1] Upon reading such a demographic, a Christian might conclude that everyone believes as he or she does. Yet that is not true. For example, Mead, Hill, and Atwood's *Handbook of Denominations in the United States* offers at least five hundred interpretations of Christianity.[2] This list of Christian denominations expands exponentially when we realize how many Christian groups are not listed there.[3] They do not have uniformity in belief, morality, rituals, or ways to organize their religion. *Christianity* seems to mean whatever the speaker wishes it to mean. The same may be said of Jesus, the central figure in Christianity. Stephen Prothero in his book *American Jesus: How the Son of God Became a National Icon* has shown us the radically differing ways Jesus is understood, utilized, and preached in present-day America.[4] The words *Christianity* and *Jesus* have little common meaning, yet Christians believe deeply in their religion, no matter what it means and how it is practiced.

This "American" religion is viewed by many as something that is chosen freely, centered upon a book and a person's feelings, stimulated by an exciting speaker, separated from politics, and centered on both book and God. This is certainly the image that dominates the media as we constantly find awestruck commentators providing pictures of people with raised hands loudly praying and singing in response to a preacher's proclamation of God's desires for this world. The commentator's awe changes to disdain when those same preachers and/or people declare God's will for the country. While a highly individualistic, experiential, Protestant-based Christianity dominates the U.S. view of religion, this is not the view of religion outside the United States. In the rest of the world, Roman Catholicism is the largest Christian religion. In more than half the world, Christianity is a minority religion, with Islam, Hinduism, or Buddhism being the majority religion. In that world, this American type of religion is disdained by some, rejected by many, and incomprehensible to most, just as their religions are to some Americans. There are many religions in our schools, many more than simple categories borrowed from textbooks and law might suggest. Maybe the subject is so complex and so filled with danger of offense that we should avoid any discussion of religion in or outside of schools?

Ignoring the complexity is impossible because we are plagued with unanswered questions. People are blowing themselves up. Why? People spend time on their knees. Why? Children's parents do or do not do religious things. Why? Shouldn't students learn about these controversial matters as a way of understanding the world around them?

Religion, as generally understood, is a prime motivator of people's thoughts and actions. Over the millennia we have seen how religion shapes the way people eat, marry, organize their week, celebrate, practice sex, think, wage wars, and give their money and clothes to the poor and many other things. Religion is also currently motivating most people as it has in the past both in its classical form and its more modern expressions. One significant modern expression is the spiritualities springing up everywhere. The paperback best-seller lists are filled with titles such as *Soul Wisdom*, *The New Earth*, and *The Power of Now*. Shouldn't students learn about how and why people live their religious lives whether in the modern or the classical form?

Within the last ten years, we have seen a significant shift in common speech from an emphasis on religion to that of spirituality. Religion is now seen by many as a life filled with blind obedience to dogmatic authorities of imam, pope, rabbi, or minister—a life constrained with unbreakable bonds of moral prescription found in ancient books and frozen interpretations of abstract past revelations by biased theologians. This life is rejected for a "spiritual life," which enables our freedom, encourages our

spontaneity, and focuses our uniqueness internally and in personal relationships externally. This book does not view religion in such a way, but
since you, the reader, may, let's for a moment shift the emphasis to spirituality, understood as an inimitable unique drive within each of us seeking
to discover our uniqueness and transcend the commonness of everyday life.
How does this new understanding of spirituality change the teacher's
responsibility for being sensitive to his or her students' spirituality?

I would suggest that we must be sensitive to students' spirituality and
thus their religion. Religion is, after all, a communal way of life that is
expressive of one's spirituality. The religions of the world offer a communion of people's individual spiritualities that share a common vision of
who they are, where they want to go, and how to get there. These religions
may differ radically on the answers to these questions of belief, morals, rituals, community, and the future, but they certainly highly influence those
who belong to them. This is evidenced consistently in surveys about happy
marriages, stress, and longevity. To neglect religion is to neglect all the
stakeholders in our cautionary tales. We cannot do that and also sustain
our educational system.

TALES, TABLES, AND CONVERSATION

A few days after writing those two tales, I was at an interreligious planning meeting with local businesspeople hosted at a local Muslim mosque.
We sat around eight tables set out in a large square. Twice during the two-
hour meeting the call to prayer echoed through the room. The meeting
began with the head of a local bank, our chairperson, describing the reactions of those he talked to about hosting a national conference of interreligious organizations. Nodding heads of the other community business
leaders echoed his tale of uneasiness, hesitancy, and sometimes outright
hostility toward bringing the diverse religions together. As I heard his
report, I wrote in my notes: fear and ignorance.

Fear

The first reaction of the majority of these leaders and their friends was
fear of the religious other. Both Muslim and non-Muslim recounted how all
they saw portrayed in the media were rabid Muslim fanatics ready to bring
death to America. Muslims said they knew no one here, or abroad, who
were like that. Several Muslims said they were not religious, had never
been in a mosque, and were Muslim only because they were born to parents
from a Muslim country. Non-Muslims said they had never met anyone who
was a Muslim. Remember the scene: a lunch meeting of business leaders
dressed in tailored dark suits, ties, shiny shoes, and with carefully cut hair.
Before they entered the luncheon, they did not know one another's

religion. Both Muslim and non-Muslim businesspeople were dressed the same way. My guess is that they had met in the past, but only because we were here at a mosque and talking about interreligious dialogue were they now aware of their fear of the Muslim religious-other. This was fear that prevented their friends, no matter of what religious origin, from supporting this and other discussions among religious people. The head of the Chamber of Commerce, who was a Jew, reminded everyone that until very recently many people treated Jews as they treated the Muslims today. Silently I recalled how Jews, Catholics, and African Americans were refused admittance to our local major university until 1960. I recalled, too, the quiet tale of a famous Indian physicist of how he saw fear in the eyes of every white American. In turn, he feared them because they saw him, a nonwhite foreigner, as a potential terrorist.

Fear causes isolation—the willful separation of one group of people from another. How do some people grow up with such fear, sometimes turned into hate, in their hearts? Is it similar to when we walk by a small group of people speaking a foreign language and laughing, and as we go by, we think they are laughing at us? Is it because they have harmed us in some way? Is it because they are different than we are and we don't feel we share anything with them? How do we adults come to fear these others?

Ignorance

Another, and simultaneous reaction at the meeting, was how religiously ignorant everyone seemed to be. *Ignorance* here is meant as a descriptive term, not a negative one. We are all ignorant in some way. I, for example, am ignorant of the basic information and skills to successfully run a business. The religious ignorance of those gathered around the table was profound. It was like when a child first learns her letters and mistakes one for the other: *b* for *d*, *i* for *l*, and *f* for *p*. These men and women knew little of their own professed religion and even less of other religions. This was not new to me. I have witnessed it over and over again at every level of education: at the graduate level, where individuals were training to be ministers; and at the undergraduate level, when students came to class to learn about "Religions in North America." Was my experience of students' ignorance the babbling of just another professor screaming, "They're dumb!" to inflate his own ego? Maybe, but I don't think so. When a high school English teacher claims her students are illiterate because they are unable to distinguish *b* from *d* and *i* from *l*, and are unable to write a complete sentence, he is describing a reality. It is such a reality that I experienced around this table—a reality continually reported on over the years. The most recent in-depth portrayal of religious illiteracy is that of Stephen Prothero, *Religious Literacy: What Every American Needs to Know—And Doesn't*.[5] Very few people know the equivalent of the religious alphabet.

Few Christians know any of Jesus's apostles or are able to identify, not recall, books of the Bible (New Testament or Old Testament/TANACK). Even Evangelical Christians were unable to recall where their memorized biblical phrases fit into the biblical narrative.[6] When it comes to the religions of the world, less than half of American teens know that Judaism is a religion, and fewer yet could identify Islam as such.[7] In a nation with a little more than 75 percent of the population belonging to Christianity, the Jesus portrayed in the gospels is seldom recognized in his reformulations to meet individual, group, or advertising needs.[8]

What are the consequences of this reality of religious illiteracy? My ignorance of business might lead to a misreading of business reports and therefore cause me to invest poorly in the stock market, and therefore cause me to lose money. If more Americans are also ignorant of business basics there will be serious consequences for the entire country. But surely religious ignorance does not have the same consequences as business ignorance? Does it?

The fear expressed around the lunch tables was one consequence. And, like a set of standing dominos, one fear of the unknown bumps against another fear, and another, and another until we are afraid to talk to one another because we don't know how to talk to that "other." We are afraid to be with each other, and because we are not with each other, we don't live next to each other, and because we don't live next to each other, we fear each other until . . . Until our children bully each other. Talk show pundits fan the flame of fear, causing more profiling and arrests, and, as in World War II, imprisonment of those we fear.

Fear of the unknown is devastating. Place someone raised in the city in a forest and they fear for their life. Place some one raised in the forest in the city and they fear for their life. Lose your way in a foreign country and you are speechless. Fear and ignorance are powerful motivators, dividers, and stimulators of hate.

CONVERSATION

As Christians, Jews, and Muslims sat around the lunch tables, we talked. We shared personal stories. We shared fears and tried to provide religious information that would help diminish some of both the fear and ignorance. Talking did make a difference. It doesn't always make a difference, but in this case, with these people, it did. A conversation that began and continued in a hospitable atmosphere by sincere people sought to face a common issue. This resulted in a common bond to go forward and continue such conversations in the future for ourselves and others.[9]

There are consequences to religious ignorance besides fear and isolation. Ignorance of religion and how religions influence people can lead to miscalculations of gigantic proportions in business, politics, and international affairs. Thomas L. Friedman, in his book *The World Is Flat: A Brief History of the Twenty-first Century*, proposes that good jobs of the future will require one to be a "good collaborator, leverager, adapter, explainer, synthesizer, model builder, localizer."[10] As you will see throughout this book, religion is vital to people's lives. We can't, in Friedman's words, "learn how to play well with others,"[11] unless we are sensitive to their religion.

Humpty Dumpty is in pieces. The flag is torn apart, and each group harbors in its pain the reality of isolation and aloneness. Only when put together again will our country, like the flag, be whole. This book is about resolving the religious ignorance and fear that separate us. It's about recognizing the religious diversity of country and world.

CAN THE SCHOOLS HELP? REREADING THE TWO TALES

Do our schools have a coherent educational policy? No.[12] Do our schools have a coherent authority structure? No.[13] All the king's horses and all the king's men don't seem to be able to put this humpty dumpty school system together. Furthermore, it seems to have already begun to crumble. "A county school system in metropolitan Atlanta . . . became the nation's first in nearly 40 years to lose its accreditation, and the governor removed four of its board members for ethics violations."[14] A school board in Texas decided to allow teachers to bring guns into class. "Country people are take-care-of-yourself people. They are not under the illusion that the police are there to protect them," said David Thweatt, the school superintendent and driving force behind the policy. If everyone follows in David Thweatt's footsteps, we are completely on our own.

The individualism of David Thweatt's country people may be matched by the seeming individuality of proposed purposes for our schools. A summary of these was provided by the Public Broadcasting Service in a national dialogue on the issue as:

- To prepare children for citizenship
- To cultivate a skilled workforce
- To teach cultural literacy
- To prepare students for college
- To help students become critical thinkers
- To help students compete in a global marketplace.[15]

However, if we all have "to learn how to play with each other," in Thomas L. Friedman's terms, then we have one, if not more, points of coherence. Citizenship and democracy are team sports. The American basketball team found out that the individualism and athleticism of American basketball could not withstand the relentlessness of playing together. Only when they realized that they had to play with one another to beat the other nations did they finally win in the 2008 Olympic Games. Humpty Dumpty doesn't have to remain broken, nor, the flag in pieces. We can put them back together again.

There is an art to fixing things. Many times they are stronger when put back together. The same can be said about our educational system. When the public school system first began, as we will see, religion had a place in that beginning. Religion reflected the culture. This adherence to one religion caused anger and riots as immigrants came into the country. Gradually, in many schools it became easier to run away from the tensions than face them and adapt to the new situation. We have an opportunity to face the issue of diversity of religions in our schools anew. If we learn how to deal with diversity of religions in our schools, we are prepared for future citizenship. If we understand and become sensitive to the religions of others, we can work with them at home and internationally. If, with time, we learn how to think critically about the various religions, we have learned a life lesson. If we can learn how to talk about our different religions and differences about religions, we will reduce the fear and ignorance that initially filled that room in the mosque. When the "maybe" or "if" becomes the "should" of school practice and curriculum, we have begun to put the flag together again not as we imagine it, but as it is.

POLITICS AND PLURALISTIC DEMOCRACY

Our country is made up of diverse peoples, ideas, and religions.[16] Diversity means difference. But it also means community. This is one of our major challenges as a nation and as individuals, since every community includes both what is common and what is different. A healthy community is not uniformity of dress, ideas, food, and so forth. It is unity in diversity. Examples of such healthy diversity within community abound. We have all experienced their benefit as we enjoy an orchestra or a band that has diverse instruments and yet creates a musical whole, a sports team that plays well together to achieve a goal, or a group of engineers solving a problem.

Have you ever been different? Most people do not like to be different, so they adopt a similar style of dress, music, food, thought, and life in general. With this style they now fit into a niche, a community of likeness where everyone nods to one another's likeness and turns away from those "different-others" who do not dress, think, and eat the same as they do. Most of the time those in similar niches live in the same place, so they also enjoy the same types of homes, front lawns, weather, and social life. These geographical areas will have their public schools. But seldom do the public schools include all the same niches. Some parents and children determine the direction of the school; others, do not. Some niches (differences) become more important and powerful than others. No one pays attention to those differences until some person or event asks why those with this certain set of differences are more important than those with that other set of differences. The pluralism of differences represents the inherent diversity of all humans seeking their individual uniqueness. It surfaces sometimes as an attempt to make one set of differences dominate other sets. This search for dominance is known as power-seeking. This will happen forever unless we discover a politic that acknowledges our diversity while highlighting our commonality. Somehow we must discover the balance between the control experienced with power obtained through war, money, celebrity, and governance and the lack of control experienced in suffering, death, and daily living with others.

THE STAKEHOLDER

The image of "stakeholder" is used a great deal in discussions of leadership and management. A stakeholder is someone who has a deep interest in the processes and outcomes inherent to an organization. The idea of a "stake" "holder" may be derived either from when a group of people who make a bet give their individual "stake" to someone to hold, or when someone holds the "stake" being pounded into the ground to mark his newly purchased land that is being "staked out." Either one is applicable here, but I would like to use the meaning dealing with land—something permanent, filled with hope for a bright future, something a person is willing to pour sweat and tears into to establish a home. This land, and the stakeholder's vision of what she intends, is rooted deep within her spirituality. It is rooted so deep that it is sacred—seldom touched, seldom dishonored, seldom challenged, and extremely important because it provides a center around which the rest of her life pivots. When we are stakeholders in this sense we can understand why we avoid the pain of challenge and the loss of our center, and why we stay joined with those who have a common vision and stake in life. What we have staked out becomes sacred to us. We must honor these sacred visions. To do otherwise is to neglect the deepest values in individuals and their communities.

But we cannot remain isolated in our sacred niche because we have a stake in a larger enterprise—our community and its common school. No matter how many gates and fences we may build around it, we cannot survive, grow, and mature if we do not face the pain of difference, both ours and theirs. The first time our kindergartners step into the school bus, they realize that they are no longer in the comfort of home. They begin to realize that life today is complete with rich and diverse experiences: each a possible challenge to who we are and have been; each containing the possibility of new values and an offer of inclusion in a new niche. Sometimes we try to avoid these experiences. Sometimes we might deny the source of these new experiences any validity in envisioning life and providing the tools for living. But that would mean denying the reality of millions, and sometimes billions, of people who live their lives based on experiences, and in this instance, religions, different from our own. To deny or avoid pluralism and differences is to deny contemporary life for what it is and what it is becoming. To learn the tools, ideas, and ideals necessary to live the life of pluralism is not easy. Anyone who says it is easy has never faced the challenge of breaking a habit such as smoking, chewing their fingernails, eating fast food, or actually not saying anything to others you would not want them to say to you. Change isn't easy. That is what makes real education difficult.

Every public school is composed of various communities, niches, and stakeholders. Each stakeholder has a vision of what is required to enable children to grow up as well-balanced individuals ready to face the challenges and pleasures of life. Each holds this vision as sacred and deserving of being handed down without modification or challenge. Essential to this vision is what we call spirituality and religion. If we scrape beyond the surface of self-identifying terms, Christian, for example, many times we discover contradictory visions of what that Christian common vision is. Most people do not want to move beyond commonly used words that provide the security of supposed communal niche-belonging—that is, until a crisis arises. How can we bring these, sometimes contradictory, visions together for the benefit of each and the survival of all? This can come about only when we develop the political will to recognize differences and accept communality.

POLITICS, POLICY, AND STAKEHOLDERS

In our schools, teachers, administrators, staff, and students represent many different spiritualities and religions. With the emphasis on students we sometimes forget that the school is a community. Everyone is the school and the school will function well only if all the stakeholders care for one another as they care for the education of the students. The school is also a community school supported by taxes and regulated by voters through the school board. School politics is the human process of conversation, ideals, actions, and arguments that hopefully produce the best education for all the students and their community. Policy is the printed norms for achieving this same end as they immediately affect everyone in the school. Because something is written down does not mean it settles the issue. Policy guarantees the minimum. Successful politics assures the maximum and provides an interpretation of policy and law. Policy is required, but politics is essential for a healthy school. When the media begins to write and show their stories, politics is usually over and negotiations over policy have begun. Politics is a matter of the communication and compromise necessary to live together. Policy is "the book," the frozen written word that becomes alive daily in the lives of stakeholders as they make school happen each day. For example, the law that states freedom of speech allows us to express ourselves through how we dress. But many educators discover that learning is hindered by certain kinds of dress. School boards, teachers, and administrators have long conversations about limiting or not limiting dress and, then, which types of dress to limit. Politics is many times not totally successful because consensus does not arise about what to do. In the place of consensus comes majority rule expressed by taking a vote. Some win and some lose. With the vote, the necessity of policy arises and, with it, codes of conduct for students that ban such dress as do-rags, bandanas, hats, and headgear that are not worn for medical or religious reasons, pants with chains hanging off of them, spaghetti straps thinner than an inch and halters, shorts above one's lowest hanging finger when an arm is at one's side, plunging necklines, net tops, clothes that promote/glorify weapons, and writing on the rear of pants. Policy is detailed. It must also be enforced by saying "no" to the banned behavior and "yes" to positive things that replace it. Always!

The religious and spiritual nature of these stakeholders surfaces in many common and not so common ways. Most of the time, however, it is beneath the surface as individuals care for one another and do their job the best they can. Sometimes it is noticed for its religious origins. In a pluralistic community, such "notice" is easier than if everyone were the same. But we are not the same and it slips out, sometimes in startling ways. For example, a grief counselor, in an effort to strengthen a 14-year-old Buddhist student's self-image proclaims, "God loves you!" A soccer coach begins the game with a prayer for victory. A history teacher finds herself avoiding the Roman Catholic Church's positive role in the Middle Ages. A social science teacher hears herself proclaiming the denigrating impact of belief upon a curious mind. Students in a biology lab discuss the absurdity of evolution outside the earshot of their teacher. A cafeteria worker wishes everyone in line Merry Christmas in a public school with a high percentage of Jews. An assistant basketball coach is a Baptist youth minister. If something is a part of you it evidences itself in your daily work and play. Politics will help ease the possible hurt caused by an offensive word or act; policy may provide a Band-Aid® when politics fails.

POLITICS BEGINS AT HOME

Politics is how people solve the everyday issues that confront their efforts to live a good and enjoyable life. Unless one lives in a narcissistic universe, one must deal with others to survive and to improve one's life. We do this every day as we work, play, love, and pray. When we include the spiritual dimension of life and its religious expression, we are also involved with others, especially in a pluralistic society. This necessary skill begins at home. We will deal with the necessary individual listening, argumentative, and compassionate skills for political action later in the book. But for now, I would like to call your attention to the fact of the diversity of religion that resides in each home. If there are children in the home, as well as teens and young adults, there is the ever-present reality of diverse views evidenced by the ordinary cognitive and emotional development that accompanies us as we mature from birth to death. Explaining "death," for example, is no easy matter wherever you are in the life cycle. You can be assured at a full Thanksgiving dinner table that, if the topic arises, all your political skills will be needed to continue with the meal—aside from the fact of whether you should be talking about death with a turkey and the trimmings in front of you!

Around the typical holiday table, there is deep religious diversity. According to the 2008 Pew survey titled *Religion and Public Life*,[17] U.S. religion is characterized by diversity within each religion and switching between each of these religions. Twenty-eight percent of Americans have left the faith they were born into. Forty-four percent of adults have switched religious affiliation. Protestants represent 51 percent of the U.S. population, and demographics suggest that they will lose their majority in the next decade. American-born Roman Catholics are among the highest of those switching religions. Sixteen percent say they are not affiliated with any religion and, for those 18–29 years old, 25 percent are nonaffiliated. It is no wonder that people talk of spirituality rather than religion. It is because religious diversity is so deep there is no common language to convey the feelings and thoughts people have. In a sort of self-defense, they must revert to saying, "You don't understand," which is another way of saying, "I'm deeply spiritual but don't talk about it." When people have deep feelings and little communication, there is great danger of misunderstanding and an important role for politics. Religious politics begins at home and gradually spreads to neighbors, playmates, coworkers, and the stakeholders of our public schools.

CELEBRATING OUR COMMON HOLIDAYS AND RECOGNIZING OUR DIVERSE HOLY DAYS: THE POLITICS OF CELEBRATION

Celebrations tell the story of a community's history, values, and relationships. Good politics result in good celebrations—bringing people together to be happy around a central, common theme. We have national holidays, state holidays, and local ones. Fourth of July parades, for example, are opportunities to show everyone our dedication to our country. Schools, elected officials, bands, veterans, and almost anyone who wants to march are found in these parades. Each of them is different in what they do and represent, but are together in the nation they value.

Every community has holidays. These are special days—days for which we take time off from ordinary pursuits to do and say special things. Some days honor people, some an event, and some a seasonal occurrence.

We have birthdays, sports days, graduation days, study days, national holidays, and religious holidays. We learn how to celebrate, why we celebrate, and the joys of celebration as we mature. Learning to celebrate is part of our education, a part we learn many times outside of school. Part of growing up is learning that you may not celebrate with others the way you do at home or if you arranged every bit of the celebration for your personal pleasure. For example, you may love birthday lemon pie while others may prefer birthday cake; you may prefer to display a straight back with one arm strongly held high to indicate "we won." Others may prefer jumping up and down and piling on one another. One modifies one's celebratory style from community to community. Learning how to celebrate is as important as learning how to understand diverse types of writing or singing. If we could come to appreciate the variety of celebratory actions, we could enter more easily into the diverse niches that surround us and come to realize their importance to people. If students in our schools should be honored with celebratory actions for sports, academics, music, and graduation, why not their religion? What about their religious holidays? Are they to be ignored? Permitted for the family? The entire school? Should students of a different or no religion know that their fellow student is celebrating a holiday, and what it means to that student and to the community the student represents? Should the students learn about celebrations of other cultures throughout the world? These are questions that cannot be ignored in a pluralistic society.

POLITICAL ACTION: ORGANIZING FOR RELIGIOUS DIVERSITY

The answers to these questions involve us in politics. The politics practiced at home, with one's neighbors and peers, begins to encompass others in an organized fashion when there is sufficient cause. It is a sad truth that many times an ideal of diversity is not a sufficient cause, while a tear shed by a small child is. But let us first describe what may be done for the ideal of diversity and then for the small child. What is done for one may be done for the other.

WHY ORGANIZE? WHY JOIN?

One person talking calmly in a large auditorium is seldom heard. A thousand people will be heard if they speak with one voice. If they yell, the building shakes. Why organize or join with others? Because that is the only way to be effective in a world of competitive voices.

What we strive to bring together are those bound by a common goal: to acknowledge the religions present in the school and to learn about the religions of the world. Diversity is inherent to such a goal, and the stake-holders will be varied. Organizing in this milieu should never be a process of imposing a common vision but of binding a people together by contin-ual dialogue. The dialogue or conversation is like a spider's web that grad-ually binds everyone together by the attractiveness of their ideas and the deep concern of their personalities. Only in organization will these ideas be heard and the concern extended to all.

Advocacy is a mutual education of those in the group and those who come in contact with it. Advocacy's classrooms are our public and private places; its curriculum is the diverse religions; its teachers are those who gather to talk about bringing to consciousness the religions in our public schools and the world at large. Advocacy is a creative activity because it must adapt and develop in interaction among people and their desire for change.

ORGANIZATION BEGINS WITH CONVERSATION

Conversations about religions in our public schools begin like all con-versations, with two or more people talking about something. That some-thing may not be, and usually is not, of a religious nature. Such conversations take place between two extremes. One is where those soon to be involved in the conversation have absolutely no idea who the other person is or what they represent; the other, is between two or more friends who have a deep affection for and a long history with each other. Every-one involved in the conversation has something important to say. Every-one involved in the conversation has a duty to listen. If someone is not speaking and someone is not listening, it is not a conversation but prattle. Conversation is ultimately always going somewhere; it has a purpose. That purpose may be, for example, serious, fun, romance, or sales, but ulti-mately, those involved go from the beginning to the end and have "done" something by the end. What happens, though, when we do begin to speak with others about religious matters?

We have certain expectations of speaking about religion that, while they may originate at home, are shaped by the media and our friends as well. If we have never spoken *about* religion, this is unfamiliar territory because it demands that we take an objective stance before another's sa-cred way of life. Some feel that unless they are religious they cannot talk about religious matters. For some reason, individuals who may have opin-ions about basketball but never played it, about government but never voted, and about music but cannot sing a note feel that they have nothing to say when it comes to religion. They may feel that way, but the fact of the matter is that anyone, no matter what their past experience, has the ability to talk and think about something that is happening around the globe.

An important thing to remember is that in these conversations *about* religion everyone is expected to take a neutral stance regarding something that many Americans view as a very personal reality. This may be somewhat threatening because it deals with a sacred content and an intellectual stance of neutrality. An "objective stance" is, in general, a learned skill since it is founded on a neutral attitude, that is, an attitude that requires we leave personal feelings and absolute conviction (facts) in abeyance as we focus on what the person is saying and what this says about their deep meanings and feelings (the sacred). In a "me" culture, to focus on another, and not on our self, is like trying to break a habit—the habit of "me-ness" for that of "other-ness." But, with practice, which we will introduce in the next chapter, it can be done. Whenever people talk about religion, they are unconscious victims of the me culture, no matter what their religious affiliation. Once done, however, and even while doing it, many people discover the exhilaration of a growing curiosity, a refreshed spirituality, and an expanding knowledge of why and how people act.

Some individuals also come to realize that *conversations about religion* many times border on religious conversations. For the moment let's say that a *religious conversation* somehow involves one in a religious process whether that process is associated with one's, or the group's, religious beliefs, rituals, moral principles, communal life, or spirituality. It is, for example, when a Christian listens to a sermon, prays, acts to help someone in need, or receives communion. A conversation *about* religion wishes to discuss religion objectively—like learning history, music, or mathematics. What happens in a *conversation about religion* is that many times it awakens echoes of one's religious feelings in the midst of attempting to pursue an objective discussion of religion. I may, for example, be in deep conversation with some Muslims, Jews, and Christians about Abraham as founder of all three religions, but I feel Abraham has meaning for only my religion. As these feelings echo through one's being, they can easily be mistaken for the actual speech of our conversation partners. When that happens, the individual may have a sense that the others are attempting to sell them a religion or that their religion is being attacked. But conversations about religion are no different than other conversations in as much as these feelings are confirmed or denied only with time and continued conversation.

Much like those business leaders at the beginning of this chapter discovered the necessity of conversation in the midst of their fear to reduce their fears, such conversations may prove to many the necessity of introducing awareness of religions into our public schools. This necessity also arises among those who have dealt with people who live a religious life different than that in their niche and found that they needed to know more about their religion to deal with them. Such a conviction may lead you to start an organization or join with others with a common desire to enhance the religious diversity in our public schools.

STARTING A CONVERSATION AMONG THE STAKEHOLDERS—SOMETIMES AN EVENT BECOMES A MOVEMENT

A slight, blond eight-year-old stumbled off the school bus sobbing. "I don't want to go to school any more. . . . And I want to be a Christian!" Her mother scooped her up and hugged her close. "What's wrong with school? Just yesterday you said you loved that your friends from the summer were there." The little girl rummaged in her backpack, pulled out a teacher's questionnaire, and thrust it at her mother. Still hugging her daughter, she slowly read the cause of her daughter's anguish: a request that the family discuss their Christmas preparations. The teacher was initiating a unit on Christmas and its meaning. She put a Christmas tree in the classroom, had the children decorate it, and began to have them talk about what the day meant to them. The "homework" was to include the family in the discussion. In this situation, the family was Jewish. The parents felt the homework was an unnecessary imposition of Christianity on their daughter. They spoke to the district superintendent. His response to the district stakeholders was to ask them a question: "Is there any reason why a small child should have a bad day at school because of her religion?" We might also add whether there may be occasions where a small child would have a good day because of his religion?

The answer to this question was a reevaluation of a school district's policies regarding religions in the schools. In this instance, the school superintendent formed a committee to help deal with the issue. In another school district, the concerns of parents for their children's religious heritage and for an increased awareness of other religions resulted in a permanent advisory committee to the school district. Some school communities have found the formation of a cross-functional and multireligious team of advisors to the school board and superintendent of schools helpful. If you, or your school district, are interested in bringing together such a coalition of advisors, I have provided some suggestions for doing so in what follows. I will use the anagram RAC to describe the Religions Advocacy Coalition.

RACs

A Religions Advocacy Coalition is formed to begin a conversation about the necessity of both recognizing the diversity of religions in our public schools and of learning about those religions. Their purpose, ultimately, is to advocate for the importance of learning about religious diversity for educational and character development of the students.

Membership should be open to all stakeholders. A special effort should be made to have teachers, staff, and administrators as part of the coalition. They will provide you with not only their professional expertise, but their knowledge of the school system: who to contact, how to contact them, and what to expect from those in that system.

Appointing members to such a team is always a political challenge. Who do they represent among the local stakeholders? Do they have a reputation of team play or personal aggrandizement? Do they feel bound to always represent the views of their stakeholders or can they be depended upon for independent thought?

Although anyone may be part of a RAC, the coalition should be aware of the politics involved in achieving their goals. Organizers must understand that there must always be a hospitable atmosphere at their gatherings, that diverse membership is central to their vision of advocacy for diversity of religious perspectives in education, and that the skills and knowledge associated with the educational profession are present either in membership or easily available resources.

Many members of a RAC participate because of their expertise and/or position in the community. They are there to both say something and to do something. They are also there to listen because to listen in a group is to understand the other members and to understand how to speak to the other members. To speak and not to be heard is a waste of time and energy. To represent and to not be accepted is a frustrating exercise. An active member of an advisory coalition demands active listening by all members.

The conversation participants must take themselves seriously but not uncritically; optimistically, yet suspicious of implicit power and the political implications of the conversation; and speak their mind, yet remain aware of who they represent. Aside from an atmosphere of hospitality, the conversation has rules.[18] Say only what you mean; say it as accurately as you can; listen to and respect what the others say; be willing to correct or defend your opinions if challenged by the conversation partner; be willing to argue if necessary, to confront if demanded, to endure necessary conflict, and to change your mind if the evidence suggests it. The drive of the conversation is the drive to understand, not to dominate, and to understand all viewpoints, not to forcefully substitute one viewpoint for the others. Conversation can only occur when everyone is sensitive to the fact that it may unfortunately become a mechanism of exercising the power of one view over others. When conversation becomes the forced replacement of viewpoints, it ceases being conversation because the drive of a RAC conversation is to share viewpoints, to come to recognition of the where, when, and who of each and all viewpoints through understanding. Conversations in a RAC recognize that listening begins, continues, and ends with listening by and to the whole person. Effective RAC discussants are comfortable, quiet when appropriate, hospitable, constantly learning, willing to suspend assumptions, collegial, inquiring, supportive, focused, and thoughtful. An effective group occurs only because of the effectiveness of its members and their process for achieving their goals. Informal gatherings may be a way of discovering concerned stakeholders, but well-run, punctual meetings with clear goals are best for developing a RAC. Since a policy change takes time to be accepted and implemented, the group must develop a sense of the achievable as it refines its skills and works its way through the process of policy change. What follows are some things to keep in mind when organizing, sustaining, and dissolving a RAC.

At the formation of the RAC, coalition members must first agree on the roles and responsibilities of each coalition member, as well as reach agreement on how the meetings will be run and how they will make decisions. The establishment of these operating agreements will help the group begin to work together and to have some initial success at developing a concrete work product. It will also ensure that all members share understanding of how the group will operate and make the work ahead go more smoothly.

MISSION AND GOALS

If a group of people are going to do something together, they must talk about it together. In order to successfully complete a year-long project, they will need to formulate and record what they intend to do. This process has many names; here we are going to use what is commonly called writing a "mission statement." This process allows the coalition to put into writing what they want to achieve.

The initial meetings should slowly move from a general discussion of what people hope for their schools to an agreed upon statement of what they wish to achieve. A mission statement for a RAC is a verbalization of the communal dream for dealing with religions in the public school. It should contain the group's sense of the RAC's purpose, as well as what they want to be and do. Most of all, it should be simple and memorable; less is always more in writing mission statements. This initial process of formulating a mission statement determines, in many ways, how the RAC will operate during its existence. This process of discussion and writing must have everyone agree to what is said. Take your time. There's no hurry. The time spent here will expedite matters later on because what is happening is not only the writing of the statement, but also the exchange of stories and hopes regarding one's community, education, and school. The cultural toolbox in Appendix B, and other material in Chapter 6, will help you discover what is actually happening in the school.

One meeting should be dedicated to formulating a mission statement. Everyone should have an opportunity to express their dream for why and how religions will be present in the schools. This is usually done in a "brainstorming" manner with important phrases and ideas written on newsprint paper and posted on the walls around the room. From those phrases and ideas, the mission statement is written. It may be that time is needed between this sharing of dreams to the actual writing. Many people find it easier if one or several people write the statement and the rest of the group critiques it.

A typical mission statement might read as follows:

> The North Pole Religions Advocacy Coalition is a gathering of citizens of different religions, political parties, and occupations who dedicate themselves to expanding our children's knowledge about religions and the skills necessary to understand and communicate with those who differ from them in important religious matters. It seeks to create a sharing atmosphere in our schools as well as classes and programs that will assist our children in learning about the diverse religions in our world.

Once the group has agreed on exactly what they intend to achieve, they need to begin to conceptualize how they will implement this mission. The group should propose steps to bring it about and define how they will know they have achieved each of these steps (some may refer to this process as identifying short, medium, and long-term measurable goals or outcomes). The real world never matches exactly what we plan, but it is always good to have plans, even though they may need to change. It will be important that, as the work of the coalition continues, they take time to evaluate their process and see where adjustments need to be made.

Meetings should be held more frequently during the early stages of group development, perhaps once every two weeks. Afterwards, monthly meetings are appropriate. It is important that everyone keeps in touch with each other by e-mail, phone, or any other suitable means. The group will only act as a team when they know one another, know what they are doing, and are doing it together.

GOALS AND OBJECTIVES

Speaking our dreams aloud requires trust in those who listen. Enabling those dreams to become reality demands action and responsibility for our actions. Goals and objectives are statements that concretely articulate (goals), and sometimes measure (objectives), our dreams. If we desire students to be aware of how those in their school and throughout the world celebrate their religious holidays, then what are the steps (goals and objectives) that we must take to satisfy that desire? These goals and objectives should be stated simply and be easily seen as accomplished. It may be that the goals implementing the vision need several sets of objectives over several years. Perhaps a school calendar acknowledging the religious holidays of the students is an objective for one year; the inclusion of units within the social studies curriculum might be an objective for another year. If a community is serious about trying to enable its dreams, it needs to clearly write down exactly what it wishes to achieve.

MEDIA

The media can be a help or a hindrance. Their interest in religious diversity is to attract attention and to sell products. If people are curious about religious diversity, so will the media. This curiosity is demonstrated in telling stories. Many times their stories do not advance the cause of diversity as a beneficial dimension of community life. That is not the reason why stories are written or shown. The reasons stories are presented is to attract attention to the paper, the newscast, the television station, the blog, or whatever outlet carries the story. Clear, easily seen differences and demonstrable energy surrounding these differences are what attract people's attention. Peace, along with shared common values and practices, is boring. So the media stories are different from what a RAC says because the purposes of the telling are different. Having said that, however, one of the major ways of encouraging people to honor religious diversity is through the media. Meeting and discussing your mission, goals, and objectives with the editors who handle education and news about religion is important. Letters to the editor may help. The media's story will always be the filter through which the RAC's mission and accomplishments come to the public. Some publicity is better than no publicity. If the RAC's membership is truly representative of the education district, any necessary clarifications of a misinformed story will sustain, rather than stop, what you are doing.

A REAL-LIFE EXAMPLE: A CONVERSATION ABOUT RELIGIOUS DIVERSITY

The religious diversity of students arriving into the town of Pittsford, a suburb of Rochester, New York, reached the point where members of the town and educators in the school system began to act. They spent a great deal of time educating themselves by bringing in speakers and providing workshops dealing with the major world religions, law, curriculum, and the teaching about religions in public schools. What follows is one of their documents summarizing who they are, what they have done, and what they still intend to do.[19]

> The Religion in the Schools Advisory Committee is an advisory committee providing guidance to the Superintendent of Schools on questions related to district policy and practices regarding religious observances or instruction and the impact of this policy's implementation across the public school environment. Its underlying goal is to support the district in maintaining a safe and welcoming environment for all students of the district.
>
> The council is made up of members representing various constituencies in the district (elementary, middle, and secondary), administration, nursing staff, Special Education, library staff, music/arts department, athletics, Food Services, the Transportation Department, parent members, PTSA leadership

and community faiths (Islamic Center, Pittsford Clergy Council, Hindu community, Jewish Community Federation, Pittsford Baha'i community and local Jehovah's Witnesses Kingdom Hall). Members commit to four 2-hour meetings per school year and agree to provide input to concerns or matters needing clarification, at other times when required. Members are expected to seek input on issues and to share information with their constituencies.

Over the last eight years the Religion in the Schools Advisory Committee has sponsored & guided the creation of the following:

- Development of the school calendar (and addition of major religious holidays page)
- Guidelines for Displays and Guidelines for Handling Absences
- Policy and Regulations review and update
- Staff Training (4-hr. program for new staff on Religious Diversity-Impact in Schools)
- Around the World Religions Summer Series (12-speaker panels sharing fundamental beliefs/traditions/practices and observances and their impacts on families during the school year; held in 2004 and 2005; followed in 2006 with collegiate circles sharing issues faced, strategies found to be helpful and discussing implementation ideas)
- Resource Network (utilized for Summer series and classroom support to curriculum)
- Board Of Education and Community Training (Vanderbilt's Freedom Forum-First Amendment Ctr.)
- FAQ sheets for Principals
- Professional Development Tips Sheet for Teacher Center bulletins
- Multi-cultural Displays, posters and Staff Bulletins (a six-year plan for quarterly or per semester displays. By building sensitivity and awareness of common ground, the Pittsford Central School District's social studies curriculum is supported with information about the cultural, civic, and religious aspects of world and U.S. customs, celebrations, and community development)
- Comparative Religions Course
- Training regarding religious expression during the Induction Program for new teachers.

Advisory committees and coalitions such as these are feared by some communities. Some communities are afraid of acknowledging the religious nature of their stakeholders and/or their religions. Past history may be a source of that fear. Some have found that when they open their doors and minds to religion, religious bullies pour through ready to force their religion upon all they meet. In the face of such aggressive behavior, it is always easier to close the doors to all religions rather than endure the aggressiveness of some. Some have found that many of their teachers and administrators are convinced that every religion is the source of ignorance, superstition, dogmatism, and exclusiveness. These very important stakeholders refuse to acknowledge the importance of religion to individuals or society because they are convinced otherwise. To acknowledge the existence of religion, without affirming its destructive nature, would be, from their perspective, evil. Extremes such as these are always difficult to encounter. That is why we need politics to demonstrate, through experience, that all religious people are not bullies and many religious people are capable of talking about their religion and the religion of others in an intelligent and hospitable manner. Until we see an increase of such politics, we have policy and law.

POLICY

Policy manuals for school districts are composed of hundreds and hundreds of pages and thousands of rules. The policies concerning religious matters may be easily discovered in some, buried amidst subheadings in others, and nonexistent in still others.

The manual of school policies may be found in the education district's central office and other places indicated by the school board. Some managers and administrators believe that secrecy is power. Those with this belief will be hesitant to share information in general, especially information that indicates what they intend and what rules them. School policy manuals, sadly, are included among such information by those who approach school leadership in this fashion.

At the other extreme from these secretive boards and administrators are those school districts that post their policy manuals online. After logging on to the district Web site, the manual may be found under administration, school board, community. The easiest Web sites provide search engines on the Web site to find items. Key words such as *religion, religious activities, teaching about religion, holidays,* and *instruction* may be used to discover the policies.

If you have an educational concern and have failed to deal with it politically, you may be interested in getting it resolved by having it become part of school policy. You may be fortunate that the superintendent and school board realize that they have overlooked your concern and realize that it is an important addition to the district's educational vision. Outside of those fortunate times, you will need knowledge, persistence, networking, and guardianship to have your concerns included in school policy. *Knowledge* will demonstrate that your concern is not an isolated opinion but a factual necessity for public school education. Thus, for example, if your RAC becomes aware that the school's library holdings favor one religion or contain no stories describing diversity of religions, knowledge first of all means you have all the facts. Talk to the librarians and look at the library holdings. If what some stakeholders are saying is true, then investigate what other schools are doing. Investigate, too, if there are any pertinent laws associated with the desire to bring more books and media into the library. Talk to teachers, parents, administrators, and students about whether this is a good idea. Talk to the school board. Keep talking. *Persistence* enables you to respond to rejection, attend meetings, remain humble in the face of bullying behavior, and to watch over the entire policy-making process. *Networking* includes both the necessary politics and the mandatory gathering of like-minded individuals to achieve change. *Guardianship*, especially in the future policy's final stages, is sometimes neglected at the end of a long struggle of policy advocacy. Guardianship means that you make sure that every comma, period, and word is where it must be. Guardianship means that the implementation of the policy is what everyone agreed upon. After the board agrees and writes an agreeable policy, check to see if the holdings are changing in the library. Check every year. Just as policy writing is the failure of good politics, implementation is the political enlivenment of policy. We must always deal with others. Their vision and interpretation make the necessary changes in individual and communal life that make living worthwhile. Politics is the name we give to humans making change.

THE STAKEHOLDERS: RECOGNIZING AND RESPECTING SACRED GROUND

The stakeholders of our children's education are many. They hold in their hands not only the destiny of the children, but also of the nation. They may be driven at times, much like those in our cautionary tales at the beginning of this chapter, to rip, cut, and pull apart that which unites us. They might also, like them, lack the willingness or responsibility to help, seek, and affirm what we have in common. They might, in prizing whatever they hold sacred, refuse to recognize and respect the sacred in other people's lives. But, then again, they might not. People inherently wish to do the right thing. Our challenge is to discover, affirm, and act on what we together affirm as right. Certainly one right thing is our children's education.

Everyone has some thing or person they hold sacred. Religions past and present deal with what is sacred. To learn about these religions and the people who honor their sacred beliefs, moral imperatives, celebrations, and communities is to learn about something we all, in different ways, possess. As we begin to recognize, understand, and respect these sacred ways, we begin to recognize, understand, and respect the sacred within each of us and those we cherish.

Learning about our own and other religions is not easy. Advocating for the freedom to learn about them in our public schools is not easy. But it can and must be done because of the inherent nature of what people hold as sacred. The following chapters help show the way to keep the conversation going, and to discover those central values that bind us together and shape our education.

CHAPTER 2

The Law: Marking the Sacred on Common Ground

When our children were eight and six years old, we traveled across the United States in a small Toyota Tercel. It took eight days. Each day we spent about eight hours in the car. At the end of the second hour, screams of "don't look at me," or "he's touching me," or "she's making faces!" would assault our ears. We tried games. We tried multiple breaks. We tried everything imaginable to help them, and us, endure the long process of living together in such close quarters. We finally put suitcases between them as a kind of defense perimeter, but it seemed that someone's finger, or some object, would always find its way across the border to the other side. Needless to say, it was a long trip . . . and a much longer summer since we were staying in a college dorm!

When "politics" such as games, short breaks, and incentives of various sorts didn't work, we resorted to policy and law. This, of course, included the necessary police protection for all involved. The sacred territories marked out by the wall of suitcases were always able to be broached by the secular word, image, or appendage from the other side. No matter how we attempted to stop the encroachment into "my" space, the "owner" of the other space was able to invade.

Sometimes it seems that the controversies surrounding religions in our schools are like my two young children were: someone is always trying to get their way with little concern for anyone else. Law attempts to calm the matter by setting strict boundaries, but it is not always enough because there are sets of human dynamics involved that seek satisfaction and satiation.

OF LAW AND FINDING OUR SACRED PLACES

Of course our children were not in the backseat of the car for their entire life. Nor were they children forever. Contexts change. They change.

This chapter will look at two things: (a) law and how it must adapt to cultural changes; and (b) listening and how it enables people to deal with those same changes. When change is occurring, people must face each other without the barrier of laws. They must talk and solve their difficulties. If they cannot agree on what must be done, laws must be changed or interpreted to deal with what is causing the controversy. There are many laws dealing with religion besides those associated with the classroom—employment and tax law to name two—that affect public education. We will focus primarily on laws associated with religion in the classroom.

Half of this chapter will provide the skeleton for the body of law regulating the classroom experience. We will review the European culture out of which it came and then the unique religious culture that evolved in the United States. It is within this historical context that our laws were written and, through interpretation, evolved. An understanding of what these laws and their contexts say enables us to know where to go next in this ever-changing world. Appendix A provides the Internet links for finding the immense interpretative literature dealing with these laws.

The last half of the chapter helps develop a necessary skill for going beyond the barriers provided by the law to the necessary skill of collegial listening. If we know how to listen, we know how to carry on a conversation. Law is the minimum. Listening enables us to engage in that authentic political life where we seek to find what binds us together. It is the foundation for advocacy, for a body politic, and for the sensitivity necessary for recognizing and discovering our and others' sacred places.

MARKING THE BOUNDARIES BUILDING BARRIERS: A BRIEF HISTORY

The distinction modern thinkers make between religion and life was, and is, not made among most people. Most people in the past and present see the world around them filled with many forces that aid and dissuade them from living their lives. Certainly "the" force, in the West, was God. God surrounded them and was present in many different ways. These ways were challenged, and in many cases rejected, by the Protestant reformers in the sixteenth century as superstition, idolatry, and ritualism. They especially challenged the principal way God was seen as present among these people for over a thousand years—as in their church and in its leaders, especially the bishops and pope. The challenge of the reformers of these religious people was to convince them to view their religion differently than how they were taught. This new approach introduced them into new ways of understanding God, God's presence among them, and what was God's will for them. One old way that was seldom challenged by the reformers was the necessity for everyone to belong to the same religion. There was only one true religion, theirs, and to allow falsehood to live next to truth was to allow evil to live next to goodness. Evil must be purged. Falsehood must be kept away from truth. Our land, our people, and our religion must be one. The king must support the church. The religion must be established; for example, supported by the community represented by the king.

Actually, they did not have a word for "religion" as we do today. They would say "church." *Religion* from about 800 CE to 1450 CE in the West referred to the type of life lived by "religious"—those men and women who take the vows of poverty, chastity, and obedience.[1] Religions or religion as something separate from life's joys, sorrows, work, and camaraderie can be understood as separate only when you have a means of separating it. It took several centuries for our idea of religion, as a set of beliefs, rituals, and morals that people lived, to develop. Once this occurred, we could make a distinction between life and religion. We could make laws dealing with religion.

Because they took the unity of communal life for granted in the sixteenth and seventeenth centuries, wars were fought throughout Europe to sustain such unity. To do so, from the reformers' standpoint, the old Catholic Christian Church must be destroyed and the new Protestant Christian Church must take its place. This didn't happen. Instead, both Protestants and Catholics fought to the death for their vision of Christianity. The result of this reform, both political and ecclesial, was the loss of the Catholic Church as the unifying political and cultural force in Europe and the deaths of millions. An attempt to stop the bloodshed and stop the spread of violent reform was the Peace of Westphalia (1648), which guaranteed that each prince could determine the religion of his own state and the people living there. The older reality of civil unity was retained, but now consciously so. What was new, however, was the acknowledgement that diverse and opposed versions of Christianity could live side by side. Now "our" sacred land existed next to "their" devil lands. God, now, blessed our land with its sacred people. Although we believed it necessary to destroy the "other," centuries of war taught us that destroying them was also destroying us. (Europe lost almost 40 percent of its population in these wars.) Westphalia said no, the killing must stop. No matter how sacred the land and the God who protects it, people must stop killing one another in God's name. Of course, the killing did not stop. As the nation-state developed, so did the key markers of national identity. By the mid-nineteenth century, the nation-state as we know it finds its fulfillment in three significant markers: national language, national culture, and national religion. Each nation had its "established" religion that consecrated their nation as God's. Baptism, church, and citizenship were all one. One became a member of both church and state through baptism. One nation and its culture were different from the other nation and its culture. Europe became an amalgam of nation-states.

In what ultimately becomes the United States of America, all these peoples, with their religions, languages, and cultures, come into the same land and nation. All these sacred, special, valuable, sensitive, identity-making things wrapped up in individual human beings were taken out of the context of "sacred land" and plopped down together on a common land. It is as if we took down the baggage between our warring children. There would be nothing to protect them from each other except themselves. A certain level of maturity and self-worth is necessary for them to live in peace. So with these diverse peoples, there is nothing to protect them from each other except themselves. The consequences could be devastating.

Fortunately, there is something to protect people from each other—the law. The law puts a firm barrier back up and makes the lines clear again so it is clearly known who "they" are and "we" are. Of course, like the children, someone is always trying to move the barrier—to change it to satisfy their needs as opposed to the others.

THE LAWS

The signers of the U.S. Constitution agreed that law, not the whims of nobility, would rule the land. They also agreed to not have an established religion, while allowing religion "free exercise." What they meant by the word *religion* and why they wished separation have been discussed by historians and legal scholars for centuries. The results of such discussions directly affect the way our taxes are collected and used, the days people work for pay, the uniforms they wear, and what and how children are taught.

CHANGING CONTEXTS; CHANGING LAW

Three cases show how people's lives are affected by how law is interpreted. One case deals with the question of whether someone must believe in God to hold office; the other two cases deal with whether students in a public school must salute the flag.

One might think that the Constitution is quite clear when it says (bold added):

> Article Six, third paragraph, of the United States Constitution:
> The Senators and Representatives before mentioned, and the Members of the several State Legislatures, and all executive and Judicial Officers, both of the United States and of the several States, shall be bound by Oath or Affirmation, to support this Constitution; **but no religious Test shall ever be required as a Qualification to any Office or Public Trust under the United States.**

Until 1961, however, the Maryland state constitution read as follows (bold added): "[No] religious test ought to be required as a qualification for any office of profit or trust in this State, **other than a declaration of belief**

in the existence of God." Maryland had ratified the U.S. Constitution in 1788. Why did it take so long to change the section dealing with belief in God? It took so long because there never was a reason to bring it to anyone's attention. No hand was poking through the luggage. When Roy R. Torcaso finally poked through in *Torcaso v. Watkins* (1961) the U.S. Supreme Court agreed that the law had to change. In addition, the Fourteenth Amendment had been passed in 1864 and begun to be interpreted by 1961 as meaning that equal protection should be provided to all citizens, no matter what state. The amendment read:

> Section 1. . . . No state shall make or enforce any law which shall abridge the privileges or immunities of citizens of the United States; nor shall any state deprive any person of life, liberty, or property, without due process of law; nor deny to any person within its jurisdiction the equal protection of the laws.

Same law, different contexts, different consequences. Since public schools are representatives of the state, it is only when the Fourteenth Amendment begins to be seen as a means the federal government has, through its Supreme Court, of judging the state laws do we begin to get Supreme Court decisions affecting the local schools.

A similar change in context occurred when children refused to salute the flag for religious reasons. In 1935, the U.S. Supreme Court ruled that it was illegal for the children to refuse to salute the flag and they should suffer the consequences. Then, in 1942, the U.S. Supreme Court ruled that it was legal and the school had no right to punish the children. Contexts made all the difference.

The first refusal happened in Minersville, Pennsylvania. Two children, 10 and 12, were expelled for refusing to salute the flag and reciting the Pledge of Allegiance. The Gobitis children were the first to refuse this new practice that had been mandated after World War I. They were Jehovah's Witnesses who considered such salutes and pledges blasphemy. To salute the flag and pledge an allegiance was, from their perspective, idolatrous. Their attorneys used the Fourteenth Amendment's due process clause to argue their case. They lost.

The same thing happened in West Virginia in 1942. Parents were prosecuted there for not allowing their children to salute the flag or recite the pledge. The children were disciplined by the school. The federal district court placed an injunction restraining the state from enforcing the school board's resolution. It went directly to the U.S. Supreme Court as *Barnette v. West Virginia State Board of Education* (1942). This time the same act of refusal was argued as an exercise of free speech and freedom of religion. The parents won. The school board lost. Same action, same law—one was legal, one was not—but different contexts. Did either side ever talk to each other and try to find common ground? Obviously none was found. The law separated the contestants.

THE FIRST AMENDMENT, ITS INTERPRETATIONS, AND RELIGION IN THE SCHOOLS

I would like to suggest five dominant models or images that guide the interpretation of the First Amendment as it applies to the public schools. The law and its interpretations have been the principal barrier preventing one group from imposing its religion on everyone else in the public schools. It reads (bold added):

> Congress shall make no law respecting an **establishment** of religion, or prohibiting the **free exercise** thereof; or abridging the freedom of speech, or of the press; or the right of the people peaceably to assemble, and to petition the government for a redress of grievances.

Until recently, the two terms I have highlighted in bold print, *establishment* and *free exercise*, were the main points of contention between those who felt some religion was being imposed on them and those who thought they were upholding the common view of religion's role in the schools. The "freedom of speech" clause has become more influential in the debate in recent decades. The models that have helped the courts, at first local and then national, deal with the controversies over religion and the public schools are *nondenominational, wall of separation, neutrality, entanglement,* and *equal access.* They are presented in historical order.

1. Schools should be nondenominational: not encouraging a denominational or sectarian position in the schools.

This view sees religion as necessary in education. But, because we have various religions in our schools, it accepts what is common, nondenominational, as the religion that must be taught.[2] There are, from this perspective, foundational religious principles and symbols that make this nation great. These should be found in all the schools. These principles and symbols would be nondenominational or nonsectarian as against those sects or denominations that would want to divide us and weaken our country.

Definition of Denominations

The term *denomination* has come to mean a group of churches adhering, more or less, to the same beliefs, rituals, and moral principles. Today the term is frequently used in reference to any Christian grouping of churches such as Catholic, Orthodox, Baptist, Lutheran, and Episcopal. Calling these churches a denomination is suggesting that they are all part of the same "Christian Religion" that includes these denominations. Thus, Christian religion would be the pie, and the slices would be denominations. As we have seen in Europe, this was not always the case. For many years, Roman Catholic Christianity and Orthodox Christianity were not accepted as denominations. Sometimes the "denomination" may see itself as "the"

Christian church and the other "denominations" as false Christian churches. Such divisiveness was also present when the colonies were established.

Historical Perspective: Denominations in America

Two things enabled the diverse founding Christian Protestant churches in the United States to find common ground: (a) a common experience; and (b) a common enemy. The common experience was the revival; the common enemy was Catholicism. A denomination might differ over some things, but it did not differ over these two things.

Except for the Anglican Church, the other types of Protestantism in the colonies were minority interpretations of Christianity in Protestant Europe. They emphasized adult baptism rather than infant baptism, as well as an adult choice for a religious way of life. They also demanded "witness," telling others why they followed Jesus. There was a great deal of diversity among them in their use and interpretation of the Bible as well as what this Christian way of life demanded of its adherents. This enthusiasm for a new way of living Christianity, however, was passed on with difficulty to their children. With time, they and their children discovered that the initial enthusiasms were difficult to sustain. What developed over time is what is called "revival" because certain ways of preaching and reading the Bible reawakened people to those enthusiasms of that faith experienced by their parents or, in the past, by themselves.

Most historians claim that the first unifying colonial experience before the Revolution was *The Great Awakening*.[3] This was a time (1730–1760) when enthusiastic preachers wandered the colonies preaching in the open air, perhaps the town square, proclaiming the sinfulness of their listeners and the need for their immediate repentance. People replied in droves— gathering around the preacher, shouting, sometimes falling on the ground, and proclaiming deep experiences of God's presence. Many of the original colonial founding churches split during the Awakening between those who felt deeply a renewed, and sometimes new, enthusiasm for their religious way of life and those who did not. But the divisiveness of the churches was matched by the unity of the experience among many colonists. They felt together the importance of the same God, the same Bible, and the same necessary commands for living God's life. What they experienced was beyond their denominations—nondenominational. Further waves of revival in 1800–1820 and 1850–1900 helped define the U.S. understanding of religion, but they never again solidified the country as did The Great Awakening.

After the Revolution, immigrants, particularly Catholic immigrants, provided another sense of unity among the resident American citizens. The original Catholics were from the English upper class, were wealthy owners of large plantations, had fought in the Revolution, and were supportive of democracy, as evidenced by Charles Carroll's signing of the Declaration of Independence. These new poor and uneducated immigrants were offensive in language, demeanor, and religious practice. Their pope sided with nobility and, it seemed, found the peoples' voices empty prattle not to be heard in church. These new Catholic immigrants needed to be, from the residents' perspective, educated. The immigrants and their clergy agreed.

Historical Perspective: Formation of Laws Mandating Public Education

A few of the Founding Fathers had expressed a need for the education of everyone at public expense, but only Thomas Jefferson in 1779 attempted to do something about it. He offered Virginia's lawgivers a plan to educate young children for three years. It was rejected. The taxpayers in general said it was a private responsibility and the clergy in particular said that the Church would care for the poor. Nothing was done to bring all the children together in the same school. That did not mean that the desire for universal education was abandoned. In 1837, Massachusetts passed a law that brought about a school for all under the authority of the state. In 1852, the Massachusetts legislature made it mandatory that all children attend school. Slowly, both the mandate and the common (public) school spread to the other states.

When a state mandates that all children attend school, things begin to happen to a community: creation of taxes to pay for the school and a bureaucracy to provide the schooling. People's sense of what is sacred and important is disturbed since now everyone is lumped together and the previous divisions have to be dealt with. When lines are drawn (or redrawn) identity initially becomes confused. Religion was central to the understanding of education at the beginning of our country. Once schooling was mandated for everyone, religion was also a necessary part of that mandate; otherwise there would have been no education. The solution to the initial quandary was to agree on what was common to religion and make this part of schooling. Religion was Protestant Christianity as it was evolving in the colonies. What was common was prayer, Bible reading, and an emphasis upon the laws of God found in the Protestant King James version of the Bible. The result came to be understood as a nonsectarian or nondenominational teaching of religion in the schools. The nondenominational nature of this solution came about more by custom than law until the immigrant Catholics, in obedience to the law and their own beliefs, began to attend the public schools.

They attended, but many did not pray the Protestant version of the Lord's Prayer, or as they would say, "The Our Father." Nor did they recite the Protestant version of the Ten Commandments. Nor did their parents and priests agree with the negative way Catholics were described in the history books. Nor did the Catholic parents wish their children to hear the Protestant translation of the Bible read to their children. Nor did they want them to learn the Protestant hymns. Obviously, this was not a non-denominational curriculum to the Catholics. This refusal and disagreement resulted in physical punishment to the Catholic students and violence throughout the cities that supported the "nondenominational" curriculum. This nondenominational curriculum, which had originally been accepted in order to enlist the support of the Protestant denominations to bring about the public school, was now seen as divisive and oppressive by the immigrants. The residents, however, saw the school as the proper instrument for making everyone an educated citizen. These immigrants, from the residents' perspective, needed to learn proper health care, proper English, proper manners, and proper religion. They attempted to force the Catholic children to become like them through law and sometimes violence. In response, many Catholics built their own school system while still becoming educated Americans. The application of school law in a nonsectarian or nondenominational manner had reached the limit of its ability to unite its citizens. The Catholic bishops opted out of the system and so did many of their fellow Catholics. Some people, however, did not opt out. Some wanted to make sure that if the Catholics opted out they obtained no help from the state in doing so. The choice of declaring that the public schools would be nonsectarian in nature did not help build community, but rather helped divide fellow citizens among themselves.

2. Schools should sustain a Wall of Separation between religion and the school.

As long as tax dollars are spent to support the public schools, and as long as those schools strive to include all of its citizens, there will be people who feel they are not treated fairly. When the Catholics formed their own school system, some Catholic taxpayers did not think it was justified that they had to pay to educate both their children in the Catholic school and their neighbor's children in the public school. At the same time, someone paying taxes and sending their child to a public school felt that all his tax money should be spent for public school children. If any of his money went for school books, bus fare, heat, water, or teacher salaries in the Catholic schools, that was almost equivalent to putting it in church coffers. For this person, the situation was too reminiscent of countries where there was an established religion and taxes went to pay for religious schools.

As cases made their way through the court system, the Supreme Court attempted to do justice for all concerned. One interpretative image that aided the courts in bringing about justice was the phrase of Roger Williams, "a wall of separation between church and state," used by Thomas Jefferson in a private 1802 letter to a group of Baptists in Danbury, Connecticut. The Supreme Court used it to help interpret the Establishment Clause of the First Amendment. Although it was first used in the

Reynolds v. United States (1878) case, it gained notoriety in the *Everson v. Board of Education* (1947) case.

This case dealt with the legality of a New Jersey law that permitted reimbursement of parents for busing their children to the Catholic school. Everson claimed that providing tax dollars to Catholic school parents was an indirect way of establishing the Catholic religion. In a 5 to 4 decision, the Supreme Court said it was a fair law. In doing so, they used the image of a wall of separation to help explain why they reached their decision.

> This Court has said that the parents may, in the discharge of their duty under state compulsory education laws, send their children to a religious rather than a public school if the school meets the secular education requirements which the state has power to impose. It appears that these parochial schools meet New Jersey's requirements. The state contributes no money to the schools. It does not support them. Its legislation, as applied, does no more than provide a general program to help parents get their children, regardless of their religion, safely and expeditiously to and from accredited schools.
>
> The First Amendment has erected a wall between church and state. That wall must be kept high and impregnable. We could not approve the slightest breach. New Jersey has not breached it here.[4]

This was a helpful image but, upon further challenges, it was found to be inadequate for dealing with the expanding and complex infrastructure necessary to support a booming economy after World War II.

3. Schools should be neutral toward religion.

This intertwinement of people and activities may be found in many situations, but "prayer" happened to be the one that was focused on in our next case. The question was raised, "People pray all the time at public functions why not at school?" Previously, we have shown how Catholics agreed with the principle of prayer but disagreed as to the form of the prayer. It was the form of the prayer, to them, but not the majority, that was sectarian and divisive.

Over the years, some states, while still mandating prayers in the schools, changed the prayers to be more inclusive of those in the class. For those who still felt offended by the prayers, some states allowed them to opt out of saying them. New York composed a prayer: "Almighty God, we acknowledge our dependence upon Thee, and we beg Thy blessings upon us, our parents, our teachers and our country."[5] Some parents felt that demanding their children to be present during this prayer was illegal. All the lower courts disagreed with the parents and supported the right of the NYS Board of Regents to compose such a prayer. By the time the Supreme Court accepted the case in 1962, New York children as well as children in other states could opt out of being present when the prayer was said; some parents claimed that was not enough because it was still imposing a religion on their children. When their children left class during the prayer, other students, and especially teachers, were antagonistic toward them.[6] To discern what was fair, the majority of justices employed a principle that it had also used in the *Everson* case. They said that the First Amendment "requires the state to be neutral in its relations with groups of religious believers and nonbelievers; it does not require the state to be their adversary. State power is no more to be used so as to handicap religions than it is to favor them."[7] For the same reason, it was held to support the parents' view in the *Engel v. Vitale* (1962) case and concluded that it was unconstitutional for state officials to compose an official school prayer and require its recitation in the public schools.

Bible reading, like prayer, was deemed offensive by some parents. Not prayer, but Bible reading caused some Pennsylvania parents to demand its elimination in 1963 in what came to be known as the *Abington v. Schempp* decision.[8] The Pennsylvania statute mandated, "At least ten verses from the Holy Bible shall be read, or caused to be read, without comment, at the opening of each public school on each school day, by the teacher in charge ... If any school teacher, whose duty it shall be to read the Holy Bible, or cause it to be read, shall fail or omit so to do, said school teacher shall, upon charges preferred for such failure or omission, and proof of the same, before the board of school directors of the school district, be discharged."[9] There was also a tradition of saying the Lord's Prayer in addition to the mandated Bible reading throughout the district. Obviously, there had been little change since the nineteenth century in the will of this school board. In an 8–1 decision, this mandate and the coinciding tradition were seen to be against the First Amendment. As Justice Clark wrote:

> ... we see that religion has an exalted place in American life because it is lived in ... the home, the church and the inviolable citadel of the individual heart and mind. We have come to recognize through bitter experience that it is not within the power of government to invade that citadel, whether its purpose or effect be to aid or oppose, to advance or retard. In the relationship between man and religion, the State is firmly committed to a position of neutrality.[10]

Neutrality does not mean that religious books, beliefs, rituals, morals, and artifacts are not present in the public schools. As both the *Engel* and *Schempp* decisions clearly state, public schools should teach about religion since it is part of everyone's life and culture. What the courts keep trying to prevent is the imposition of one group's religion on those who do not believe in that religion by making it unconstitutional to have state-sanctioned prayer and Bible reading in school.

Much like the children in the backseat of our car, however, something always gets through the barrier. New challenges to former interpretations occur. New times demand new views of the law to make these interpretations.

4. Schools should sustain a minimum entanglement between religions and public schools.

Does tax exemption result in the establishment of religion? *Waltz v. Tax Commission* (1970) dealt with the challenge of Frederick Waltz to New York City's exemption from taxes of all religious buildings. Mr. Waltz and his attorneys argued that the fact that these institutions did not have to pay taxes was an indirect subsidy to these religions, thus an establishment of them. Chief Justice Warren Burger helped formulate the guiding principle when he wrote that "No perfect or absolute separation is really possible; the very existence of the Religion Clauses is an involvement of sorts—one that seeks to make boundaries to avoid excessive entanglement."[11]

This image of minimum entanglement was developed further into a three-part test that helps understand whether establishment is occurring or freedom of religion is being disallowed. It is stated clearly in *Lemon v. Kurtzman* (1971): "First the statute must have a secular legislative purpose; second, its principal or primary effect must be one that neither advances nor inhibits religion, . . . finally the statute must not foster an excessive government entanglement with religion."[12] If any of these three conditions is violated, the government's action is unconstitutional. In this case, a law was passed in Pennsylvania in 1968 that permitted the state superintendent of public instruction to reimburse nonpublic schools for teachers' salaries, textbooks, and instructional materials. Rhode Island also had a Salary Supplement Act that provided funds to nonpublic elementary schools. In both cases, most funds were spent on Catholic schools. The laws were judged unconstitutional because, using the Lemon Test: first, the texts and teachings were religious; second, it supported religious schools; third, 25 percent of elementary students in Pennsylvania attended private schools. Of these, 95 percent were Catholic. Consequently, these laws violated the Establishment Clause of the Constitution.

5. Schools must allow Free Speech and Equal Access.

Contexts change. Images blur in their ability to interpret life, while others take their place. The context of many legal decisions was institutional, or as some might say, communal. American society has continued to become more individualistic,[13] or, as others might also say, narcissistic. This shift of context is seen somewhat in the increase of research, writing, and involvement in contemporary spiritualities as well as law. Such a shift occurs in the interface between religion and public schools when we move away from discussions of religion understood as an institution imposing its will on a minority and more into discussions of freedom of speech understood as expressing one's spirituality. The speech may now be an individual's spirituality, but also a community of spiritualities, also known as religion, present in the school. Once the interface between school and religion is expressed as an exercise of free speech, the Court's former means of interpretation surrounding "establishment" and "free exercise" of religion is not as helpful. What can be said about exercising one's free religious/spirituality speech? Does it make a difference if that someone is a student, a teacher, an administrator, or a caretaker? The questions multiply just as one of my children's fingers, a probing toy, or words tried to reach through to the other side for whatever benevolent or malevolent purpose. Perhaps the whole issue would be solved if Congress would pass a law enabling students to speak their religion in the school through prayer and reading of sacred scripture. Maybe this would resolve the difficulties of religion's place in the public school.

This "maybe" becomes a reality with the *Equal Access Act* of 1984 and the upholding of that act by the Supreme Court in the *Board of Education of Westside Community School District v. Mergens* (1990). What the act did was emphasize and bring into prominence the image of each individual student having an equal opportunity to speak their ideas and/or beliefs in the public school building. As the law reads:

> It shall be unlawful for any public secondary school which receives Federal financial assistance and which has a limited open forum to deny equal access or a fair opportunity to, or discriminate against, any students who wish to conduct a meeting within that limited open forum on the basis of the religious, political, philosophical, or other content of the speech at such meetings.[14]

This statement and its accompanying explanations opened the door for new ways in which religion would enter into the school—and, of course, further laws and court cases. This will continue forever because behind each new law and interpretation are viewpoints that both provide an understanding of what may be done as well as what is considered religion and education. We know that Catholics opted out of the public schools because they felt violated by what was happening there. We now see more and more people home schooling their children because they sense that the education that occurs there does not represent their values. Obviously, individuals and groups of individuals are willing to live with the barriers, and sometimes decreased educational opportunities, rather than the politics of communal life. It says something about people's sense of ownership of the common destiny of the nation and the means to achieve that destiny when they do not participate in its formulation or celebrate its achievement.

In the spirit of public education, the following "pop quiz" will test your ability to apply what you have read. The particular court cases that lie behind the answers would fill volumes. The answers are found in this endnote.[15] Answer: "True," "False," or "See a knowledgeable attorney."[16]

Table 2.1
Religions in the Schools: Pop Quiz

1. So long as they are not disruptive, students have the right to pray individually.	
2. Students may read their Bibles or other scriptures with other willing students.	
3. Students may pray either out loud or silently in informal settings such as the hall—subject to the same rules of order that apply to all speech.	
4. Students may pray aloud during a silent film shown in history class.	
5. Schools must rent their facilities to privately sponsored religious baccalaureate services even if they have rules against renting facilities to private groups.	
6. School officials may organize a religious baccalaureate ceremony for graduates.	
7. Schools must allow graduating students to pray aloud at graduation ceremonies.	
8. Teachers may not engage in religious activities with their students if they are doing so in their official capacity.	
9. Teachers may engage in private religious activities in faculty lounges.	
10. Students may be taught about religion.	
11. Teachers may not teach religion in the public school.	
12. The U.S. Supreme Court has repeatedly said that one's education is not complete without a study of comparative religion, that it would be difficult to teach art, music, literature, and most social studies without considering religious influences.	
13. Schools may teach about explanations of life on earth, including religious ones, in social studies classes.	
14. Students may not express their religious beliefs in their reports, homework, and artwork.	
15. Religious or antireligious remarks made in the ordinary course of classroom discussion or student presentations are permissible and constitute a protected right.	
16. Outsiders may not be given access to the classroom to distribute religious or antireligious literature.	
17. Student participation in student-sponsored religious events on school grounds is permissible either before or after school.	
18. Students do not have the right to speak to, and attempt to persuade, their peers about religious topics, just as they do not have the right to do so about political topics.	

Table 2.1 (Continued)

19. While it is constitutionally permissible for a student to approach another and issue an invitation to attend a religious service, repeated invitations in the face of a request to stop constitute harassment.	
20. Public schools may teach about religious holidays and celebrate their secular aspects.	
21. Schools should generally excuse students who do not wish to participate in holiday events.	

BEYOND THE CLASSROOM INTO THE COMMUNITY

One significant context for the discussion about religion in the schools is the classroom and what happens there. Classroom activities are central to contemporary education, but cannot accept responsibility for a student's total education. Parents and peers also have a significant role in each student's education. In the twenty-first century, a child has the world at her fingertips with computers, television, and other electronic devices. The world outside the classroom is, and is being used by some as, an instrument of education. An intimate part of that classroom world is the school building and those who work there: teachers and teacher's aides, cafeteria servers, bus drivers, the people who clean the halls and grounds, secretaries, and administrators, and so forth. Their religious expression, or lack thereof, may also be a means of education for the students. Their freedom of expression is limited and allowed according to the laws of the workplace, not the classroom.[17] For those who were educated in the twentieth century, it is so easy to think that education consists of a teacher, a student, and a book. It does not. We will talk about various means of enabling the student to work with this total environment later in the book.

CROSSING BOUNDARIES; BUILDING COMMUNITIES: THE SKILL OF LISTENING

Laws and court decisions regarding religions and schools provide secure boundaries between warring peoples. Hopefully they also provide a sense of fairness for all concerned, or at least a sense that one's emotions need to be tempered by the use of both reason and necessity. If, on one hand, these court cases reflect a sense of hurt and injustice on both sides, they also indicate, on the other hand, the necessity for means of accommodation and respect in order to sustain a common economic and cultural life.

A healthy pluralistic community must somehow design mechanisms to deal with people encroaching onto the sacred space and way of life of the other. The fact is that once we encounter, through media or personal contact, someone who is really different from us, we run away, fight, adapt, or are bored. We may run by building larger barriers so we do not have to meet them. We may fight by aggressively trying to change them to fit our expectations. We may talk, listen, understand, and compromise so we may live together in a tense peace. We may yawn and pay no attention to what they say and do. One thing it is extremely difficult to do is deny that those who are really different do exist and will continue to exist in our pluralistic democracy. We cannot return to the wars of religion and the consequent death and destruction.

Legal decisions and legislative action are ways to settle things between people who need some resolution to seemingly insoluble human situations. Religious people get caught up in defending, and at times imposing, their sacred way of life and its various symbols on nonbelievers. These sacred symbols, and their personal eternal consequences, are seen as unchanging. No compromise. Get a law passed, or interpreted, bring in the police, send the perpetrators to jail. And . . . and is there less controversy? Does the religious way of life prosper? Does the social community heal and nourish what is necessary for prosperity and healthy living? Much like my children in the backseat of the car, the only words spoken in such situations produce negative responses from the other side; the only words heard are those causing pain or imposing someone's will. Maybe we can prevent the controversy or at least reduce its pain among sincere people by setting an atmosphere of respectful and collegial listening in matters concerning religion before the controversies begin.

Respectful listening is key to building such an atmosphere. It seems that the most publicized method of talking and listening in our culture is adversarial—where we listen only to demean the other, catch the other up in word games, and paint an image of the other that is repulsive to the audience. That is why they speak in loud, short sentences for brief periods of time, repeating the same message over and over. Respectful listening by everyone in the conversation honors the words, ideas, and feelings of the speaker and the listener. Respectful listening begins by honoring the speaker as valuable and unique both to him and to us. Such listening can begin anywhere.

Except in a very few instances our initial meetings, for example, with stakeholders in public education, do not center on religious matters or for that matter, on education. We might meet them in the supermarket, taking out the trash, walking the dog, or on the sports fields, ignorant of their stake in public education.

Such meetings are usually short. Yet, they provide a mark of identification as a "school person." This stakeholder-realization, however, is usually subtle and centered around the students. It may be parent-teacher meetings, sitting in the gym during a basketball game, waiting for the arrival of a school bus, or kids knocking at your door for cans, a contribution, or a request to purchase candy. In all these instances, you realize that here is someone who has a stake in what happens at the school.

It is so easy to write and/or read these words, but so extremely difficult to put them into action. So much of our quick-paced world seems caught up in doing what must be done now without taking the time to set the context for what comes later. Whether taking advantage of the moment next to someone in the gym or settling into a longer session at a PTA meeting, listening is central to establishing a context of mutual concern that is necessary for a fruitful life together. If someone senses that you are interested in her as a person, then when other matters arise, she knows your primary aim is her—not religion, money, or anything else.

To establish an atmosphere of mutual concern, we first listen to their words, then to their meanings and feelings associated with these words, and then to their hopes, dreams, and fears that encompass them. Depending on the situation, it may not be easy to listen to a person's words. Continual loud cheering in a gym usually leaves room only for additional loud cheering. But we can't cheer forever, even during a basketball game. There are times for conversation and times to listen to the other person. If we do not talk and listen when there are no controversies, all we will do is scream when there are.

When you sense you know how the other person feels and are able to repeat the ideas of what the other person says, you know that you are listening to him. When you can "read" her body language and find value in whom the person is, you know you are listening to her. When you are not interrupting, giving advice, jumping to conclusions, arguing, or letting the person's words or feelings stimulate yours too quickly, you know you are listening. Listening is a learned skill. It must be practiced. With practice you gradually realize you do not need to constantly defend yourself, and that receptive silence does not indicate you have nothing to say. Respectful listening is a skill that demands continual practice with children, coworkers, friends, and the significant people in your life to do well. Here are some methods for building the skill of respectful listening as it becomes, with the stakeholder, collegial listening.

BUILDING THE SKILL OF LISTENING TO AND FOR EACH OTHER: COLLEGIAL LISTENING

By the time we can talk we have learned ways of both listening and talking. If we find that we are not listening well, that means we will need to break those habits associated with bad listening skills and build new ones. Good listening is essential to building a good community. If all we have is people speaking their opinions, no matter how learned and loud, all we have are individuals uttering sounds. Words spoken without words heard are vibrations. When spoken words are both heard and listened to, they are collegial—they convey meaning and nourish communal life. What follows will help you build the skill of collegial listening.

When conversation is going well, we never think of words, of meaning, of how a person gestures, their facial features, or even who they are. When things are going well, we enter into a zone of collegiality and understanding that may produce laughter, sorrow, joy, and, even hate, since collegiality may have many forms and purposes—good as well as evil. When it is not going well, we find ourselves oozing negative attitudes toward the speaker such as anger, hate, and destructive competitiveness. We find ourselves not hearing what they are saying now but, instead, reacting to what we have heard or we have expected to hear. We find ourselves dismissing the speaker as perhaps a fool, an ignorant lout, or a provocateur. In any case, the speaker is "opposed" to me.

How do we practice collegial listening when we do not like the person and find him offensive in every way? We can listen only if we have reasons to listen and hopes of building a positive attitude toward the person.

This optimism is based upon your conviction that you have the necessary listening skills and that the person you are listening to is as valuable as you are—capable of good, a source of learning, a link to others, or someone who possesses an important story. With such a positive and inclusive attitude, you are prepared to learn how to begin to engage in collegial listening. *Collegial listening is an ability to attend to the whole person: body, mind, and spirit. It demands we be silent and listen to silence; we hear the words the other utters as valuable; we see the actions that a person makes as conveyers of meaning; we honor the thoughts he expresses as sacred to him. It demands we honor his ideas as well as his feelings.* Such an attitude, and the skills that accompany it, are always essential to a happy and successful life. We should already be practicing collegial listening with friends and family. If we are not, then we should change our attitude and learn new skills. If we are, what follows may still be a way of refining the skills we already have.

I have developed one minute drills to enable you to slowly build new or review old skills. The nature of building any skill is that you are replacing old habits with new ones. This is difficult, but if you have the proper attitude it can be done. Also, the nature of building a skill is to learn a little at a time. If you are able to learn the skill offered in each of these One Minute Collegial Listening Drills (OMCLDs), you will then be able to build each of them into a solid collegial listening approach for dealing with advocacy of religions in the schools. A summary is provided at the end of the description.

ONE MINUTE COLLEGIAL LISTENING DRILLS

Preparations for all the drills:

- Choose a timer that will make a sound at your chosen time
- Choose a place that is comfortable but not restful, away from as many distractions as possible.
- Choose a time that provides you with an atmosphere of concentration.
- Determine your response to distractions. Some suggestions are provided below.

OMCLD for Breathing

Listening to your breath

This is a foundational skill for all that follows. At the same time, the continued nuanced skill of breathing can be the foundation for many forms of stress control, meditation, and yoga. Here we are limited to developing something we do every day into an effective tool for community building.

When we breathe, our chest rises, our diaphragm rises, or both rise. We will call each of these a breath: chest, diaphragm, and whole body. We also breathe through our nose or mouth. We suggest that you always breathe through your nose for what follows, and vary your initial minutes to first chest breathing and then diaphragm breathing.

Listen with your whole self: mind and body; body and mind. This "wholistic" listening emphasizes something every good conversationalist is aware of and all mystics know—our body influences our mind and our mind influences our body. Listening for sounds is hearing only part of what the person is saying.

Week One

Sit in your chosen place. Set the timer for one minute. Relax, and breathe using chest breathing until the timer sounds. During that time, listen to your breath. Your goal is to hear your breath during this one minute. Remember, this is wholistic hearing. After the alarm sounds, rise and walk to the end of the room. Return. Sit. Set the alarm for one minute. Breathe using your diaphragm for one minute. This exercise should be done for one week, two times each day.

Week Two

This week you will perform the same exercise, breathing now with your whole body. Instead of listening for your breath, listen to the silence. This may be extremely difficult to do. Distractions may be overwhelming. If you find this is so, concentrate on counting the breaths and listening to the silence. For some, this may be the beginning of centering prayer or meditation where you focus not on a number, but on a phrase from some writing that is important to you, or a significant inspirational figure. Our intent is not to lead you to meditative prayer, but to build the skill of listening. This should be done for one week, twice daily.

Week Three

Repeat what you have been doing, except change the timer from one to two minutes. By the end of this week, you may be ready to begin building the next skill—listening to words.

Week Four: OMCLD—Sounds

Once you can hear your breath as well as the silences associated with it, you are ready for listening to sounds. The purpose of this skill is to be able to attend to various sounds as well as words that accompany any conversation. Although you must be able to focus on the speaker, it may be helpful to hear other sounds, even if briefly, before discounting them. They may provide a context for what the person is saying. This practice also enhances your ability to concentrate on one sound in the midst of many. It may be the sound of her chair shifting, his leg shaking, or the music playing. Words, and the contextual sounds, help listen to the whole person.

Sit in your chosen place. Set the timer for one minute. Relax and take whole breaths. As you breathe, listen to the sounds that surround you. How many can you count before the alarm sounds? Do this twice a day for four days.

Pick another place, preferably outside. Find a quiet place. Set the timer for two minutes. Relax and take whole breaths. As you breathe, listen to the sounds that surround you. How many can you count before the alarm sounds? Do this twice a day for three days. If you cannot go outside three consecutive days, do this inside.

Week Five

Repeat sitting either inside or outside for one more week. But now concentrate on one sound: perhaps a bird singing or a car speeding. Next week you will begin to listen to words rather than sounds. You begin by listening to your own words.

Week Six: OMCLD—Your Words

How we speak not only influences others, but the sound of our own voice sometimes sets a pivot around which we listen to others both in its inflection and modulation. To listen to our own speech helps us listen to others. This is a short exercise with the intent of helping you grow aware of how you sound, before going on to review how to listen to another person.

Pick a favorite paragraph you would like to read. It may be a poem, song lyrics, or a passage of something you have read. You will also need an audio copying device of some kind, since you will make a copy each time you read for one minute.

Prepare yourself as previously, and read aloud for one minute breathing rhythmically. Take a two-minute break. Listen to what you have read. Read the same passage again. Listen. Do this twice a day for three days. Are all the readings the same? Repeat, with a different paragraph for the next three days.

Week Seven: OMCLD—Someone's Actions

For this exercise, you will need to have a video of someone you can see and hear talking. Your will need two minutes of video. You will use one minute of the video for three days and another minute for three days. Breathing rhythmically, watch the soundless video for one minute. Write down what you think was being conveyed. Do this again. Repeat the next day, but this time listen to the words. Write down what you think was said. Do this again. The third day, listen to the entire minute exactly as it was recorded. Write your impressions. Compare all your responses. Repeat using another paragraph for the next three days.

Distractions

Distractions move us from our goal, distract us from the present, and prevent us from attending to our past. Certainly we are individuals with an individual identity, but sometimes it seems like we are a coalition of biological, mental, and spiritual communities each pleading for attention. The One Minute Listening Drill may find us feeling a sudden itchy toe, an ache in the neck, or thirsty, or remembering a long-lost friend or something we forgot to do—distracted!

One immediate response to a distraction is to say to yourself, "listen!"—thus acknowledging the distraction and returning to what we were doing. Some have also found it helpful to set a time each day when they would take care of everything that distracted them. That means that during the OMCLD you think, "I'll do it then," knowing there is a time for taking care of distractions.

Do not let distractions discourage you in doing an OMCLD. Distractions are overcome by continuing what you are doing, not by giving in to them. Dealing with distractions is actually part of the drill since they are part of any attempt at collegial listening.

Table 2.2
Overview of OMCLD Drills

Week	One	Two	Three	Four	Five	Six	Seven
Skill Goal	Training yourself to take whole rhythmic breaths	The same	The same	Training yourself to listen to the whole environment	The same	Training yourself to listen to your whole self	Training yourself to attend to another's conversation
Practice	Listening to chest breathing; diaphragm breathing	Listening to whole body breathing	Listening to whole body breathing	Listening to a multiplicity of sounds	Listening to one sound	Listening to one's voice	Listening to the other
Technique	2 times a day. Each time: one-minute rhythmic breathing, listen to chest breathing; next minute to diaphragm breathing.	2 times a day. Each time one-minute wholistic, rhythmic breathing, listening to one's breath; repeat.	The same as week two except you will perform the task for two minutes instead of one.	4 days, twice a day, inside. Rhythmic breathing while counting the sounds you hear. 3 days. Repeat outside.	The same as the previous week except concentrate on the same sound for the entire week.	3 days, 2 times a day. Read and record a favorite paragraph. Breathing rhythmically, read for one minute; listen for one minute. 4 days. Repeat with another paragraph.	2 times each day for one minute each time; breathing rhythmically. One day: without sound, watch, write impressions. Next day: with sound only. Write impressions. Next day: with sight and sound. Write impressions. Repeat with another recording for the next three days.

Goals and Repetition

The purpose of these OMCLDs is to make you aware of the necessary parts of listening to the other. We listen with our whole self to their whole self. This listening takes focus, memory, and responding to be done well. You are listening well when you have a positive attitude toward the other person. You can repeat back what he says. You check every now and then to see if you do understand what he said. You can understand both his words and his body language. When you do ask him if your understanding of what he says is accurate and he says "yes." You know you are not listening when you bring distractions into both your listening and the other person's speaking by jumping to conclusions, allowing the other person's emotions to affect you, interrupt, and argue.

Good breathing is always important, but is especially helpful when under stress. To take whole body breaths before responding in a stressful situation both provides you time to think of the appropriate response, and also places you ready for what happens after that response. Repetition and perhaps extending the minutes of these OMCLDs may be helpful for your advocacy here as elsewhere.

COLLEGIAL LISTENING: A NECESSARY ART TO BUILDING A POLITICAL COMMUNITY IN A PLURALISTIC DEMOCRACY

A pluralistic democracy is one of difference (pluralism) and commonality (democratic process). But it must be more to survive—a sharing of difference, common actions, and sets of values. A community, a school, a nation are not built upon divisions enforced by hateful words and deeds inflicted upon each other, nor by running away from those we ultimately depend on for the basics of life, nor through a sustained boredom that rots the fabric of individual and communal identity. Our community, of which education is one expression, must be built upon collegial conversation in tandem with collegial action. In Chapter 1, we described one type of collegial action, the Religions Advocacy Coalition. Here we saw the legal boundaries within which such an organization must operate. At the same time, the development of listening skills enables us and the RAC to begin dealing with the question of fairness, justice, and education that lie at the heart of the law. At the heart of the law also lies the question of individual sacredness and religious identity that we discuss in the next chapter.

CHAPTER 3

The Individual: Those Who Live on Sacred Ground

ME

I'm important!

I'm valuable!

I'm sacred!

Who am I?

American society holds the individual as central to everything. Such centrality demands every consideration in discussing the religions in our schools because it is each of these stakeholder experiences, expectations, and views of religion that determine the politics associated with acknowledging religion's existence and supporting the necessity to recognize and learn about it. In this chapter, we will look at how one gains a sense of religion, becomes socialized into a religion, matures in a religious atmosphere, and develops sensitivity to listening to religious talk. We look at the entire life cycle because how all of the stakeholders experience religion is vital to the entire school. We begin with what many describe as a religious experience—the experience of the sacred.

THE BEGINNING OF THE RELIGIOUS INDIVIDUAL

A truly awesome event happens to each of us—we are born. This awesome event is followed by many others, each just as important as birth in our development as a human being, and each, in its own way, connected to the development of our individual importance and sacredness. When something is sacred we are afraid of touching it and, at the same time, attracted to touching it—feeling that somehow, if we do touch it, something amazing will happen. When we get up enough courage to actually touch it, walk upon it, or enter into it, we shake in fear, yet feel good because we've done it. We have experienced the sacred. Reflecting on the experience, and deciding whether to try it again, we realize we might have been killed, yet are tempted to do it again. As Rudolf Otto said in *The Idea of the Holy*, it's an experience that is both *mysterium tremendum et facinans* (both frightening and attractive), we feel we're involved with something totally different than we are, that is capable both of destroying us and gifting us with many benefits.[1] Yet we want more.

While not conscious and reflective, the awesomeness of birth is not lost on the one born as he begins to breathe, eat, and defecate. If birth gave him breath, something else seems to care for his eating and defecating.

Gradually, the infant "learns" that certain sounds, touches, and smells produce food; certain sounds, touches, and smells produce comfort; and still other sounds, touches, and smells stimulate nervous systems. If patterns associated with the fundamentals of life develop and become predictable, consciousness develops. But consciousness develops in the midst of, and as a result of, predictable patterns that produce positive feelings of comfort, most of the time. No caregiver is perfect, consequently the baby also experiences moments when the pattern seems broken, when food will not be provided or pain will not be destroyed. Negative feelings are mixed in with the good. This broken pattern sometimes results in a broken baby—death. But most of the time both positive and negative, attraction and repulsion, are mixed into the same awesome expectations. The awesomeness of birth gradually begins to develop into the awesomeness of life and its accompanying fears associated with the powers over food, water, comfort, and love itself. To be with such power—awesome! Some would claim that we are always trying to return to the womb; I would suggest that we are always trying to return to the predictable awesome (*mysterium*) patterns of life that provide us with identity and the ability to say "me."

Many commentators would argue that religion develops because of death. I am suggesting that the core of the religious experience, and thus religion, begins with birth and early development in which the dialectics of fear and attraction, destruction and gifting, and uncertainty and mystery begin. Whether or not a person belongs to what our American culture terms a religion, each of us has experienced the sacred in some way.[2] What we call "religions" build on that primitive experience.

HOW WE LEARN TO BE RELIGIOUS[3]

Religious identity, as all human identity, depends upon the people with whom we live. In a previous chapter, I referred to these people as our niche. They are usually more than that, of course; they are our community, society, or culture. We learn about our feelings, how to talk about them, celebrate them, and norm them in this community.

Community is what happens to a group of people over time. Whenever people live and work together, they form patterns associated with their life

and work. Their words, actions, and relationships become repetitious, patterned, in such a way that words have a common meaning, actions are a
common way of responding to the adventures of life, and the gathering,
directing, and interacting of peoples take on expected routines. These patterns are expressive and formative of foundational attitudes that are necessary to live their lives. These foundational attitudes are those of meaning,
belonging, fairness (purpose/justice), and well-being. Without some sense
of meaning, belonging, purpose, and well-being, our individual and communal life withers. The technical term for describing our entry into this
community is *socialization*.

Religious socialization is most easily understood without paying attention to the meaning of religion. When we specify, by definition, the meaning of the term *religion*, or the specific religious group one is being
socialized into, the description of the socialization process becomes more
complex. An example of this complexity is when a religious group believes
that the afterlife is composed of only those who are members of the group.
Socialization, in regard to that particular group, would necessitate talking
about becoming part of those elite who will live after death. We will leave
the definitions of religion and their consequent complexity upon socialization for later in the chapter. Here, we first describe the essentials of any religious group, then the manner of entry into this group, and finally the
levels of socialization as they occur within a religious group.

Every religious group has a way of speaking about that which is important
to them. We will call this *verbalization*. Every group has a way of doing that
which is important and sacred to them. We will call this *action*. Every group
also has a way of assuring that the words and actions are systematized and
the group itself is organized. We will call this *institutionalization*. These verbalizations may be found in stories handed down from generation to generation, in significant books, songs, and creedal formulas. What is common to
these verbalizations is that they use words to express the religious reality
that enables some sense of the sacred. Action has two major divisions: moral
or ethical behavior and ritual behavior. Every religious group has a way of
indicating what it considers to be right or wrong. Every religious group has a
way of ritualizing birth, marriage, and death, and has regular gatherings
throughout the year. These latter celebrations are usually gatherings of subgroups within the larger group. The institutional element is the organizational structure that assures that the words and actions have a coherent
form or pattern from day to day and from generation to generation.

RELIGIOUS SOCIALIZATION: LEARNING
TO BE RELIGIOUS

Religious socialization is the process through which people learn to
engage more deeply in the verbalizations, actions, and institutions of a

religion. Anyone who becomes a member of a religious group learns how to say the religious words, do the religious actions, and acknowledge the accepted pattern for religious life recognized in its institutionalization. The recognition and description of the actual socialization process will depend on which religious group we are attempting to describe. The socialization process of Baptists would be different than that of Roman Catholics because their concept of membership is different. Baptists believe in adult baptism; Catholics believe in infant baptism. This fundamental difference results in two different ways of describing officially recognized membership in these groups: one becomes a Baptist through a deep experience of Jesus as Lord and Savior recognized in the ceremony of adult baptism; a Catholic becomes a Catholic when faith itself becomes part of their life through infant baptism. A description of the socialization process of a Baptist will see the born-again experience as a significant marker in one's entry into the group; Roman Catholics' socialization process is gradual; conversion is usually described as a lifelong process. The socialization process is well underway by the time one is baptized as an adult in a Baptist church. Socialization usually begins with one's infant baptism in the Catholic Church.

If we put aside membership considerations, we can describe religious socialization based on group development theory. For this description to be accurate, we must take for granted that we are born into a stable family environment. Our religious socialization would take place in the following manner. Early in life, we would learn how to act or behave in the religious manner of our family. We learn basic patterns of behavior. For instance, in church we learn when to stand, sing, and be quiet. We learn the words of the prayer before meals. We learn what to do on significant festive days. Our socialization into our family is socialization into the religion of our family.

We next learn how to feel about what we do. From our parents, our friends, and the people gathered around us we learn what it feels like when we say the words "I am a sinner" or "love your neighbor," or "praise God," or "Amen." When we pray our thanks before a meal we know what it is to feel thankful on this occasion, and we do feel thankful. That feeling we described before using the word *sacred* now begins to have association with food, family, friends, neighbors, and God. Feelings become linked with behaviors. Although commentators generally identify a sense of the sacred as central to religious words, actions, and associations, we must remember that many other feelings are part of the socialization process such as obedience, justice, discipline, hope, power, guilt, mystery, compassion, and the supernatural.

But life is more than doing and feeling. It is also thinking. Socialization into our family's religion means that we gradually have ideas and concepts associated with what we do and feel. We begin to arrange these ideas and abstractions in certain common ways. "God," for instance, becomes more than a sound we say that is associated with a certain feeling; now it becomes an idea we can question, argue about, and clarify.

In the process of thinking and clarifying, we recognize that our religion recognizes certain ideas as correct ideas, and certain behavior as correct behavior. We become socialized into the norms of the group. We accept what we consider to be normal for ourselves and for all those who belong to this religion.

Some individuals are able to make a further entry into religious group life by accepting leadership positions. These positions will require them to be able to adjust the group to changing conditions. They will become accustomed to recognizing the behavior, emotions, ideas, and norms, and projecting new ways for all this to occur. In order to deal with the changes of life, they come to understand various ways the religion may be verbalized, acted, and institutionalized. A successful leader is one who enables the religious group to adjust its socialization process to changing times and therefore continue the traditions of the religion.

Most people are socialized into a religion through the religion of their parents. Some reject the religion of their parents and become part of another religious group. To be fully socialized into the group they will, over time, repeat what we have said previously about socialization.

Conversion is the word that describes one's accepting a religion to be one's own. One can be converted to the religion of one's parents or to another religion. One is socialized into how to convert and what conversion is like. Each religion has a different way in which conversion is expected to happen; for some it is an intellectual experience, for others a deep emotional one; for still others it is a formal acceptance of a way of life. Although the meaning and manner of conversion differ among religions, every religion has a way of recognizing one's acceptance of this religious way of life in contrast to another way of life.

WHAT "RELIGION" ARE WE SOCIALIZED INTO?

The real-world application of what we have described as religious socialization depends on one's definition of religion.[4]

Religion is one of those topics everyone thinks they know a great deal about until they start talking with those with a different understanding of it. Because we live in a culture that has its roots in Christianity, many of us equate religion with Christianity, or at least with some of its principal features. For those with this view, religion will always have to do with a God, a book, commandments, and going to church on Sunday. From this perspective, religious socialization is a process in which one comes to a gradual realization of God and what God has told us to say, do, and expect. If people do not believe in God, they cannot be a member of a religion.

When we examine non-Christian religions we find some that share many of the same roots that Christianity does. Islam and Judaism are two of these. Other religions, however, do not share some of the same presuppositions. Other religions may not have a God, believe the world was created, or that humans enter an eternal individual afterlife when they die. When religion means a group that has verbalizations, actions, and institutions like ours, then those religions that are not like ours are usually called pagan religions, ways of life, or philosophies. Religious socialization would not apply to them.

Most experts in studying religion do not accept such a narrow definition of religion. Some of them look at all the religions of the world and claim that what is common to all of them is an involvement with and recognition of the supernatural. The supernatural, from this perspective, is that which is beyond and not subject to what our senses and ordinary knowledge show us. Religious socialization, then, is an acknowledgment of the roles we should play in the face of this supernatural reality. Certainly this view of religion recognizes many of the religions that existed before the sixteenth century. If one grants this definition of religion, many styles of life that have developed in opposition to supernaturalism would be dismissed as philosophies and ways of life, just as the first definition did of all non-Christian religions. Consequently, other theorists find a need for a broader definition of religion, such as the following: A *religion is a way of life that promises and promotes total change for the good*. Religious socialization is the process by which we share with others the common conviction of such ultimacy.

We are religious, from this perspective, as long as we share verbalizations, actions, and institutions that provide us with a sense of wholeness and a way of understanding our existence. Religion enables us to make sense of personal and universal existence.

The last definition builds upon the fact that each of us has a unique vantage point—a position from which we see and act in this world. This point of view is physical, we take up space; is social, we live with a certain group of people; is emotional, we feel life in a way unique from others; is intellectual, we think and act differently from others. Our socialization into our culture and its various groups provides us with this point of view. Citizens of the United States will see things differently than citizens of Canada or Japan. Their points of view are different because of the culture into which they have been socialized. When this point of view is their only way of understanding and dealing with life—when it becomes the ultimate viewpoint—then it is their religion. Everyone has a point of view and thus everyone is religious.

This broader definition of religion also enables us to understand a pluralistic world where there are many competitors for that ultimacy that seeks our total dedication. It also enables us to evaluate the development of new religions and compare them with the older ones. At the same time, it acknowledges that the various competitors for our limited energies seek to convert us to their way of life and are constantly engaged in a process of attempted socialization and conversion.

In the past, the role of religion was to legitimize the truths, morals, and institutions of a society. The religions that did this, such as Christianity, no longer function in this way in contemporary modern society. The question could be asked, granted the last definition of religion, "what does legitimize our laws, literature, and institutions?" That which legitimizes our culture may be seen as a civil religion.[5] We enter into this religion at birth and are socialized into it along with our socialization into our culture. Our schooling, work, sports, politics, and media are all instruments of that process where we learn the roles to play in this civil religion that shapes our point of view. Nationalism would be when the civil religion provides ultimacy to our point of view.

Social sciences have always had a difficult time with religion. All the social sciences do. Most of the social sciences were born with a fear of the absolute nature of religion and a rejection of religion's claim to provide answers beyond the empirical world of the social sciences. If one takes the religious socialization process seriously, the end result of the process is an entry into a world different than the one we presently see, feel, and touch. For Christianity, "heaven" or "the Kingdom of God" is when one is totally socialized into this community; "nirvana" would be the equivalent for Buddhism; "life, liberty, and the pursuit of happiness" may be seen as an end for American nationalism. The majority of social scientists claim that religion is having less and less influence in the modern world. Because many define religion in the first or second sense, they look around and formulate the questions of their research using these definitions and the instruments of socialization associated with these definitions. Many opinion polls will describe contemporary loss of religion according to their author's highly personalized view of religion. A typical evangelical Protestant concern is weekly church attendance, reading the Bible, effective prayer to God, and belief in some sort of miracle world. Much sociological research dealing with religion is shaped by a very narrow view of what religion is. The typical headline reflecting these polls will usually declare the death of religion.[6] But what actually is happening is that the questions asked were based on one understanding of religion, and it is this type of religion that may or may not be dying.

Secularization is the process whereby a religion loses its legitimizing role in society. Because some social scientists and church leaders accept only the first and second definitions of religion in their discussions, they claim that this is a secular society. The way this is usually reported is that religion is losing its influence over society. The fact is that Christianity, and usually only certain forms of Christianity, are losing influence over society. One's definition of secularization depends upon one's definition of religion. One's discovery of the role of religion in society will depend upon what one sees as tools of socialization of that particular religion. If one begins with the conviction that to talk of religion is to talk of Christianity and to talk of Christianity is to talk of the Bible, then one becomes a Christian only as one becomes socialized into the value of the Bible, its reading, and use for directing one's life. A researcher then will make claims about religion based upon people's socialization into the value and reading of the Bible. If people do not deal with the Bible in this way, then the conclusion will be reached that people are not religious. But verbalization does not have to take place by reading a book, even in Christian religions. It can take place by telling stories about famous individuals (saints) in the religion, by telling stories about one's grandparents and how they were persecuted because they were pacifists, or by singing songs that have been passed down since the beginning of the religion. One must always remember when reading research of religion how the definition of religion will determine both the questions asked and the answers provided. This is especially important when talking about bringing the knowledge of the various religions into the schools. Most of the advocacy and consequent controversies revolve around what are called world religions or at least those that have existed for centuries. Any of what might be called new religions either are not attended to or are not allowed into the schools because they are not recognized as religious. Upon further reflection, it might be seen that they also provide verbalizations, rituals, moral imperatives, and community life founded upon an experience or experiences of the sacred.

DEVELOPING A RELIGIOUS PERSPECTIVE

If socialization is the gradual matching of internal experiences and feelings with our surrounding milieu, that matching happens in a dialogical or developmental process of thinking, engaging with others, and sensing what is right and wrong. Descriptions of this process are usually given in various types of stage theory models. Although I will follow some of these, I would like to emphasize that few things in life move in step-like stages, one following the other and never going back. It is best to see these stages as a set of values and ways of thinking that we gather as we age. They become part of our identity. Sometimes one stage provides a direction for life's choices; at another time, another stage does. A fact of life is that sometimes we act and think like a baby even though we may be 70 years old. We should also recognize that the "final" stage almost invariably reflects the bias of the investigator for what the climax, or final stage, of development should be. What the investigator searches for will reflect her point of view. These theories provide a framework for thought. A quick literature search will provide you with the intense discussion surrounding all these theories. What follows provides a way of looking at the community we deal with in gathering a Religions Review Coalition (RAC), the various stages of development of the stakeholders we are associated with, and, most importantly, how students will view the religions they encounter in their schools at various times in their development.

BEYOND BIRTH: FACING LIFE'S CHALLENGES

We begin life, the psychologist Eric Erikson[7] suggests, with the tensions and challenges between trust and mistrust. If we experience consistent and continuous love in our early years, we will probably become hopeful and mature. We also experience tensions and challenges between autonomy and doubt. If we have opportunities to try out new skills, we will probably develop a mature will because we will not be afraid of acting on our own. The ability to deal with these tensions and challenges at this stage of development enables us to enter into the next stage well prepared to meet its challenges. According to Erikson, this is the same with all subsequent stages.

Later in our childhood, tensions and challenges between initiative and guilt offer us an opportunity to accept life as purposeful. Solving the tensions and challenges between industry and inferiority during our school years allows us to have a sense of competence. If we have been praised for our appropriate actions, we will have this sense of accomplishment.

The resolution of these tensions and challenges gives us a good start in facing the adolescent tensions and challenges between identity and role confusion. An ability to recognize continuity and sameness in our personality in different situations and with different individuals enables us to know who we are without depending consistently upon others for our identity and as guarantors of our actions. We can have a sense of fidelity to self and others as we have a sense of who we are.

Knowing who we are, of course, isn't everything. How we interact with others is also a sign of maturity. A resolution of the tensions and challenges between intimacy and isolation in early adulthood leads to a mature ability to love. Gradually we are able to fuse our identity with another person in such a way that we are able to be intimate with other persons.

Yet love also is not everything. How do we compete with others? An overly competitive and combative relation with others only leads to isolation. How do we face the tensions and challenges between becoming absorbed in ourself and our own goals and being concerned with others? Solving these challenges results in either our being a caring person, one who can reach out and help others for their good and the good of the world, or being a narcissistic individual—one who is only concerned with his own good.

Finally, all of us are faced with the tensions and challenges of giving up hope in the face of suffering, injustice, and incomprehensible death. These tensions and challenges always surround us, but they begin to dominate much of our life in the later years. To be able to face disintegration is to be one who is wise. A mature old person is one who has the ability to look at disintegration in self and world and choose wholeness and life. This is wisdom.

Table 3.1 on the following page summarizes what we have said so far.

Table 3.1
Development of Values and Self Identity

Core Value (What's Important)	Value Conflict	Vision of Self
Hope	trust vs. mistrust	Forming *There is more to life than I experience right now, and I can obtain it.*
Will	autonomy vs. reliance	Beginning recognition in things and others *I want to do it myself.*
Purpose	initiative vs. guilt	Inside/outside (fantasy) *I will do it myself.*
Competence	industry vs. inferiority	Action and friends *I can do it.*
Fidelity	identity vs. role confusion	Ideals *Doing it is part of who I am.*
Love	intimacy vs. isolation	Goals *Here I am. Treat me with care. We can and will do it.*
Care	generativity vs. self-absorption	Relationships *Look at what I/we did. Keep it going.*
Wisdom	integrity vs. despair	Memories *Everything is disintegrating. I'll keep it all together as long as I can.*

Maturity is never made in a moment nor celebrated by a birthday. Maturity is a constant challenge of life—a challenge that is never complete. We are always growing older. How we meet the previously mentioned crises determines our way of life. Each of us may be mature or immature depending upon how we deal with these tensions and challenges.

If we begin life in a situation where we are not loved—where our pleas for warmth, for food, and for cleanliness are not heard regularly—we will probably grow up not trusting our environment. The first stage of Erikson's theory suggests that if we do not experience trust in those first months of life, we will not be able to develop as a maturing person. From a Christian religious perspective, for example, we will have a difficult time accepting a trusting God or living a balanced church life. If we never experience trust and love, we will never know the meaning of the symbols of love and trust. To describe a "loving" God is to describe a reality beyond our experience if we never knew human love. Our religious way is always influenced by the way we are human.

Developmental theory, however, does suggest that we can "make up" or catch up on our development at a later stage. It is possible that during adolescence, for instance, we can struggle through trusting again. All the challenges of past stages of life can be relived and won at another stage of life.

The consequences of understanding developmental theory are many, but certainly one is an ability to understand the all-too-common experience of being bored with our everyday religious life. Some people notice that at times their church is boring. It does not respond to their concerns, or even rejects what they hold dear. It may be that in some of these situations our present developmental needs are in tension with those of the religious community into which we were socialized. A young family, for instance, going to a church where everyone is over 60, cannot expect to share many of the same interests as their coreligionists.

The same can also be said of the mixture of intelligences and life cycle stages represented in every classroom—not only among the students, but also the aids, teachers, and the approaches represented in textbooks and media presentations present there. An essential part of acknowledging and learning about different religions is also the acknowledgment and learning about how others differ from us in understanding and sensitivity to one another. Sometimes this sensitivity is especially difficult for those in our elementary and high schools. We will look at some of these things in the chapter on bullying.

THINKING ABOUT OUR RELIGION: THOUGHT PROCESSES

Emotional and developmental needs are one thing. The same developmental concerns are demonstrated in our intellectual abilities. The following schema (Table 3.2) outlines Piaget's "cognitive" developmental model for childhood development.

If we accept Piaget's approach to human learning, we realize that someone between 7 and 12 can easily have a very difficult time conceptualizing the meaning of many symbols. Then, too, we cannot accept responsibility for our actions until we can foresee the consequences of our actions. In order to accept responsibility, we must be able to think forward and backward. We gradually learn to think forward and backward. Thus, levels of abstraction and causality present different ways of thinking about our values.

Learning and affirming one's own and another religion will reflect the person's cognitive stage. If someone cannot accept responsibility for actions, their view of religious moral imperatives is significantly different from those who do. If one cannot think symbolically, one is caught up in a literal interpretation of one's religious, as well as one's secular, world. We must remember, too, that although stage theorists always place one's physiological age next to a stage, that a birthday is not necessarily an indicator

Table 3.2
Piaget's Model of Cognitive Development[8]

Age (Years)	Period	Developmental Characteristics
0–2	Sensorimotor	Focused on senses and motor abilities; learns objects exist even when not observable and begins to remember and imagine ideas and experiences.
2–7	Preoperational	Development of symbolic thinking and language for understanding of the world.
7–12	Concrete	Applies logical abilities to operational understanding of concrete ideas; organizes and classifies information; manipulates ideas and experiences symbolically; able to think backward and forward; notion of reversibility; can think logically about things experienced.
12+	Formal	Reasons logically about abstract ideas and experiences; can think hypothetically about things never experienced; deductive and inductive reasoning; complexity of knowledge; many answers to questions; interest in ethics, politics, and social sciences.

of one's cognitive development—especially pertaining to religion. Many people have experienced 40-year-olds acting like 14-year-olds.

Some authors have taken Piaget's theories beyond preteen years by seeing cognition as more than a process of logic and critical thinking, but also of constructing affirmation of what is true or false, right or wrong. We will look at this expansion later in the chapter.

WAYS OF RELIGIOUS THINKING

Ronald Goldman, in the style of Piaget, did research with children at various ages of religious development.[9] He discovered that what children say is not necessarily what they mean.

In discussing the story of Jesus's temptation in the desert, Goldman asked one child what Jesus said to the devil. The young child replied that Jesus said that we do not live by bread alone. The author thought this a very educated answer, but decided to push further. "And why is it that we cannot live by bread alone," he asked. "Because we need peanut butter and jelly, also," the child replied.

The mental ability of those who live a particular way of life is significant because we usually convey our faith through our understanding of it. "Understanding" brings into play our ability to conceptualize and think critically as we get to know the mystery of the other.

Piaget's theory suggests many consequences for those who share a way of life. At least two of these consequences are that we will be at different points of conceptualization throughout our lifetime and, secondly, that we will be associated with those who think differently about our religion throughout our lifetime. This leads to a need to share the various conceptualizations of our religion in order to have a broader idea of what it is. We should also realize that "unity" within a religion means just that—a common acceptance of the symbols that make up the religion, not a unity in how these symbols are understood. There can be, therefore, one lifestyle, an agreement on what symbols and values constitute that lifestyle, but many ways of understanding the lifestyle, symbols, and values.

DOING WHAT I THINK IS RIGHT

Over the years I have noticed that some people have great difficulty in distinguishing between what is legal and what is moral, and what is the law of social and religious organizations and how they should act as a consequence of their own system of values. The following story may help you discover your approach to law and morality.

Helen's mother was very ill. The doctors indicated that she would die in the next few weeks. Helen had been caring for her for the last week when, quite to her surprise, she called her to her bedroom. "There," she said, "There, beneath the sheets in the drawer. There's a bag. Take it. It's yours."

"But what is it mother?" Helen asked.

"Those old coins your brother collected when he was young. He gave them to me a long while ago. Take them. Give them to your children for their education."

Helen paused. She could use the money. But it was her brother's money. Yet no one would know. What *should* she do? What *would* you do? *Why* would you do it?

A review of the results of recent investigations dealing with ethical decision making such as Helen's should help clarify our choice in the story. These are not normative descriptions of actions, for example, their application to the Ten Commandments, but rather descriptions of people's motivations for action and why they think this is the right thing to do.

One of the principal researchers in this field was Lawrence Kohlberg.[10] He suggested that we should look at the reasons why we think an action is wrong rather than at our behavior or talk about what is right and wrong. To know a person's reasons for action is to know the direction of their way of life. For example, upon observing a child named Billy, we notice that he never does anything unless it makes him feel good. We suspect that Billy does things only for pleasure. That is his way. Let us look at some of the other reasons why people see some acts as good and others as bad.

WHO OR WHAT DETERMINES WHAT IS RIGHT?

The first way is what Kohlberg calls *pre-conventional*. Here the concern is for ourself as the center of action. There is generally a lack of identity with anyone beyond ourself. There is no feeling of identity with society or with a group. To move out of this type of egoism, we must be able to put ourself in the place of another. To be a part of society, we must understand that rules have a purpose. Those who act in a pre-conventional way do so because they are afraid of punishment. Reward and punishment are the basic motivators for their actions. Everything is viewed in terms of what makes them feel good or will hurt them. A good action, from this perspective, is that which gives us pleasure. Fairness is more a sense of "you scratch my back and I'll scratch yours."

Another way is the *conventional*. Here we see that meeting the expectations of our family, group, or nation is perceived as valuable in its own right regardless of immediate and obvious consequences. Here the attitude is not only one of conformity to the social order and to others' expectations of us, but of loyalty to it, of actively maintaining, supporting, and satisfying the order, and of identifying with the persons or group involved in it. To do something good, in this instance, is to do that which pleases, helps, or is approved by others. We do it because we want others to think well of us. Right behavior is doing one's duty and showing respect for authority. We must be able to think abstractly to act upon these motivations. To appreciate the existence of a group requires an ability to think in an abstract way and to be able to see ourself as a member of a group. We realize that an ordered society and membership in this society demands that we give up immediate pleasures for social order and security.

The *post-conventional* approach to moral action makes a clear effort to define moral values and principles that have validity and application apart from the groups or persons holding these principles. Here we see ourself as good if we act independently of our own egocentrism and the society in which we live. "Good" transcends ourself and society. Both society and ourselves, as members of society, must match our behavior to that which is beyond us. The "beyond" may be, for example, a set of rational principles, or a set of norms implicit in all human action. It is upon these transcendent principles or norms that we base our actions.

People, obviously, have various reasons and motivations for doing good. They may act for immediate pleasure or pain, to meet the expectations of others, or to adhere to principles. We see, in other words, that there may be one way of acting, but many reasons for us to act the way we do.

A brief summary can be seen by asking why someone should go to church on Sunday, granted, of course, that they are Christian. Your answer shows you where you are in Kohlberg's developmental theory.

I go because someone will punish me or I'll go to hell.
I go because God or someone will be good to me.
I go because everyone goes.
I go because it is my duty.
I go because a person should recognize his or her relationship to God.
I go because this is the best expression of love to God and neighbor.

IT'S ALL RELATIVE: TRUTH, RIGHT, AND RELIGION

A great deal of writing, many times under the heading "Spiritual Development," occurred toward the end of the twentieth and the beginning of the twenty-first centuries, which expanded Kohlberg and Piaget. This writing was in response to many deep changes in the culture, especially the experience of school counselors in secondary and postsecondary education who reported a significant increase of students searching for meaning and purpose in life. Most of these writings used William Perry as a jumping-off point for their reflections. The first stage, dualism, is usually understood to occur in late teens.

Intellectual Development and Core Values (W. Perry)[11]

1. Dualism

What is important and true are given to us by authorities who know more about these things than we do. Our task is to make them part of us. They teach us these things because they are true and, consequently, we should expect no conflicts. *The teacher knows what's correct. I'll learn it and use it.*

2. Multiplicity

There are a plurality of values and truths, but there seem to be no established criteria for evaluating them, or for establishing that a certain set is better/more appropriate than another. The critical reasoning we apply to these things seems to provide only limited sense that there are solid norms for anything. *Teacher's don't know what they are talking about. They constantly contradict each other. I'll tell them what they want to hear, but I'll never use that stuff.*

3. Relativism

There is no right way of living because everything is relative to the context and people who are living them. We live in a confusing world with little mutual support for the way of life we were taught and value. I live my way. You live your way. That's it! It seems that the best way to live with others is to accept everything as relative. *Nothing is certain. It's all opinion. Their word is as good as mine. I'll give them what they want to pass the test.*

4. Commitment in relativism (no cheap relativism)

Indeed there are many systems of values, but some are more appropriate than others; some provide a better way of life than others in specific situations. We must strive to discover these for ourselves and those with whom we live. We must discover, strive for, and build common truths and values to enable us to live together in difference. *It seems that things may not be absolutely certain always and everywhere. But some things are and I have to base my life on these. If a teacher can show me why something is true and I understand it, especially compared to other claims, I'll do it.*

Once again we see various levels of development. Certainly there will be a tension between those in the community who see the reason for accepting law as punishment and others who see law as love, as there are those who claim absolute truth and relativity in thinking. But notice that this is not only an argument about religion, but also an argument as to whether there are developmental stages of thinking and feeling. Is one argument "better" than the other? The answer to that question is too easily found by those who argue that all the developmental theories presented so far are normative for individual growth rather than descriptive of it. Authorities disagree over whether the last developmental stage of Erikson, Piaget, Kohlberg, or Perry should be thought of as "best." We do not have to get into the argument here. If we accept developmental theory as describing the different ways people change, we realize that every religious way of life is made up of many individuals at various stages of living their changing life. We should not presuppose that an ecclesiastical position or a certain number of birthdays necessarily includes emotional, conceptual, or ethical maturity.

WHAT IS RELIGIOUS IDENTITY?

We have been talking about "identity" since Erikson's time, and the creation of "teens" as a separate part of the life cycle, and, more importantly, an identifiable age group with money. Our identity is basically our ability to remember the past, be aware of the present, and have hopes for the future. It is when the answer to the question, "Who am I?" is a consciousness that affirms that past, present, and hope as "me." Religious identity, much like the questions of religion as a research category, depends upon one's understanding of what "religion" is.

I would suggest three levels of religious identity: (a) that into which we are initially socialized; (b) that which we become aware of through our experiences (often through the media and education; and (c) that which we awaken to at certain moments throughout our life. This last level may be called "spirituality." All three of these provide a means for us to identify our religion.

We have already described how one enters into this first level of religious identity. For most Americans, this is an initiation into some form of Christianity, a form that has left symbols of its presence in the arrangement of the week, holidays, literature, music, language, and everything else that constitutes American culture. Words such as *God, Bible, Jesus, sin, heaven, commandments, Sunday, Christmas,* and *Easter* are all symbols marking our socialization process, if we think we know what they refer to. Our awareness of their deep meaning and how they norm our life indicates how well we have been socialized into our religion—if we are Christian. Other religions will socialize their members, but, as part of that socialization, there is always the awareness of the American form of Christianity to which they are "other." Even if one is socialized into being a nonbeliever, that *non* is in relationship to the views of belief that are part of the socialization process. Most of the time when we talk about religion this first level of identity is present either explicitly—this is what we mean by "religion"—or implicitly—it forms the norm by which we try to understand other "religions." In either instance, this is "my" religion.

The second level of religious identity usually occurs when one mixes with other religions either by watching television, reading, or meeting people outside our niche. In a heterogeneous society, this may happen at any time; many times it happens when we go to school, engage in sports, or some other pastime. These are those historical ways of life titled "religion" in normative cultural texts such as encyclopedias, dictionaries, and Library of Congress cataloguing. Some call them world religions. In everyday life, it's what may characterize the uniqueness of other people we meet.

I once had a long conversation with an older Italian immigrant. He said he discovered he was an Italian only when people in the United States started saying he was. Until then, he was Neapolitan. A similar occurrence was seeing the speechless shock and amazement on the face of a young lady from the Deep South when a Canadian, in all innocence, upon meeting her proclaimed, "She's a real Yankee!" She was born and raised in the Deep South and spoke pure Southern. In both instances, they discovered that their personal way of identifying themselves was not the way the rest of the world did. In religious identity it is moving from "my" religion to "our" religion, or, from the perspective of the listener, from listening to "my" religion to listening to "their" religion.

The third, and last, level is the "spiritual." It is the awakening to the sacred experience of those first minutes, days, months, and years after birth. It is awareness that "I" am unique, important, valuable, dependent upon others, and capable of dying—that deep feeling of being balanced on the edge of nothingness and everythingness, that resonates through many symbols of language, action, nature, and artifacts, that leads us to seek a deepening of authentic religious ties as we seek meaning and fulfillment in our lives. Because of our socialization process and the formal descriptions of religion, we expect that religions are where we find this sacredness. We may or may not discover this in our birth religion. If we do not, the search for a sacred locus continues. In a religious conversation we may also be listening for the spiritual.

When we meet, discuss, and advocate for religions in our schools, all three of these levels are operative. Listening for each one helps facilitate a productive conversation.

LISTENING TO THESE RELIGIOUS IDENTITIES

A gathering of people reflects their unique identities. When a school's stakeholders gather to discuss the diversity of religions, it helps to remember that not only are you talking about religions but also about religious people. Those present, as well as not present, each has a story to be heard and to be told. Listening to that story is essential to learning about another religion. But it is not everything.

The religious other is sometimes like a mirror—reflecting to the observer or listener the religion he is socialized into and/or the stereotypical U.S. religion. To break the mirror, to encounter the person, one must perfect and practice the listening skills offered in the last chapter. But knowing a religious other (first identity) is not the same as knowing the particular religion. As we have also said, before each religion is a way of life that promises and promotes total change for the good. We need those intellectual skills necessary for dealing with large social structures, abstract ideas, and universal norms to begin to understand the religion that shapes the identity of a person, a village, or a culture.

Religious listening, in this instance (second level of identity), is attending to the individual's and community's way of life without judgment as to truth or falsity, good or bad, or superstition or sacrament that have provided people religious direction throughout the centuries. Although our personal feelings may be those associated with our socialization process or recent spiritual awareness, we must focus on the sacrality of this person's religion plus their religious words, actions, and sense of community, how it all fits together in an objective manner. Many times this listening "about" religion will be the principal focus for all stakeholders, especially the students. We should note, however, that such disciplined ability to see others and their religion in an objective manner is a learned skill and reflective of being at certain stages of development. But it must be learned not only to know others, but to know one's self.

Religious listening in the last spiritual level is listening to discover this individual's spirituality and yearning to change the self and the world for the better as evidenced in their way of life. It may be a way of hearing the resonances of the beginning of all spiritualities or how that person's religion expresses their spirituality. The skill here is that not only of a reflective listener, but also of one in tune with spiritual experiences as they occur at different times and circumstances throughout the life cycle.

A PARENT'S RELIGIOUS IDENTITY AND THE SACRED CHILD

When a teacher confronts a student's tantrum, a mother struggles to comfort her three infants crying in the middle of the night, and a baseball coach of six-year-olds explains to his two outfielders that they should stop picking flowers and start playing, it may be hard to experience these children as sacred—someone who is both frightening and attractive; capable of destroying us and gifting us. Yet to parents, especially those parents socialized into and accepting of a formal religious way of life, the children are sacred. Forgetting this while advocating for the recognition of diversity of religions in our public schools may lead to serious conflict.

The sacred pattern-making that began at birth continues throughout life. Gradually these patterns become entwined with those of other people. Significant others, especially one's children, play a special part in such entwining. The newly born infant held in the palms of our hands, the three-year-old held close after a fall from a bike, the parent's sudden eruption of joy as the young teen scores a goal—all become part of the developing patterns of the sacred for both the parent and the child. Those patterns of life that develop as the source of the sacred as we age easily become materialized in the child himself.

To those formally socialized into a classical religious way of life, parenting is part of that socialization process. This formal sacralization of life becomes part of the more informal processes mentioned previously. One's formal and informal religious ways of life are integral to personal identity. The growing child's religious development becomes a living mirror of the parent's religious world. For the parents it is so easy to look into that mirror and see their own religious development rather than that of the child. Common family life many times hides the unique development of each of the family members. So much "seems" the same. In those mutual exchanges of the sacred, and the religious world they encompass, both the adult and the child are subject to the inherent tensions that are part of the world they are creating. For those adults who attempt to realize the meaningfulness of their religious world through their children, these tensions may be especially fearful and sometimes exaggerated. The adult, who has lived with these tensions and strengthened her religious bonds over the years, knows the possibility of breaking these bonds. She may have broken them at one time. She may have seen her peers leave their religious way of life and been tempted to do the same herself. But she has not. Now she sees that her child is experiencing the same tensions. To feel the possibility of one's sacred world, which now includes the child, collapsing, is itself fearful and painful. To feel the possibility of the child's religious world being destroyed is even more so. To avoid this dangerous possibility for self and child is a natural response of every parent.

When the curious child takes home bits and pieces of another sacred world in thought, imagination, or actual artifact, the pattern of sacrality building between parent and child is challenged. "Others" experience the sacred different than we do. As is often said in our dominantly Christian culture, "They don't believe in God" or "They don't worship God like we do." Teaching about religion is never as objective and unemotional as it may seem to those who advocate it. The mere fact that this child is learning about another religion and its manifestations of the sacred offers the possibility of desecration of that personal sacred identity nourished by her parents and their religious way of life. It scares them that this "sacred-to-someone-else" may become sacred to their child. Their child will lose his innocence. Their child will no longer reflect the values that they, the parents, have struggled to sustain—so many possibilities of hurt in an idea, a video, a song, a picture of a foreign god. It is unlikely that such desecration will occur. Usually it is just the opposite. But the "possible" hurt may lead some parents to strenuously object to bringing other religions into the school. Unaware that they already exist, many times within their own religious way of life, they fear what will happen.[12] The following chapters will deal with many of the responses of these fearful parents. But we cannot forget a possible cause of their responses— the desecration of a sacred child. Desecration many times leads to awful consequences when a sacred flag, building, person, idea, time of year, sports team, music, political, or economic ideology are threatened. Change always brings the threat of desecration and the options of new patterns of sacralization. A human being is always growing up. Sometimes we forget that.

RELIGIOUS IDENTITY AND THE SACRED INSTITUTION

The pattern making that results, for many parents, in an intimate relationship with their child also expresses and provides that sense of togetherness and belonging that is essential for community. Our identity is very much dependent upon those who provided and provide this sense of community. Before our modern way of life, when we lived in a small isolated village or island, there was one community that provided this fellow-feeling experience. We have seen that this experience is very much tied in with our developing sense of the sacred. In the premodern situation, this development was spread throughout the entire community within which the religious institution played an important part. This is not so today for us or the religious institutions. In a pluralistic society the religious institutions are viewed as the sole possessors of the sacred as it is experienced in word, action, and communal gatherings.

Today we are very much aware that not one of us has exactly the same identity as someone else. We find ourselves living in many communities at the same time. Consequently, the clear identity of both individual and community may be difficult to discern.[13] Those of us who grow up in a pluralistic society take this for granted and pay little attention to our multiple identities as we move from community to community.[14] Institutions that span the centuries, such as the classical forms of religion, are not so fortunate. Most of the sacred words, actions, and institutional forms that are currently part of their tradition developed while they were a state religion—everyone did and said these sacred words and actions; everyone had a sense of togetherness when they did and said these things. The religious institution's identity, much like the individual's, is constituted by its patterns of sacred words and actions. In the modern world, however, individuals have pretty much adapted to the movement in and out of various communities. They know how to speak and act in the various communities they are part of. Many religious institutions have not adapted to the variety of communities, especially to other religious communities, in our modern world. They are ill at ease at how to deal with them and what is expected in their interaction with them. This is many times witnessed when possibilities of mixing together with other institutions in common sacred word (e.g., prayer), common action (e.g., sexual matters), and common communal gathering (e.g., use of the same building) present themselves. A sensitivity to the, sometimes subconscious, unease of these religious institutions is necessary for those advocating for recognizing religions in our public schools.[15]

If the identity of the classical forms of religion is challenged by a pluralistic democracy, so is the identity of those religions that have grown to maturity in American culture. A business mentality based on free market and competition guides many American decisions. Just as the classical forms of religion matured as established religions in their native lands, so some Christian religions have grown up in the business culture of the United States. Just as the classical forms of religion adapted their original words and actions to a state-supported religion, so these Christian groups adapted many of their words and actions to an American culture. *Evangelization* is one of those actions and words that evolved from its ancient roots to become, in the U.S. situation, "get out there and sell your religion." This sense of aggressive evangelization has become part of many American Christian religions' identities. They, too, are ill at ease in what to do in a pluralistic culture. Much like the classical forms of religion, they are discovering what to do when their sacred words and actions are expected to commingle in the public events. As with the classical forms of religion, great sensitivity and political acumen is necessary to deal with them.

It can be expected that the threats to institutional and personal religious identity will result in tensions among community members especially when it comes to the public school and its role in learning about the religions of our nation and our world. Some will reject the image of their religion as equal to all others because they do not recognize such equality—thus they demand reasons for their superiority be given in the school itself and/or the curricula. Others also convinced of their superiority and socialized into the aggressive sales processes inherent to their religion, demand that these processes be allowed in the school as well as the curriculum. The processes as well as the purpose of evangelization are seen as inherent to the religion. To portray it otherwise is to be inaccurate in the presentation. Conflict will be the theme of Chapter 5. But before moving on, let's talk a little about the institutional spokespersons and then about the stakeholders.

SPOKESPERSONS, CLERGY, THE SACRED, AND SCHOOLS

The spokespersons for these institutional religions are the result of a long socialization process in which their identity and the identity of the institution are fused in such a way that they identify themselves with the institution and we, many times, do the same. We must remember that every religious institution contains the variety of thoughts, feelings, and adherence to its ideals as we described at the beginning of this chapter. It also contains some leaders who sustain their power by looking backward and others by adaptation to the present and possible futures. Some of these will advocate for religious diversity in our schools, and others, not. A RAC must be able to enlist the aid of those who favor its goals while respecting those who do not. Many spokespersons for religious institutions are also clergy. Within each institution the clergy hold a special place and role in that religion. The pressure of the American religious atmosphere has made many of them take the role of preacher and/or spokesperson even though this may not be part of their ancient tradition. In any case, the clergy are special people. Many times when we have been socialized into a certain way of feeling and acting toward a clergyperson of our own religion, we tend to project onto one from another religion our personal expectations and feelings. Many American Christians, particularly Catholics, see their clergy as having a special relationship to God, thus clothing them with a tinge of sacrality. It is also to be expected that when clergy have been socialized into thinking they are God's messengers, they would have a difficult time not being treated as such by those who never think of the clergy in such a way. This role confusion can be difficult for all concerned.

The spokespersons for the religion and the various religious clergy are important parts of an advocacy program. A RAC must make a concerted effort to enlist their aid in any attempt to advocate for religions in the schools. At the same time, remember that if some people in the religion would be opposed to such activities, there are others who would not be. The challenge is to find those who share your advocacy of diverse religions in the schools.

THE STAKEHOLDERS: THE CHALLENGE OF THE ONE AND THE MANY

Every society faces the tension between the individual and the communal good, the rights of the majority and the minority, and the values of the majority and of the individual. Some individuals easily find room for their spirituality within a religion; others spend their entire lives seeking a match. What both separates and unites us in these continual tensions is the fact that every individual is also part of a community of some sort: each "I" is always part of a "we."

Advocacy for religious diversity participates in, and sometimes intensifies, both these tensions and the necessary choices associated with them. We cannot escape the choice or the tension. Instead, we must acknowledge and engage this tension in order to foster the growth of ourself and our community. Subsequent chapters will reflect upon the ideas and practices associated with community, conflict, and teaching about religions in order to foster this growth. Let us first look at community and then at the necessary conflicts associated with this growth.

CHAPTER 4

The Community: Live and Grow Together, or Survive Apart?

Have you ever traveled across the United States by car, train, bus, or plane? Over the years, I have been fortunate enough to do so. One of my favorite trips was a train ride going to Los Angeles by way of New York and Chicago. It was not done all at once, but gradually and for various reasons. The gradualness enabled me to see the country and experience its communities.

Three enormous cities and their metropolitan areas marked the beginning, middle, and end of the trip; hundreds of smaller cities and still smaller towns touched the route along the way. It's quite a contrast—the three metropolitan areas continue to grow in population, economy, and creativity; the other cities and towns continue to get smaller. As you look out the window of the train you see old canal towns in upper New York State slowly shrinking into decay, waiting for the tourists to provide an influx of money, while their young flee across the country looking for jobs. The rusting steel plants of Buffalo, New York; Cleveland, Ohio; and Gary, Indiana, are now dark where sparks of melting steel and iron formerly lit the skies. The big cities continue to grow; the small cities and towns continue to decline.

The cause of the decline? Many causes are suggested, but if you look closely, it's because of sameness—the sameness of occupation resulted in sameness of people resulted in sameness of everything and everyone.[1] The lessons of nature are easily forgotten as we claim knowledge and control of it: diversity provides survival; homogeneity guarantees destruction. When we farm only one product with only one type of seed, then one thing will destroy it, be it disease, weather, or insects. If we grow many types of things in different ways, then there will always be something to eat. Nature suggests that diversity increases the probability of survival, and that sameness increases the probability of death. The cities and their metro areas continue to survive because there is great diversity there; small towns continue to shrink because there is not.

But while some major cities' economies and populations increase, most of the schools in our entire country continue to worsen. Edward Fiske's *A Nation at a Loss* (2008), which reflects on how things have gone downhill since *A Nation at Risk* (1983), reminds us of some of the damning statistics. Only 70 percent of students entering high school graduate. The United States ranks sixteenth out of 27 industrialized countries in the proportion of those graduating college. "We are failing to provide nearly one-third of our young people with even the minimal education required to be functioning citizens and workers in a global economy."[2] There are so many more statistics indicating our educational decline over the years. Yet, we repeat the same facts, arguments, and decisions year after year while the decline continues. To reawaken the feelings of helplessness and anger while advocating for dealing with the diversity of religions may seem mystifying. To neglect peoples' religion, however, is symptomatic of a culture that is producing a loss of community, an increase in destructive individualism, and a decrease in mediating social structures—a culture in which many people seem so narcissistic that they never view another person in a positive way. Only complaint, criticism, and derogatory remarks escape their lips. There is no willingness to gather with others to achieve a common objective without obtaining some immediate personal reward. There is no sense of community because community is dependent upon spending time with others for the sake of the common good. No wonder schools are in trouble. Schools reflect their stakeholders who, in turn, reflect those who support the schools. Most of our U.S. schools are global failures because they are failures at being an academic community within a pluralistic democracy. A common, public school is dependent upon what we have in common—a community. Without community, we have no schools.

FINDING AND BUILDING COMMUNITY

This chapter offers several descriptions of how theorists define community. In doing so, you are offered an opportunity to clarify your goals for family, town, and school. In clarifying these goals, you are reminded of the foundational human need to be with others, to belong. This sense of belonging may be found in one's school as well as one's religion. Sometimes severe tension results between these two feelings of belonging.

Central to this tension, and its possible lessening, is our understanding of the role of symbols in individual and communal living. Recognizing how symbols function within religious and school contexts enables us to understand how many people of differing religions can work together within the context of a public, common, school.

It also enables us to recognize varying contexts for how students learn about diverse religious people and their respective religions. Religious dress is used as an example of how these multiple religious perspectives are expressed within an educational setting and may become an opportunity for learning rather than for debilitating controversy. If learning occurs, then one of the values of the school and its stakeholders is affirmed and community is enhanced.

AN IDEAL COMMUNITY: DISTINCTIONS AND CLARIFICATIONS

Discussion about community usually begins with the distinction between community (*gemeinschaft*) and society (*gesellschaft*) made by Ferdinand Tonnies.[3] The distinction is helpful because it forces us to reflect on what we mean and expect when we say, "community." Tonnies suggests that contemporary life finds us in two different types of permanent or quasi-permanent associations: one, such as our family, which is tight knit, affectionate, and loyal (*gemeinschaft*/community); and the other, which is formal, reasonable, and more contractual in nature as to the interchange of effort and affection (*gesellschaft*/society).[4] Understood in this way, "community" is a way of life incapable of being understood in a purely modern sense of competition and narcissistic individualism where it is incomprehensible for a wife or husband to remain with an adulterous spouse, parent to love an ungrateful child, or a Roman Catholic to proclaim church membership while violently disagreeing with papal pronouncements. Tonnies suggests that *gesellschaft* is the expectation in our modern society where people move in and out of relationships and associations dependent upon whether their expectations are being met and their sense of self is substantiated. *Gemeinschaft* fits into a more stable culture of few choices and narrow societal expectations. Theoretically then, every modern society should be *gesellschaft*, yet we find a deep yearning in contemporary industrialized societies for community, *gemeinschaft*, something beyond contracts and shifting associations.[5]

Beneath the shifting associations of *gesellschaft* is the simple human experience of saying, "we." This declaration of "we" indicates some bond with the others to which it refers. It builds upon that first unuttered "we" experienced with one's mother, father, and siblings. This feeling of belonging, as much a part of us as our belly button, reflects our most primitive experience of connectedness. Although, for various reasons, it is not part of everyone's consciousness, the necessity to be part of a "we," to belong, is part of being human. To neglect this reality is to leave ourselves open to easy manipulation by those providing instant community for our quick-paced world.

The sense of "I," "we," and "you" grows together. This sense of community, "we," is especially dependent upon the awareness I both provide and receive from others. This sense of community grows as do the feelings of respect, trust, truth, commitment, interdependency, and shared values (importance of persons, things, and ideas). We live community. When we like and seek to be with certain people, we experience community. Community also exists when we can do things over and over again with another or others whether we are bored or not.

Communities are time bound. The community as a whole and those within it grow, mature, and die. Community is constituted by time. There are some who promise instant community and many times can provide individuals with an overwhelming sense of trust, honesty, and openness among a group of people for a day or several weeks. But this is a fleeting instance of wholeness and belonging; it is a wonderful, brief feeling, but not a community. A community writes a common story composed of various characters whose plot, while headed in a certain direction, goes in many directions because of the individual stories of all of those in it. The story, while being each person's story, is still more than each of them or the sum of all of them. The community affects them as, over time, it creates events and artifacts unique to them. Large communities, over decades and centuries, create impressive cultures that are a source of wonder to all humanity.

Communities are variable. They ebb and flow in their ability to sustain a sense of belonging and life to their members. At the same time, the members vary in their attachment to the community. A great deal of research and discussion about community seems at times based upon a homogeneous community isolated from all others. Discussions about community may give one a sense that it requires a permanency of membership and relationships among its members. In our contemporary society, however, this permanency of community, membership, and individual contribution of total energies to any one community for one's entire life seldom, if ever, occurs. In a pluralistic democracy, there are always many communities present, each vying with the others for total adherence or belonging of both soul and body. While each of these communities may remain vital in providing to its members the characteristics of a community, each individual's contribution to the whole varies as does one's sense of the community of the whole to the individual. On one extreme we find many people bouncing from group to group on the eternal search for a fulfilling community; on the other we find some remaining in a community, which, while destructive to their physical, psychological, social, or economic being, they adhere to for fear of being alone, isolated, and alienated from those they derived so much joy, support, and energy from in the past.

In a pluralistic democracy communities are both homogeneous as well as heterogeneous. Simple examples are found in the diversity of families present in the United States. Stanford University sociologist Michael Rosenfeld calculates that more than 7 percent of America's 59 million married couples in 2005 were biracial.[6] In 1997, Catholic commentators claimed that 25 percent of all marriages sanctioned by the Catholic

Church in the United States and 19 percent in Canada were interfaith.[7] Generational differences have become starker with the advancement of technologies and niche marketing. Works describing these differences highlight how people with different images of work, leadership, family, and authority can not only work together, but live together in the same house.[8] Many may even have the experience of family homogeneity and political heterogeneity. These family experiences demonstrate that we may have the commonality of family ties paired with the heterogeneity of values, dress, politics, gender, and so much else. Mature families, as mature communities, foster growth, stimulate creativity, and provide a deep sense of belonging through sharing foundational values while supporting diverse expressions of those values. Values, from this perspective, are those people, things, ideas, and ways of life that are important. Importance is demonstrated by the way we spend our time and money. If we do not do it, it is not important. If it is not important, it is not a value. It is possible to make community if we discover our commonalities in the midst of our differences. Certainly mutual respect and trust are important for people to live and work together for their children's education.

There is always that reality seen along the railroad tracks—small town and city sameness and disintegration; metropolitan growth and diversity seeking a common will. And, in all these instances, our schools, are an essential instrument in finding a sense of belonging by providing and receiving respect, trust, truth, commitment, interdependence, and mutual values. The questions here are: What type of community or communities constitute the foundation of our schools? What values do they share? Are our stakeholders representatives of these communities? Who seeks and/or sustains the communal nature of the school? What follows seeks to answer these questions.

THE SCHOOL AS COMMUNITY

There are many types of belonging. Community is one of them. Although many stakeholders, especially principals, teachers, and staff, may claim to have a school community, but a school community as I have been describing it may not exist. Most of our towns, cities, and school districts, to return to Tonnies's distinctions, may reflect the necessary modernism of our culture that functions best as a contractual type of belonging (*gesellschaft*) rather than community as we have been idealizing it. After all, *gesellschaft* is the world we live in—work for pay, play to win, and go to school to make money. This is the world of "if you do this" then "I will do that," a world of contracts both written and implied. Becoming a "professional" is a goal, a role, and an expectation among people working together to reach a goal. Most stakeholders expect everyone in the school to be professional, to apply the knowledge and skills of their craft to those in need of those same skills and knowledge. They expect them to do that based on the objective nature of the situation, not their feelings—to grade and interact with students based on what they do, what they earn. Everyone in the institution is to keep the rules and the rules, once kept, will bring the educational institution to its designed goal.

Indeed, such professionally run schools do achieve a great deal. If run by well-trained and up-to-date people, they provide their students with an education that will enable them to achieve a great deal. Yet, as many commentators would suggest, they can be better; they can enable their students to not only excel at test taking, but also excel at life living. To have them function as a school community within a school district will enable them to excel at both tests and life. For it is the quality of relationships in general and caring relationships in particular that determines the quality of the school and of life.[9]

Nel Noddings, in her book *The Challenge to Care in Schools*, says that within the context of community, four things are necessary to build a caring school: (a) students should stay in a school building long enough to acquire a sense of belonging; (b) the teachers and staff should stay with the students for at least two to three years; (c) the curriculum is such that everyone's abilities are recognized and respected; and (d) students are accepted for who they are not for what they can do.[10]

What is the communal nature of a school? It is when all the stakeholders have a sense that this is *our* school. This school community provides us with a sense of common caring, purpose, and concern for one another. Among these people there exists mutual respect, trust, truth, commitment, interdependence, and sharing important values in a safe environment. It is demonstrated by caring for the halls, the restrooms, classrooms, offices, and other places in the school. It is shown by students helping students, teachers helping teachers, and administrators helping administrators—everyone aiding everyone according to need and ability. It is demonstrated by good grades, creative challenging ideas, and successful whole-school activities. It's felt. It's seen. Community is us.

For ten years I held focus groups, investigated, interviewed, visited, and dug into central and school archives of the Roman Catholic Diocese of Rochester, New York. After awhile, I knew when a school was a community. It happened in many of the ways I have already mentioned, but it was always felt as the principal, without prompting, rose from her desk and proudly asked, "Do you want to see *our* school?" And, then, she showed me the students, the teachers, and what they were doing. If there was one repeated complaint from all these principals, it was their pain-filled utterance that because of paperwork, they did not have as much contact with the students as they wished.

Among the many things I also learned during those years was how a school building evolved. Seven of the schools in the city of Rochester were very old. They were so old that as the principals showed me around the building, they were able to point out additions to the original building: a gym here, a cafeteria there, space set aside for computers and Internet access, and modifications for the safety and protection of students, teachers, administrators, and staff. These buildings were living testaments to cultural trends and mandates over the years. At the same time they gave witness by their actual size and expense as to their relation to the original classrooms and auditorium. How easy it can be, because of current trends and expenses, to forget the core mission of our schools: education. The purpose of all these additions was to foster a better education for the students—the same with the school as community. The purpose of engendering the community is education. This must never be forgotten because one of the many dangers of building community is to focus on the well-being of the group over everything and everyone else within or outside the group. We do not want to fall into the trap of sacrificing education for only feeling good toward one another.

RELIGIOUS COMMUNITIES

In a pluralistic democracy there are many means to satisfy the desire to belong. Listening to the same music, wearing the same clothes, and cheering for the same sports team offer a sense of belonging to many. At the same time there are numerous groups that, depending upon our association with them, provide us with a true sense of togetherness (*gemeinschaft*). Perhaps it is our family, a volunteer organization, or a neighborhood watch team. Modern society offers the individual a whole range of opportunities "to belong." How much they satiate this desire depends on a wide range of psychological and social variables.

In modern society a religious group is one of these many opportunities to experience togetherness. It has not always been that way, but today many seek religious membership as a source of intimate community membership.

In the past, for most of the religions, religious activities were only one part of the community's activities. One religion, one community; yes, but also the same community worked the farm, fished, and so many other things. Religion was part of communal life. It was not the sole purpose of the community's life.

In modern life, communities as well as people are specialized. We have people doing various things for pay such as cooking in a restaurant, policing the neighborhoods, or teaching children. These people belong to various other communities such as soccer leagues, Girl Scouts, Catholic churches, and Jewish synagogues. This process of specialization has been occurring over the centuries in the West and, especially in regard to religion, has not even begun in other areas of the world. This specialization, or narrowing of purpose, sometimes is called "secularization" by religious groups, as modern society narrows the purpose and acknowledged role of each religion in a pluralistic society. The particular religion and its clergy no longer provide the central ethical, ritual, and life cycle norms for the society at large as it did when it was an established religion. These norms may be instilled by journalists, philosophers, politicians, celebrities, and business organizations. Both society and religion are in the process of working out this relationship. Tensions in regard to this "working out" abound within the lives of religious individuals and the religious traditions themselves as contemporary religions attempt to bring the values of the past into the present while retaining the authenticity of the religion—for exactly what does a "religious" community do?

Understanding the present and preparing our children for the future is difficult. But certainly one aspect of the future is our present need for pluralism and the implicit and explicit choices inherent in a pluralistic, modern society.[11] If religion is important to people, as evidenced by their membership in religious organizations and the role of religion in individuals' lives, then the question is whether the public school should bring to its stakeholders, and especially the students, an awareness of the diversity of religions in our country and our world. The answer, from our perspective, is that they should be made aware in the most professional way possible.

SYMBOLS: EXPRESS AND MAKE COMMUNITY—RELIGIOUS AND OTHERWISE

The principal way to become conscious of another person, community, or culture is to become sensitive to their central symbols. This may seem easier than it is because many times we think of symbols as signs; however, a *sign* has one meaning, like a stop sign says, "stop," and nothing more. But a *symbol* has many meanings; a *sign* usually is devoid of feelings, a *symbol* is enmeshed in feelings; a *sign* has little connection with a community, communities are built around *symbols*. Just think of some famous symbols: the American flag, the Notre Dame fight song, the Star of David, or a football. People love and hate the American flag. Some will die to express either the love or the hate. Sing the Notre Dame fight song at a bar near the University of Michigan campus, and you take your life in your hands. The Star of David is many times identified with the Jewish state of Israel, but Jews at the time of David would not recognize it while others might not see it as a star at all but, if encircled, recognize it as a pentagram used in occult rituals. It is illegal to catch an Italian football, and its shape is different than an American one. You may also be familiar with the way certain body, hand, or facial gestures mean one thing among some people and another thing among others. Every language is in itself a symbol, and as a composite of letters and words, is a system of symbols.

Each of our lives has its own language and symbols. Think for a moment about certain words that make you feel better, or angry. Perhaps these are words you share with someone close to you or a family member that have a certain meaning to you and to no one else. A song from your teen years may spark memories and stir hope. A certain item, for example, a toy, may have been very significant in your early years, which, if discovered now, would flood you with memories. Many times we keep symbols of someone who has died—a piece of clothing, a photograph, a letter, or a small stone gathered on a seashore while on vacation. Symbols may be easy to recognize or may only be noticed when their appearance or disappearance are felt.

Symbols, of course, vary in their ability to draw people together as well as to stimulate emotions. A national anthem may find most inattentive at a sports event, while providing a deeply felt experience at the funeral of someone who died in a war. A school might easily change the configuration of all its rooms, but never change a small garden next to a side door where many students and teachers sit to talk. Some symbols, in other words, are sacred—they continue over the generations, seldom change, and provide the same experience to those in the community from generation to generation.

Religious symbols are expressive and constitutive of a religious community and, much like a language, take a lifetime to learn and manipulate. More importantly, they also connect their practitioners not only with the community past, present, and future, but also with various types of religious experience. In Judaism, Christianity, and Islam, for example, they are seen many times as expressive of God's revelation to the religious community. So the Tanakh, Bible, and Quran are understood to be in some way God's word(s) to humanity. Worship rituals acknowledge God's presence and power. The ethical commands provide God's norms for a good life and community. Religious rituals are usually centuries old, bringing into the present the experience of previous generations and awakening the community and individuals in the community to that experience in a new way as a child is, for example, circumcised or baptized.

RELIGIOUS SYMBOLS, CONTEXT, AND COMMUNITY

Context determines the symbol's meaning and ability to sustain and/or gather a community together. An endearing word of love at the beginning of a relationship becomes something different when that same relationship has gone sour. An action of religious reverence can become one of defiance at another historical moment as the early Christians found when they refused to offer sacrifices to the gods and medieval English Roman Catholics discovered when the king demanded they stand to receive communion. The word *wiener* disappears from general usage during the American wars with Germany as it becomes the mark of an enemy, to be replaced by hot dog. Many curse words during the mid-twentieth century are part of public discourse in the early twenty-first century. Symbols, particularly religious symbols, need their religious community for the fullness of their meaning. The symbol of communion is significantly different in Protestant, Catholic, and Orthodox Christian churches. No religious symbol is "only" a symbol. People have died over them. What may seem like an insignificant symbol to a nonbeliever may be very significant to a believer. Without belonging to the community, one's understanding of another religion may be limited, but it is not, through the use of imagination, impossible.

THE EDUCATIONAL CONTEXTS OF RELIGIOUS SYMBOLS

An educational context is a state of mind made actual by multiple methods. The state of mind is a desire to learn about ourself and our world. The multiple methods are what we describe as the academic disciplines. Both state of mind and methods come into play throughout the school year and, hopefully, our life. When we learn about our religion among coreligionists, education occurs in one way; whereas when we learn about that same religion among a diversity of believers, education happens another way. While education is happening in both instances, the context makes a difference.

Among coreligionists who believe in God, for example, both teacher and students take for granted that everyone believes in God and that God has shown humans things about the world, its direction, conclusion, and their relation to God. It is within this context that they learn about their religion using history, logic, and ways of reading literature, legal reasoning, music, and other disciplines. Bring just one nonbeliever into the class, and the context changes because now everyone is aware that one person does not see the world the way they do. Explanations may begin to be more detailed. Statements of "fact" may be proclaimed louder, as if loud is true, or, perhaps, constantly couched as items of faith, that is, cannot be questioned, rather than fact, that is, can be proven.

When a religious leader speaks to those not of her religion she must speak in a way different than when she speaks to her coreligionists. Because those of different religions do not have the same symbols as she does, she must take on the symbols of the common community of discourse that embraces both the speaker and the listeners if she is to be understood and, even more, if she wishes to persuade her listeners. A deep theology occurs when a religionist chooses to speak in the language of the listener—to use words, images, and actions of the listener's context must become the avenue of understanding and empathy to the speaker's way of life.[12] Our public schools offer a challenge to a believer, which is not as difficult as if they were speaking in a totally different language, but a challenge nonetheless—to speak in an objective rather than a "believing" manner. The public school context demands one teach as objectively as possible about religion. It can be done with some imagination and training; however, many religions do not take up the challenge because they are so accustomed to speaking in their faith context. If the religion has never provided its own thinkers and communicators an opportunity to wrestle with the difficult task of communication in an objective manner, they have neglected an important tool of modern discourse and retained only those educational methods developed within their religion. This is similar to a company that hopes to sell a product in a foreign land but refuses to learn the country's language and culture.

Into the empty space provided by the religions that are unwilling or unable to communicate in a common language step those trained in religious studies or a subspecialty within a discipline such as sociology, psychology, or history. They deal with a variety of religions and thus must act as nonbelievers in all religions. They have learned the religious symbols and imagined their context such that these specialists many times know more about a religious way of life than those who practice it. What one practices as a result of the socialization process these specialists have learned through long years of linguistic training, reading of official religious texts, and living with members of the religion. Much like anthropologists they have mined the depths of the religious tradition so as to provide those not of that tradition with an understanding of it. It is these people who formulate many of the texts used in the public educational system, from kindergarten through graduate school. Consequently, when religions are described or analyzed in the public school context, the description and analysis is an "objective" one. Or, as the Supreme Court says, the teachers and students are learning "about" religion. Many times, when the religion being analyzed and described is one's own, the objective presentation seems to leave something out. This "something left out" may be because of your ignorance (you do not know your religion as well as you think), the ignorance of the teacher who does not know a fact about the religion or interprets the facts she knows from her personal religious bias, or, the shift of context from private religious community to public school.

In a public school the context for learning about religion changes in many ways, but it especially changes depending on whether the context is one of *gemeinschaft* (community) or *gesellschaft* (society) and "belonging" is the difference. In those schools that are a community, a student, teacher, administrator, or staff member may have a deep sense of belonging to both the school community and the religious community. What happens in this instance, especially for younger students, is a sense that some of the same feelings they have among coreligionists are also found among those not of their religion. Thus, if the feelings are the same, the education is the same; the authority as to the validity of equal presentation, in this instance, is the same. It is a similar "logic" found among those who, when they have a religious experience outside a recognized religion, claim that the two experiences are the same. Or, to put it another way, because I hear (experience) a scream in a dark room there must be someone screaming in a dark room. Or, just because I have a deep experience of togetherness with fellow co-arsonists while making a fire means that making a fire together is like praying together in church, synagogue, mosque, or temple.

Because of the similar experiences, and common false logic, some would say young children should not be exposed to diversity of religions in our public schools. To expose the immature to diverse religions before they have a foundation in their own religion is, according to some parents, undermining parental authority and destroying the religious certitude a child must have before being able to sustain exposure to pernicious relativism. According to this logic, a school of religious diversity is a school of relativism, and relativism is destructive of individual and communal life, which must be founded on the certitude of religious authority.

Certainly we see here that the educational context of religion matters both in how the information is conveyed and, in some instances, the possible communities within which it is conveyed. But there is more at work here than parents being uncomfortable with teaching about religions in our schools and the idealized community these differing views represent. What is present are two different views of education and how to interact with those who differ from us. Each of these views sustains a community, providing it with a coherent sense of meaning, value, and purpose. This results in multiple communities using the same symbols such as books, computers, tests, teachers, and classrooms, but understanding them differently. These two communities are found in the common/public school. If they never deal with their divisions, they opt for a school divided, an issue dealt with in the chapter on leadership. If they do deal with their divisions, they face the challenge of forming a new community with sufficient diversity for growth.

THE EDUCATIONAL CONTEXTS OF EDUCATION

Two theories of teaching and learning are present in contemporary education. These two theories result in differing classrooms, teachers, administrators, statements of best practice, and means of evaluation. There are significant bodies of literature defending both educational perspectives. I think both are needed in providing an excellent education. For our purposes, however, it is easier to reflect on them as contrasting ways of teaching and learning. Although these two contexts of education have their contemporary supporters, their basic paradigms are familiar. If recast into statements by a teacher they would be: "I have the knowledge and skills you need. I'll help you learn the skills and information." The other, "I wonder what we need to do and know in order to solve this problem? Let's figure it out. Let's work the problem."

I Teach; You Learn: Active Teaching, Direct Learning, Direct Instruction

This is the prevailing mode of education in many schools, with its governing pedagogy of lecture and/or demonstration. Research produces the knowledge and skills. These then are conveyed through thoroughly researched pedagogical methods to the students. Every class is highly scripted. Every student is challenged to learn because the presupposition is that everyone can learn if the teacher has the proper methods. You know that the students have learned what was taught when they can replicate the skill or information the teacher conveyed. One of the best motivators for learning is competition among the students. Each student must be seen as an individual learner whose own skills and information will prove, once learned, sufficient to solve any problem. Once the student learns something well, she can apply it in any situation.

We'll Teach and Learn Together: Constructivist Learning, Progressive Education

This is the dominant theory taught in most college and university departments of education. It emphasizes connecting current learning with real-life situations, getting the students actively involved with the problem at hand in order to learn the necessary skills and information to solve it. It holds that the student's current understanding influences how she learns. This mode of understanding must change in order to solve the current problem. In working together with others to solve this problem, the student will slowly change the way he thinks and the skills he practices so the problem may be solved. Teachers facilitate the student's learning, which is usually content and context specific. One of the best motivators of continued student learning is her innate curiosity enabled with the proper knowledge and skills for success. Success is indicated when problems are solved. The answer to four questions help a student reflect on her learning: What do I know? What do I want to know? What have I learned (am learning)? How can I learn more?

RELIGIOUS VIEWS OF THESE EDUCATIONAL CONTEXTS: A CHRISTIAN EXAMPLE

Although it may seem that academic disciplines develop separately from one another, this is not true. The atmosphere of research and discovery pervades a university and seeps into all disciplines. What was described earlier as two views of teaching and learning developed within a context of changing views of truth that also influenced thinkers in many disciplines, including those in Christian theology.[13]

Until recently, the dominant view of truth, teaching, and learning in the major schools of Christian theology was that of the German research universities. Truth was something "out there" that we discovered. The teacher-scholar understood what was discovered in the past, participated in discovering it in the present, and handed both past and present on to one's students. A teacher, therefore, must know the material (truth) and the methods to advance the gathering of this material. A good teacher was one who was able to convey what she or he knew to others so they, in turn, might do the same. Truth and knowledge were, therefore, advanced. A parallel theory of revelation projects God's word "out there" in Bible and/or Church teaching. We were to understand it and pass it on to others. Teaching was preaching . . . with footnotes.

As the years passed, another view of truth began to dominate theological discourse. Truth was not so much a thing separate from the human person, but rather a relationship between people. Critiquing the earlier view, what good are abstract facts (truth) when people are starving, dying, loving, and hating? People *know* the facts and *have* values, but still act contrary to both. Truth, as mentioned before, was like the proverbial fallen tree in the forest. The whole forest had fallen, but we had not heard a thing. Truth, in this second view, is a wholistic and personal relationship. Only when people's lives are affected is truth real, and we have the tree. A good teacher, therefore, enabled the students to link heart, mind, and action such that they both felt and did the truth. If we were not hit by the falling tree, then it didn't fall. God's Word was real and we held it in our hearts to pump the blood of action wherever necessary to build the Kingdom of God. Revelation occurred principally when we helped those in need. Teaching was like leading a protest march.

Finally, truth is not found so much in thinking, doing, or feeling, but in thinking, doing, and feeling *together*. In this conversation between thought, feeling, and activity, we keep the truth alive. Truth is the product of our continued conversation. The trees keep falling as long as we keep listening and looking. The good teacher helps keep the conversation alive. Revelation originates and is held within the community of those dedicated to building God's kingdom. Teaching is like a group of friends who keep in contact with each other over the years by letter, phone, e-mail, and visits. Shared experiences, ideas, and motives result in an ongoing conversation, which enables all those who are conversant to discover and live their lives.

These three views of truth, revelation, and pedagogy each formed their own community and ultimately their own church. Each church community has chosen to survive apart from the other and avoid the painful process of challenge, confrontation, and compromise. The result is obvious to a neutral observer: a religion that symbolizes division and dogmatism.[14] One can only hope that in a nation where more than 78 percent of its citizens belong to one of these churches, there are some of these same citizens who can learn the political skills necessary to live creatively together rather than survive apart.[15]

EDUCATING FOR A FLAT EARTH

Thomas Friedman's book *The World Is Flat: A Brief History of the Twenty-First Century*[16] argues strongly that we are in easy contact with everyone on the globe and that we must interact with everyone to prosper as a nation. To be able to speak objectively and with sensitivity with those who think and believe differently than we do is essential to interacting on this flat earth. Both sensitivity and objectivity can be taught. One of the best situations for learning these skills is in classrooms and schools in which different cultures and religions are honored and learned about. As described next, one example of such learning is the discovery of the variety of religious dress in our world since dress is a symbol expressive and constitutive of a community.

WORKING THE PROBLEM: RELIGIOUS DRESS IN OUR PUBLIC SCHOOLS

Religious dress in our public schools highlights the challenge of community (*gemeinschaft*) and the capability of society (*gesellschaft*) to solve a complex human problem of how to dress in a particular context, that of the public school.

How we dress is important. Everyone knows this and spends time thinking about, buying, and actually dressing appropriately. We have proper dress for the military, a baseball team, a marching band, and formal dances. To not dress appropriately may result in embarrassment, a fine by the NFL, a possible night in jail if we have no dress at all, or death if we wear the wrong colors in a gang's territory. Dressing appropriately is a survival skill.

Religious dress is also important. It marks one off as a leader, a teacher, a member of a religious community. Religious dress, as with all dress, is a symbol. It has many meanings and feelings associated with it whether it is the ceremonial headdress of a Roman Catholic bishop, a yarmulke or kippah for a Jewish man, the robes of a Buddhist Bhikkhuni (nun), or a hijab worn by some Muslim women. Usually the symbol has developed over the centuries. Sometimes its origin is lost in the communal or ethnic past, thus enabling some member of the religion to dress one way while others dress another way.

Dress is important not only for the individual but also for the community. A symbol is always connecting people, ideas, and feelings. As such, dress, as a symbol, connects people together and helps make community—whether it is the community of a sports team, military unit, gang, or religious group. Those types of dress that both reflect one's community and sustain one's identity in the community are generally treated with respect by the members of the community.

A symbol outside its context does not convey the same meaning, communal adhesiveness, and feelings. When the dress is worn by someone not of the community it may be very offensive (Boston Red Sox fan wearing a Yankee jersey), death dealing (American soldier wearing a Nazi uniform in Germany during WWII), or completely empty of its entire original meaning (rosaries and crosses around a rock star's neck).

Dress in our public schools is controversial even when it is not religious. Certainly the way students dress is a symbol of their understanding of why they are in school. Some public schools have reverted to having their students wear uniforms because school uniforms call attention to the educational context of the school and avoid the distraction of the multiple types of dress and their accompanying cacophony of meanings and communities they represent. With the availability of so many different types of dress and the various niches they represent, it would seem religious dress is the least of everyone's worries. Yet this is not true as court cases and challenges attest. Obviously politics has not worked since every school has its dress policy and the courts have their history of cases.

LAW, POLICIES, AND RELIGIOUS DRESS IN OUR PUBLIC SCHOOLS

Our discussions always include all the stakeholders in the public school because we believe that education happens in the entire building and grounds of the schools. Consequently, when we talk about dress we are talking about dress of all the stakeholders, but mostly about administrators, staff, and students. This brings into play not only discussions about education law and policy, but also about workplace law and policy. These must also be part of our investigation into what to do about religious dress in our public schools.

The bottom legal line regarding religious dress in the public schools is that it should be permitted as long as it does not disrupt the educational process.[17] Workplace law reminds us that our initial discussion about the meaning of religion was not wasteful because the courts' understanding of religion in these situations is very broad, very individual, and quite expansive. For example, some tattooing may be considered religious. Most employers are trying to make as many accommodations as possible because it is good for business. From an educational perspective, it is also good for education.[18]

Most schools have a policy regarding dress in general and sometimes as an indicator of the importance of diversity, religious dress in particular. Every school should have a policy on dress because of its symbolic importance, and on religious dress because of not only its symbolic importance, but as being distinguished from ordinary dress.

WORKING THE PROBLEM: WHAT CAN YOU LEARN ABOUT RELIGIOUS DRESS; WHAT CAN I LEARN ABOUT RELIGIOUS DRESS?

All school problems are local with local sensitivities, local stakeholders, and local solutions; however, in today's global environment, education must also be more than just local. It must provide everyone with an opportunity to learn things that will benefit them in the present and the future. Religious pluralism means that everyone's religious dress should be recognized, described, respected, and, possibly, understood. To honor one, we must honor all; to describe one, we must describe all. To respect one faith, we must respect all faiths in a pluralistic society. What follows is offered as a list of key considerations when going about dealing with the issue of religious dress, but these considerations may also be used for any issue associated with religions in the schools.

Let us begin with a possible news report dealing with a student's suspension for bringing a knife into his high school in a suburban neighborhood on the edge of a small Midwestern city. Let us add a coalition member (RAC) as being on the faculty of the high school. While in the faculty lounge, she hears the principal talking about this young boy who, on his first day in school, was caught with a knife. He was described as belonging to some religious sect in India that carries swords as protection. The RAC member, on overhearing the conversation, made a point of contacting the principal to hear what had actually happened. The member is beginning to "work the problem," which requires four necessary steps to be completed effectively: (a) *Doing your homework* by gathering as much information as possible about the situation. The goal here is to provide a detailed description of who is involved and the necessary data to begin to fairly evaluate the situation. Certainly this is a time to practice the listening skills offered in the previous chapter. (b) *Looking it over* takes the description and prioritizes what will be done, why it will be done, and who will do it. (c) *Taking it to work* refers to implementing the plan for dealing with the situation. (d) *Grading it* brings into play the very necessary evaluation of what the RAC did. Before offering a mnemonic for each of these steps, it may be helpful to review slogans that are foundational to a successful job.

Trust the person with sensitivity and the information with professionalism

Every individual must be honored for who they are until proven otherwise. We never know the multitude of layers involved with anything dealing with religion. What at first might seem religious may, with a little investigation, be found to be very personal. The boy's father, in this instance, was a primary care family doctor who had just begun to work in this town. Who knows the ins and outs of how people react to someone with a turban and Indian English accent coming into a town that, perhaps, has lost jobs to India? Everyone must be listened to is part of "doing your homework." At the same time, all the information about the situation must be considered as objectively as possible in order to provide an authentic description of the situation. Part of the information gathering, of course, would be to discover the exact nature of the religious dress the student is wearing. Here it was the *kerpan*, a small, decorated, sheathed sword, which is a symbol in the Sikh religion of the person's struggle over evil.[19]

Honor their uniqueness within the school, the society, and the religious community

Uniqueness here brings to mind the reason for the sensitivity mentioned before, but it also highlights the necessity of not lumping everyone together into categories before it is appropriate for decision making. While each of us is unique, we play different roles in a variety of communities. It is some-times within these roles that we see the common values held by everyone involved in the issue. *Uniqueness* is another word for *difference*. Each of the communities involved in a problem have their goals and their variety of in-ternal and external roles in various other communities. The media, many times, in writing their stories about a situation, forget local differences and force them into some overarching myth played out over and over again in recent or past media stories. Your emphasis upon the local uniqueness of people and/or concerns makes this story unique, this community unique, and thus different from the urge by some to forget those real human beings and their communal lives that will exist after this problem is long forgot-ten. Because we have lost many of the mediating societies that brought us together in the past, we must discover those that bring us together today. There may be many such communities, such as sports, music, work, and the school itself. These, and their combination, are unique to this problem. Concentrate on this uniqueness because it makes this problem this com-munity's challenge to solve. What was unique here was the many returned veterans from the Iraq conflict. They were accustomed to their all-white community. Their recent experiences led them to fear those with unfamil-iar head covers and who speak another language. Their uneasiness, while unrecognized as to its cause, spread among some of the other parents. Then, too, this town was on the edge of a large metropolitan area that had recently undergone violent gang conflicts. When the school principal called a colleague in the city to ask what he would do, the colleague exclaimed, "No way! No weapons in school! Allow one, you allow more." At the same time, the many college-educated parents in professional jobs tended to wel-come the diversity represented by this one young man and the necessary medical care provided by his father. Obviously there were many communities here—unique in their concerns and united, sometimes unknowingly, in many ways still to be discovered.

Move toward political not legal resolution within an educational context

Because we are interested in dealing with people as people and the communities they form, we take every step possible to reach a political solution rather than a legal one. This takes time. This takes talking. This takes a great deal of energy. Every time one problem results in a political solution, the context is built for further political solutions. The first is always the most difficult. The town had recently faced the possibility of total destruction following a spring flood. Because of their hard, exhausting work, they built sufficient defenses against the possible flood and were already planning for the future. Then, too, most of them had supported and funded the search for a local primary care physician. They did have recent community experiences of success. Now they had to deal with another challenge.

What's controversial is important, but what is important may not be your controversy

This is a matter of setting priorities and recognizing that sometimes what everyone is talking about may not be the cause, or network of causes, that has everyone talking. It is easy to get distracted when various media personalities want to write their story devoid of the facts of the problem. Especially in religious matters, the stoking of the fires of controversy occurs with the wood of prejudice and ignorance producing stories of imagination and fiction. What was the focus of controversy here was the knife. Naturally the media, both local and national, chose this as the center of controversy as commentators and experts solved the town's problem in public and filled their streets with news crews.

Yet behind the screen of noise and controversy was a young boy who had recently left his homogeneous community to live in another homogeneous community. Except now he was different than them and they were different than him. There were men and women weary from second and third tours of duty in Iraq. Civil and religious leaders faced one another and the controversy with mixed emotions.

Don't let your wishes get in the way of your necessaries

Throughout the problem-solving process this is a constant temptation. Especially when the team is evaluating what is or has occurred it is easy to lose sight of what is really happening in the light of the RAC's goals and desires. It may be, for example, that after a prolonged period of time a policy and/or legal decision must be reached for the good of all concerned. Politics has failed. But that was not the case here. National attention is always short lived. The streets were silent after a week. The veterans were uneasy but not revengeful—they recognized a lonely child when they saw one. They had recently experienced deep loneliness themselves. Religion and civic leaders, in an unusual demonstration of ignorance, saw this as an education issue. As a consequence, the town established a committee similar to the one found in Chapter 1.

A mnemonic that is helpful in working your way through the necessary steps is offered here as an aid for remembering that each of these considerations is necessary for working the problem at each step of the process. By keeping them in mind you will be assured of giving your time and energy to what is necessary for success—judged as the agreement among all parties that your resolution is a proper one to the problem at hand. Remember the five "P's": People, Principals, Paper, Principles, Possessions in common.

The *people* are the stakeholders in this particular problem. The school *principals* are central to any solution. The *paper* is the sources of information necessary to successfully accomplish the step at hand. This includes people, books, journals, and media of every sort. *Principles* refer to the foundational ideals and ethical rules that guide your RAC in dealing with interreligious issues. *Possessions in common* are those values that will surface as unifiers that will constitute the educational community capable of supporting the diversity of religions in this school within this society. These may be ideas such as freedom of expression or a safe space to express one's religious ideals and ideas. These must constantly be attended to in every step of the process because it is so easy to be sidetracked by problems other than the building of a political community reflecting a pluralistic democracy.

The people in our idealized example were able to step out of the isolation of their base communities to see that their common growth was being challenged. They recognized that if they wished to grow they had to go beyond local resources to get professional medical help. The first step, without knowing it, was a realization that deepened with the veterans' experience of another culture and its religion. The majority of local religious leaders understood that the freedom of this young man and his family in their community and its school was essential to the freedom of their religion in this town and provided a moral argument of fairness for their attempts to bring their religion to other cultures. The vast majority of people opted for growing together rather than living apart. At the same time, they all learned a great deal and grew together in their respective base communities, choosing a positive road for community building rather than the negative one of hatred of the other.

Conflict is inherent at each stage of the process and every part of life. It must be expected in dealing with any attempt to bring further knowledge about individual religions and individual religious people into an educational setting. For this reason, the next chapter is dedicated to reflections about contemporary religious conflict in general and practical steps to resolving it in our schools.

CHAPTER 5

The Conflict: My Sacred Ground, Not Yours

Judaism, Christianity, and Islam claim Jerusalem as a sacred, holy place. Each has conquered it from someone else. Each has ruled undisputed over it. Yet today it takes great concentration and imagination to see the city as belonging to only one of these religions. Since many do not have such concentration and imagination, conflict is always a word or gesture away as these religious people vie to re-create their sacred past by occupying and governing the city. No one has found a solution to this sacred symbol of God's presence. The "solution" offered by many is to repeat the formula of the past for solving conflicts over sacred ground: violence to enforce the will of one of these peoples over the other. No one looks to religious diversity and its consequent pluralism among equals as a solution to this multiplicity of sacred lands.[1]

In contemporary society every land is a Jerusalem. The pace of travel and instantaneous communication enables a culture, and the things it holds sacred, to be trampled underfoot more quickly than in the past. The beat of the hooves of the warhorse has been replaced with the thump of music and the thunder of warplanes, with the whine of pundits proclaiming the advance of new ideological and lifestyle fads. The slow, ponderous pace of change of the last two thousand years now explodes into our lives with the tap of a finger on the power button. Instead of the three religions of Jerusalem seeking the return of their sacred ground, there are the ideologies and religions of the past and the present declaring ownership of the cultural landscape.

It is on this cultural landscape that our schools are built, with various peoples declaring their vision of their sacrality. As we face the future, it is in these cultural Jerusalems that the threat of conflict is always just an offensive word or action away. To advocate for diverse religions in these schools is to embroil ourselves in conflict at both the macro and micro levels. At the macro level, we witness a culture undergoing deep change and the necessity to deal with it in ourselves and our schools. We sense within ourselves the need to cope with this change in order to sustain and develop our identities. Advocacy demands the knowledge and skills to deal with these changes. We will first discuss what is happening at the macro and micro levels and then provide suggestions for dealing with conflict as it arises in the development of a RAC and in striving for diversity of religions in our schools.

CULTURAL CHANGE

A culture is changing when the words, beliefs, rituals, and normative behavior of former generations no longer provide a sense of meaning, belonging, and fairness to current generations. Something serious is happening to a culture when, for example, there is confusion as to relationships between genders and races; a lack of confidence in scientific, political, and religious authorities; and, people's words cannot be understood and/or trusted.

When does a culture turn from one way of interacting with its physical and social environment to another? When are the patterns of words, actions, and communal relationships clearly turned from one culture to another? Looking back over a one thousand-year history we can see two clear patterns of social structure, one called medieval and the other modern.* You can see from this dichotomy that they are two very distinct cultures; what we don't see is what it took them to get there and how muddled the transition period would have appeared (see Table 5.1).

We know that embedded within each culture, and the people who are part of the culture, are remnants of the previous ones found in the languages, music, art, science, religions, and practices of everyday life. As things slowly, in those days, changed from one culture to another, their cultural symbols slowly changed with them. That does not mean there was no conflict—the religious wars are evidence to the contrary—but it does suggest that change happened more slowly in those days than it does today.

The means of communication and education play an important role as a culture moves from one to another culture. In medieval culture, word-of-mouth communication sufficed for providing what was necessary for fulfilling one's role in the society. Education was by imitation and memory. In modern society, communication was through the printed word and

---

*For an excellent discussion of traditional, modern, and postmodern cultures see Ronald Inglehart, *Modernization and Postmodernization: Cultural, Economic, and Political Change in 43 Societies*. (Princeton, NJ: Princeton University Press, 1997). Their continued updating of their world values survey may be found at their Web site. The table that follows is dependent on some of their ideas.

Table 5.1
A Comparison of Two Recent Cultures

	Medieval	Modern
Norm	That which we have done before that resulted in survival	That which is logical, scientifically proven, rational, and results in economic security
Dominant mode of elite reasoning	Deductive and a priori	Inductive and a posteriori with an emphasis upon the method to be used for both modes of reasoning
Work Organization	Farmer (hunter, gatherer) Inherited or "ordained" status	Industry Rational bureaucratic authority
Government Distrust	Feudal The new, the outsider, unbridled reason and analysis	Strong central bureaucracy The old, supernatural norms and experience
Dominant Status	"Religious"—as God-speaker/actor, e.g., pope, king	Scientist (e.g., doctor) as objective discoverer of truth
Core values	Sharing, work, loyalty	Individual accumulation, hard work differentiation, choice, pluralism, relativity, reductionism, empirical (rational), this worldly. It is dominated by instrumental and pragmatic reasoning and usually demeans tradition.
God Threat to status quo	As king Occult: dark and hidden works of the devil	As machine Parapsychology, the "spiritual"
Vision of Universe	The earth in the center surrounded by spheres of perfect circles that are the stepping-stones to heaven, the farthermost sphere. Some retained a biblical view of the universe, with the earth as the center and God in the clouds above the earth. Mountains were a means of touching the heavens and God.	The sun is the center of the universe. Established upon the laws discovered by Kepler and Newton, seen by people like Galileo, the Copernican revolution changed how humans understood themselves in the universe.
Power	Coercive as local or transcendent. The transcendent is available to all, but many times controlled by clergy.	Coercive, usually associated with mechanical; elicitive associated with professional knowledge; leaders.
Religion	Part of everyday life, and its authorities are powerful agents of culture stability.	Separate from everyday life, and its authorities one of many responsible for cultural stability.

education was built around learning to read and write. Without reading and writing one could not advance in modern society. All of this has changed, of course. Today, one can push a button and obtain information through radio, television, and other electronic means. That information is immediate. It must be dealt with immediately. Individual and/or communal existence depends on such quick response. Societal change, therefore, occurs more quickly in contemporary society as communication becomes instantaneous and information gathering demands less preparation.[2] Consequently, the communal response patterns in preparation for a response to the changes will be happening more frequently today than in medieval society where the human psyche and community had more time to absorb the offered change and its consequences.

These response patterns occur in four ways: (a) *accepting* the change as beneficial and needed; (b) rejecting it as hurtful and unneeded, and responding by *fighting* it; (c) rejecting it as hurtful and unneeded and *moving out* of its influence; and (d) something we see more recently as the speed and choices increase exponentially, people react by being *bored* or numb to the change that surrounds them. Let us briefly review in detail these four responses.

Change, of course, has at least two levels: deep change, which is currently happening in American society,[3] and superficial, or faddish, change that is part of daily life in our commercialized world.[4] The two are not necessarily bound together, and sometimes cultures that easily accept a fad a day cannot accept the challenge of deep change, while those lacking all modern ways of life change more quickly. For example, after several generations most Americans have not yet begun to face the consequences of the energy crisis, while many Africans are moving from a hunter-gatherer culture to a computer culture within one generation.

Adapting to deep change takes time even though the change itself may be such that one has no choice but to accept it. An individual may have a sudden change of heart that suggests a new future. But that change of heart must slowly enter the rest of the body. A community may be suddenly destroyed in war (Nagasaki by the atomic bomb) or by nature (Indonesia by a tsunami, New Orleans by a hurricane), but the rebuilding will most likely take years to complete. Of course we must remember that there are the changes that slowly creep into individual and communal life that reverberate in such a way that the consequent change they cause can be either accepted or rejected (e.g., the technology of the automobile, prepared food, or niche marketing).

Adaptation takes place slowly. It begins with an important affirmation such as "I need this." "I/we will survive!" "Running away from it won't help me or us." We need these other words, ideas, actions, or communities. We need these new patterns because they will enable us to survive and, perhaps, improve our lives. This "need," in turn, is usually recognized in the following ways. First, I need these new patterns to exist as equal to what I have and live at present. This minimum in a pluralistic society is called "tolerance," which is an atmosphere that allows culture to grow by itself, alone. But nothing grows alone. Plants need water and air. People need food, intellectual challenges, and recognition. We need others to live. Others are different. Second, I need your differences. Differences allow the survival of the whole while some ways of life wither and others die. A multiplicity of cultures allows the survival of some cultures while a few die. Third, I need to have some of the other culture as mine. I need some of its ideas, words, actions, communal styles to make my way of life better. Fourth, I need to change my life and accept all of the change that surrounds me.

Adaptation is sometimes the means of last resort. Instead of adapting, people either fight the deep change that surrounds them or run away from it. Many times people gather together in groups to form a movement that *fights change as evil*. These movements may focus on certain stereotypical people, ideas, technologies, and so forth that they affirm as evil and they seek to destroy. Sometimes war and terrorism are initiated as ways to reject the cultural changes that threaten a group's culture. Violence between groups within a changing society is not uncommon since the society as a whole must face the challenge of whether and how to change. A constant search for security is reflected in stereotyping those who do not share one's cultural ideology. Many times this stereotyping has nothing to do with the agents of change that threaten the culture—witness the role of Jewish stereotyping and scapegoating throughout Western history. As part of this stereotyping and violence the community usually turns to leaders who offer clear lines of thought and witness to past certitudes. These leaders are invested with total power over the community and its relationships with others. Safe in the security of such powerful stereotypes of the past, the community faces the present and future confident that their powerful leader will reject the evil of the surrounding change. Cultures seem to have their own second law of thermodynamics that states that when a culture becomes isolated it achieves a configuration of maximum internal power such that it no longer can change. Of course cultures are groups of humans, not exchanges of energy. When humans no longer grow, they die.

In the presence of a dying culture, or in the face of an aggressive culture, another way people react to change is to run from it. When we are the weak other, we may fight back, but we may also run away, *flight*. People run away from threats to destroy them. The threats may be those that threaten actual bodily harm or, more often, they are more subtle. For example, threats to steal their children actually or culturally. Stealing children many times is done under the guise of improving their condition in life. In nineteenth-century America, Native American children were sent to schools that stole their identity; and Catholic children were sent from the city to Protestant farm families to give them a chance to grow up in a healthy environment. From the standpoint of the weaker way of life, however, the stealing happens in other ways, as the dominant culture entices the children by its perceived, selfish values and materialistic softening of the cultural shield that defends against evil. If not *fight* or suicide, then it must be *flight*.

The initial part of cultural change involves conscious choices as to speak this way rather than that, act this way rather than that, get together with these people rather than those. Choice by individuals is a vital part of the initial entrance of one culture into the other. Once the other culture is into the dominant culture, by adaptation by many of the citizens, the socialization process takes over. Once the other culture is part of our socialization process, the choice is not as conscious.

If choosing is an essential part of the mature human being, then *boredom* associated with choosing is a neurotic/psychotic response to choosing and mature growth. Why don't people want to grow up? What is there about one's way of life that prevents them from choice and growth such that they are bored with life? What is it that produces boredom with life such that, as in the movie *The Matrix*, we live in our own cocoon and become excited only when someone accidentally kicks our cocoon? What is it about this "whatever" response to deep choices that ignores the significant choices that surround an individual and/or culture?

Jay Lifton[5] coined the phrase "psychic numbing" that occurs in the face of overwhelming and/or foundational choices. People can't choose. They only can continue with the style of life they have lived in the past. They can't face the present or the future. "Whatever" may be that nonresponse. This "whatever" response seems particularly associated with many in the industrialized West. It may be that there are so many trivial responses associated with the capitalist need to sell everything that produces too many mini choices. This choice overload results in the "whatever" response as an ego-coping mechanism. To the changes that are currently being offered, the fight, flight, and adapt of the past are joined with the "whatever" of the present when we begin to look for further patterns of response in the cultures we have offered for observation.

What we find in a changing culture, therefore, reflects all four of these responses that are manifested as significant shifts in the former signposts of the culture—words shift their meaning. It is extremely difficult to know what others are saying until, at times, we stereotype them. The same goes for certain bodily gestures of hands, face, feet, and body. Actions are taken that formerly all agreed were good or evil. All at once, one community interprets them one way; another community interprets them another way. Slowly one sees people "flighting" in many ways, for example, to communes, gated communities, monasteries, or other countries. In religious matters, it should be mentioned, a type of flighting has always been a move from outer to inner norms, or spirituality. In their inability to deal with the changes threatening the religious culture of the past, present-day individuals seek to deal with something they feel they can attend to—their inner spiritual life. This is especially true in societies such as the United States that from their beginnings projected the myths of sudden change brought about by internal conviction (born again) and easy stages to personal and social change (the self-help movements). Violence occurs within one's own community as various subcommunities vie for power with the hope of establishing a secure environment for daily life, work, and leisure. Boredom is found in lessened productivity, declining creativity, increased drug and alcohol usage, and a reluctance to challenge established institutions and their leaders. Gradually, a culture is entering into what is described as the time of "liminality."

CULTURAL LIMINALITY

Victor Turner coined the term *liminality* to describe the in-betweenness of puberty rites[6] among the cultures he studied. The children in these cultures lived with the expectations associated with their role in society. They were comfortable with the mode of speaking, acting, and relating to those around them since they knew the expectations and limits associated with their role.

At a certain time, some children, the pubescent, are suddenly taken from the general group of children. Through ritual they are transformed into adults. This "in-between time" of the puberty rite is the time of liminality, of disorientation. All the former signposts of a child's way of life are gone. One often has a sense that one has died.[7] The rites themselves many times include a portrayal of dying to one's old self and coming alive to one's new self. Once the children become aware, through ritual, of this new self, they enter back into society with new roles in the society and the corresponding language, actions, and relationships that are part of that new role. The concept of liminality has been used by many scholars to describe other struggles individuals have when facing difficult transition moments in the life cycle or movements within one's social hierarchy.

This concept can also be used to describe what happens in a culture. A culture, of course, is made up of people. In this chapter I am suggesting our culture is undergoing deep change from one temporal culture to another temporal culture. Certainly the people responding to the change will experience individual liminality with a corresponding transition of identity and self. The question here is whether the culture undergoes a time of liminality and whether we can discern its happening. I would suggest that it does. The marking events of such a transition are: transitional political events, such as the death of a king, a war, or a national election; transitional ideational events, in which new and old patterns of ideas face off against each other through publications, conventions, and granting systems, and through state, monarchical, corporate, individual sponsorship, or other ways ideas advance or wane in a culture; transitional technological events, as a certain technology gains dominance; and transitional religious events, such as conferences, formation of new religious groups out of old, ecumenical councils, an increase of interreligious activities, and the acknowledgment of diverse religions.

These marking events form a dialectical pattern in which the "new" breaks through at a certain moment in time to seemingly dominate the culture, only to find, within a short time that it was an illusion because the "old" returns with a vengeance. Now, conscious of what is happening, the old begins to exercise its power to destroy the new. This dialectic sometimes occurs quickly, and sometimes over centuries. This illustration may help visualize this dynamic:

"OLD/OLD...NEW/old.....new/OLD.....New/OLd.......NEw./Old......NEW/ old.....NEW/NEW"

The numerator indicates the culture of less influence, the denominator the culture of most influence—as visualized within the culture! The dialectic is such that there is a continual contest over the language spoken by the culture, the normative ethical and ritual actions of the culture, and the proper empowering modes of decision making in the culture. Slowly, what is new becomes part of the way people speak, act, and gather; slowly, these ways of speaking, acting, and gathering provide a sense of meaning, belonging, rightness, and well-being to the change agents of the culture; slowly, through trial and error the new way sustains peoples' lives; slowly, a new culture becomes THE way of life. Of course, we see this dialectic only from the rearview mirror of the now dominant culture.

One might ask, "What is going on among the various subcultures?"[8] What is happening is a great deal of activity as people cross over from one way of living to another. The subcultures are composed of varying generations. Each new generation into the culture easily finds many of its members shifting from one way of thinking and acting to another. The definition of a cult as a one-generation revolutionary movement highlights what occurs within the subcultures. The generation that reacts to the new by fighting, flighting, adapting, or boredom quickly finds, as it attempts to socialize its children into the way of life consequent to that reaction, that the children do not feel the same about what was "new" to the parenting group, nor do the children react in the same way to it. This is to be expected because the world has changed since the initial reaction of the parenting generation. It is this changed world that this particular generation is reacting to and it may easily see that the proper reaction is any of the four options in the face of change that we have offered. A quick look at a recent example of generational difference in the United States as provided by R. Zemke, C. Raines, and B. Filipczak [9] demonstrates what I mean.

Take leadership as an example. From the beginning of the century to the end, it flows in this sequence from generation to generation: leadership is by the "boss" telling us what to do, leadership is by all of us agreeing what to do, leadership is by those who know what to do, leadership is teamworking together to accomplish a goal, part of which is our mutual appreciation of each other. What we see here is an important part of any cultural life—its view of leaders. Such movement within a culture is an example of what is happening within the subgroups because people are being socialized into various patterns of leadership as well as ways to react to larger shifts of words, actions, and social relations. This movement of subcultures and generations within them is the expression of the larger culture's liminality, the larger culture's attempt to stabilize itself in the face of "the new" of deep change.

Because we are talking about one culture with many subcultures, there must be something that brings the various cultures together to form one culture. I would suggest that within each culture there are transitional subcultures that act as agents of transition and translation of what is new and what is old—change agents that act as interlocutors between the old and new in a culture. Much like immigrant children who translate the language and actions of the new land to their parents from the old country, these transitory subcultures translate the old and new to each other.[10] The public school can have an important role in helping each generation deal with generational change. Exposure to the diversity of religions is one of those particular changes that both allows reflection upon change and also encourages an examination of a variety of ways of dealing with it, because every one of the world religions has dealt with deep change over the centuries.

PERSONAL CHANGE

This cultural change represented in the conscious presence of diverse religious peoples in our country and throughout the globe may be part of who we are. We may or may not have absorbed this diversity into our identity. If we have, then the movement toward admitting and advocating for diverse religions in the public schools may be an obvious choice. If this diversity was not part of our socialization process, we may have a more difficult time since it represents a more shocking awareness of difference among the world's peoples. Perhaps diversity has not yet become part of our identity, causing us to feel some of the negative emotions mentioned previously. But even for those who think themselves acclimated to the diverse religions and the cultures they represent, their identity may be more one of "I"—"them" than "I"—"we." Any sense of identity change is unsettling, and we react to this change in many ways.

The question of personal identity is not an easy one to clarify or describe. We have already seen how our religious identity evolves as part of whom we are, not something separate from everyday life. Yet our ability to say "I" somehow gives us a sense that the past, present, and future are all connected in some kind of "forever self" that is beyond change.[11] —a self that is indestructible and heroic and does not need to depend on the mundane minutiae of life. This "forever self" is protected in many ways as we cope with life, especially anything that would challenge this sense of who we are. Some call these protectors ego-coping mechanisms, while others call them defense mechanisms. I will use ego-coping mechanism because it best describes what happens to us as we live our lives. A sense of what they are and how they function in our lives is helpful in dealing with both personal and social conflict much like fight, flight, adapt, and boredom did in the previous discussion. Some of the most important mechanisms are the following:

- *Altruism* is a type of unselfishness that allows people to see their own needs in a context that includes the needs of others. My need to be loved finds me helping build a house for Habitat for Humanity.
- *Humor* allows people to defuse the anger of the moment by focusing on its comical elements. Telling jokes intuitively allows us to see that life is funny, not always serious. In the brokenness of life there are cracks of dissimilarity that allow us to laugh in the midst of terror and deep hurt. The humor is a shield that protects us from the lance of terror and the arrows of pain.
- *Sublimation* directs the energies produced by conflict into constructive and socially acceptable channels. Therefore, instead of the United States invading a country, they try to beat the country at a sport the United States is good at.
- *Anticipation* is the capacity to perceive future danger clearly and thus minimize its effects. For example, one might remind one's self, "When I go into this meeting there are four people who will shout loudly and aggressively that religion is a delusion that only keeps people immature."
- *Suppression* is the ability to cope with conflict by temporarily putting it out of our consciousness. Suppression is a conscious action. For example, "I won't think about it and it will go away" or, "I won't think about how lonely I am."
- *Denial* is when we unconsciously ignore or refuse to acknowledge disagreeable realities by procrastinating or disregarding reality. It helps resolve emotional conflict and allay anxiety by disavowing thoughts, feelings, wishes, needs, or external reality factors that are consciously intolerable. There are many types of denial. We can deny facts and the implication of facts. We can even deny the reality that we will die (annihilation). Denial is a mask we develop when we are very young, and we see it appear in normal children before they are five. In adults, it may be worn in hopeless situations and provides them with the time to persevere, explore, and survive in the face of this

hopeless situation. Notice this is unconscious. We do not realize we are denying whatever it is that may harm us.

- *Acceptance* is recognizing what actually happens. Acceptance is not tolerance, putting up with what happens to us, bearing it without complaining. Acceptance basically says: "That's it!" "Now what should I be doing about it?"
- *Crying* is a physical expression much like language. We learn how to cry from our parents and our culture. One must have experience with the person and the culture to be able to interpret a person's crying. We do know that it is one of the first modes of expression that we learn as an infant. In early life, it is an expression of pain or discomfort, but it can quickly become an instrument for getting the parents' attention.
- *Fantasy* is when a person both denies unpleasant realities and constructs a new world composed of a reality he or she would like to see. This is not hallucination. We pretend company is coming when they are not.
- *Delusion* is a false belief based upon a misinterpretation of reality. Delusion usually has a basis in reality. Some common delusions are *persecution*, when the FBI keeps deleting the files for this book because they are after me; *influence*, when some hacker deletes the files for this book; *grandeur*, when members of my department are deleting the files because they realize the importance of what I am writing. Oh, the reality is that a file was deleted because I pressed the wrong key. This, of course, may have resulted because of fixed delusion, my paranoia or schizophrenia.
- *Hallucination* is a false sensory perception characterized by a lack of external stimulus. Common types of hallucination are auditory, when I hear someone dictating what I should write, or visual, where I see the words appearing on the wall next to my computer screen. (Don't I wish!)
- *Depersonalization* is when I make my own self or people into things in order to deal with them with greater comfort. I see a needle rather than a nurse hurting me, or quietly and calmly pick up my finger that was cut off by the lawn mower and rush this part of me to the hospital.
- *Projection* is when you assign to others the urges and wishes that your own ego repudiates. You transfer blame, failure, misdeeds, unacceptable impulses, and thoughts to others rather than own up to their presence in you. "Those liberals/conservatives are always thinking about sex." "Those men/women are trying to run my life."
- *Hypochondria* is when we are habitually preoccupied with our physical health and/or defects.
- *Passive-Aggressive* is when we control another person by seeming to allow them to control us. A student who continually says, "Yes, sir.

How do you want me to do this, sir? Is this the correct answer, sir? Do you want me to use the spell check twice or is once enough— sir?!" Or, a "work to rule" that is done to achieve a specific objective.

- *Acting Out Behavior* reduces the anxiety aroused by forbidden desires by actually expressing them. A middle-aged, married man whispers in the ear of a female guest that he wants to take her into the bedroom for sex. A widow solicits money from her friends in order to go on a vacation.

- *Intellectualization*, sometimes called rationalization, is when we attempt to justify actions or beliefs while ignoring inconsistencies or contradictory evidence, or we substitute socially acceptable reasons for antisocial motives. "I have to take care of J.J. who is in the hospital. The kids can take care of themselves" (The kids are driving me nuts!) "The doctor is so intelligent. She takes the same amount of time with each of her patients. I trust her completely." (I don't understand a word she says, and she seems to never let me tell her everything that is wrong with me.)

- *Displacement* is when I transfer an emotional reaction from one object or person to another one. My boss yells at me. I yell at my wife. My wife kicks the dog. The dog bites the cat, and the cat chases the squirrel. (And the squirrel eats the tulip bulbs in the boss's yard.)

- *Reaction Formation* is when we both deny certain unacceptable feelings and, at the same time, develop the feelings opposite to these repressed ones. My leg is cut off, and I begin to be very happy that I do not have to tie my shoes any more.

- *Somatization* is when we convert psychological anxiety or fears into physical symptoms. A woman's husband dies of a stomach cancer, and she begins to have pains similar to his. I get a headache every time I do my income taxes.

These ego-coping devices keep us from being overwhelmed by change and conflict. They enable us to keep a sense of continuity as deep change occurs in our life. If they become hardened into habits that defend us from never changing, they may result in continued infantile behavior and an inability to deal with others. When our sense of religions in life demands that we change by intensifying our hospitable attitude toward them, they will influence our thoughts and actions. But it should be remembered that these reactions are not only present in each of us, but in all of us. We notice this particularly when conflict occurs as the shields of defense (defense mechanisms) are raised to protect each individual. We must make a conscious effort to be aware of whether our response is appropriate to the stimulus of the conflict or the other person's ego-coping mechanisms. For example, a minister begins to cry when he becomes aware that his religion is only one of many that will be dealt with in the global studies class.

RELIGIOUS CHANGE: CULTURAL AND PERSONAL

Religious change occurs and is manifest through religious people as they live their cultural and personal lives. The deep change that is occurring affects the people and their institutions. They enter into advocacy coalitions in the midst of changes within themselves—tentatively trying to deal with the change that is occurring to both religious individuals and institutions, while advocating for other causes such as the environment, social justice, or religious diversity. No two institutions are the same in this adaptation, as no two people are the same. Some religious people and institutions embrace change totally, some reject it totally, and some accept parts of the change that is offered while rejecting other parts of it. Historical examples abound in all the major religions, for example, Judaism's three major branches of Reformed, Conservative, and Orthodox; Christianity's Protestant, Catholic, and Orthodox; and Islam's Shiite and Sunni. It is not uncommon that those outside a religion see similarity among these various expressions of the same religion, while to those of one of these expressions the others are heretics or infidels. Historically, each of these reformulated religions is a response to the change demanded to the status quo; no existing religion is the same as previous to the challenge. The medieval Catholic Church, for example, had to deal with reform. *Reform* was the word used for deep change in worship, devotions, moral imperatives, spirituality, and organization. Some Christians responded by changing a little (Roman Catholic), some a little more (Anglican), a little more (Lutheran), and more (Presbyterian), and even more (Quakers). The point here is not the substance of the changes that occurred, but that all of them changed, each claiming continuity with the "authentic" Christianity. They may call their fellow religionists who did not make the same changes as they did "heretics" or "infidels." Yet the fact of the matter is that the religion itself changed in the face of this historical necessity for change. It has in the past and it will in the future. Religions are undergoing such change today. In asking the religions to participate in the mutual learning that must occur in today's multicultural world, we must be sensitive to this tender moment in their history. For, just as an adolescent or older person may seem uncomfortable or angry without seeming cause, so the diverse ancient religions may institutionally respond in irrational ways to the new reality of religions in the public schools and/or to allowing someone not of their faith to teach about it.

CONFLICT

Religious conflict abounds in our world while many interpreters still hesitate to see religious issues as the source of these conflicts. Instead we hear of economic deprivation, lack of education, language skills, or some well-used interpretative category in the social sciences as an explanation of past and present wars in place of the religions themselves as the cause of the war. The reasons for conflict of any kind, war included, are always multiple. Because the conflict originated for various reasons, the means to resolve it are also numerous and many times demand multiplicity. But when war between religious people is at hand, the spokespersons for the religion must accept the responsibility for dealing with it through religious means. After all, it is their people who are fighting.

Conflict in advocating for religious diversity occurs on the micro and macro levels. The micro level includes the interaction of peoples within the RAC as well as between the RAC members and others. The macro level is conflict that occurs because of consistent and persistent structural factors such as ignorance, clergy, and media formulation of issues.

Experience demonstrates that all change does not bring conflict. This is seen in advocating for religious diversity as it is for everything else. The thrill of understanding another, of those who differ in politics and religion uniting for a common cause, of seeing children prepared for the global economy, and the sense of peace within a community are all positive experiences. Yet conflict does exist and we should look at a few ways to reduce it. First, ten general observations are presented, and then applications to the micro and macro levels.

TEN NECESSARY ATTITUDES FOR CREATIVE CONFLICT/CONFRONTATION

1. *If there is no will there is no way.* Aaron David Miller in his article "America's Elusive Search for Arab-Israeli Peace" was reflecting on the difficulty of resolving the conflict when he said: "There can be no bricks without straw. . . . unless the raw material is there, the political will and the urgency among the Arabs and Israelis, we can try all day long without success."[12] No conflict will be settled unless everyone concerned believes it must be settled. The challenge is how to enable all stakeholders to see it is to their common interest to resolve the issue that causes disruption at a RAC meeting, school meeting, or policy discussion.

2. *Things take time.* We Americans always want an instant solution. There is no instant solution where people's historical feelings are involved. Conflicting habits must be recognized and new ones embraced and practiced. Habits relating to gender, to race, and to religion have been engrained in culture and psyche over the millennia. Things take time to change. Relax. Be patient with yourself and others while being stubborn in your dedication to advocating for religious diversity.

3. *Keep talking, but not in circles.* Because change takes time does not mean that we should not keep pressing the issue. Communicate, communicate, communicate—but realize too that in communicating

people may disagree or oppose what you are saying. With such opposition, it may not be the communication that needs clarifying, but the substance of the communication that needs review. Do the reasons for opposition make sense? The process of talking with those who oppose you is a process of finding common ground. Common ground does not necessarily begin with foundational ideas concerning the universe. Common ground, in its beginning, may easily be common difficulties with teens, the high price of gas, taxes, a good place to fish, a sports team, or the weather. Small talk does not necessarily make you small. Many times it is the mutual discovery of a common ground upon which we stand that makes it possible to resolve our differences.

4. *Everyone is in opposition, not just some.* When you present an idea, some will support it, and some will not. Those who do not support it, obviously, oppose it. It is easy to forget that your idea is also in opposition to theirs. Everyone present is, in some sense, an opponent. Remember to look at things through the eyes of the opposition to help understand how your ideas are seen by others.

5. *Leave time for argument, and respect the time dealing with opposition.* We usually see opposition through our eyes—who is opposed to us. Remember the one we are looking at sees us as his opposition. When and how you deal with those who oppose you tells everyone, allies included, who you are and suggests your motivation for pursuing an issue. It also suggests, unknowingly, how you want others to treat you in opposition, which, of course, you are.

6. *Argument is necessary; opposition is helpful.* Group decision-making literature has been consistent over the years in emphasizing that a diversity of ideas results in better results than when everyone thinks the same.[13] Diversity of ideas means that people will disagree and oppose ideas as they arise within the group. Disagreement may mean shouting, or even walking out of the room by some people. Knowledge of participants' arguing styles is helpful, but not necessary, in bringing an issue forward. It is important that you realize that peaceful agreement does not mean the best agreement; shouting does not mean loss. How you deal with both situations will determine whether what is done benefits the school's stakeholders.

7. *Keep your cool without creating a freezing atmosphere.* Of course if your argumentative style is eruptive, you should make a point of reminding everyone that just because you are emotional about the topic does not mean that you are unreasonable about it. Something like, "Okay, now that you know how I feel about it, maybe we, including me, can talk about it calmly." It may also be that your role is such that you must remind individuals that people may be offended by their behavior. Such reminding is best done privately unless, as chair of a meeting, you have no other choice.

8. *Keep things comfortable and confrontations will lessen.* One business executive held meetings in the coffee break room where there were no seats. He said that they were more efficient that way. Perhaps that was true in his type of business. One should be sensitive to the physical accommodations provided for the meeting. Sometimes people get angry, uncomfortable, and irritable because they are too hot, the seats are hard, and they cannot hear what is going on.

9. *Make the person personal and the issue impersonal.* Separate the person from the issue. Bad people do good things; good people do bad things. Our advocacy has nothing to do with the individual's character, but with what he is or is not supporting. Once we begin continual personal attack, we have adopted the way of the bully trying to force our view upon others. Their only response is to reject us and our views.

10. *You always have something in common no matter what your differences.* Seek out those common values, concerns, and stories that bring you together because they form the bedrock of the community within which you live. There are many ways to look at a situation. Is there one you can agree upon? Try not to reject a conflicting position, but rather try to reframe the issue to find common ground.

MICRO CONFLICT

Micro confrontation is what happens among those working together to achieve some common objective. This includes not only the RAC, but those with whom RAC collaborates to achieve some common objective. When two groups or committees begin to work together, they are actually beginning a new group. It is not unusual, especially in the beginning, that they seem to get bogged down with continual confrontations, long-winded orations, and laziness. A review of group development and effective meetings will help make your advocacy more purposeful.

Group Development

An article by B. W. Tuckman on small-group development forms the basis of most discussions about such conflict in small groups. I will use it here while keeping in mind the unique nature of a Religions Advocacy Coalition.[14]

Tuckman suggests that as people do things together they go through four stages of development toward achieving their objectives: forming, storming, norming, and performing. Although I am going to describe these as if one follows the other, it is not necessarily true that everyone in a group is at the same stage at the same time. If life were so easy! Instead, you might find yourself responding to various conflicts within your group when just a moment before it seemed everything was going along well and you were about to finalize a project. Also remember that part of what is happening during this entire process is that the members of the group are getting to know one another: how they express themselves, how much they understand about the topics at hand, and how devoted they are to getting the task done (who is part of the 20 percent of a team that does 80 percent of the work). That said, here is how a group gradually forms into an effective advocacy coalition, and areas in which it may be derailed.

Forming

When you first come together, you are there because you heard that people were gathering to discuss the role and presence of the various religions in the public school. Some may come because of interest, others because the organizers asked them, some out of curiosity, and still others because they feared views opposite to theirs would take over the school system. These and many other motivations may be present among those who come to the first few meetings. The objective in these meetings must be clarity of purpose. As mentioned in Chapter 1, the role of a mission or vision statement, along with goals and objectives, provides such purpose. Those who attend the first meetings gradually begin to work out why they are doing what they are doing, what they intend to do, and how to do it. At the same time, they are also gradually becoming an identifiable team. A team name and regular meeting times, such as the second Thursday of the month, help express this identity. Some conflicts will arise as clarifications of mission and goals rise to the surface and are agreed upon. Recipes for dealing with such conflicts will be provided later.

Storming

These conflicts can be a result of personality differences ("She seems to never have taken a shower in her life."), as well as differences in group expectations ("He only wants world religions taught!") Mutual expectations also may cause confrontation ("No, I will not make the phone calls!" "I will talk to the press."). It may be that some people should, or must, drop out because they disagree totally with the group's mission. Every effort should be made to remain in contact with these dropouts. Because they disagree with you is no reason to not remain in touch with them and find common ground for this or other projects. It is important to remember, as stated previously, that conflict (storming) is a natural part of group development and can be useful in moving a team toward the stages of norming and performing. If dealt with correctly, these storms will help the team to become more cohesive and more focused on their goals. We will discuss how to achieve this in the section on "creative and destructive confrontation."

Norming

Members gradually become accustomed to what they are expected to do. Offer opinions with the expectation that they will be treated fairly and, whether accepted or rejected, taken seriously. This is much like when a basketball team knows where every member is on the court, and can be trusted to be where the ball is thrown, and that the ball will be thrown to one of them. In the same way, everyone on this particular advisory team can be trusted to do their best and work toward the common goals.

Performing

After the coalition has both successfully and unsuccessfully dealt with a school or a school district, it has a sense of past success, present creativity, and future expectation that its mission will be accomplished. The stakeholders experience a positive feeling of performing together. These are the moments to be savored in our busy lives.

People come and go in coalition building. Time passes. The group changes. Success, failure, and change bring new experiences to those who are members of the group. The dynamics of group formation are just that—"dynamic," changing, and in flux. If the coalition is fortunate enough to retain most of its members, it will probably be able to sustain a level of performing over a long period of time. Its greatest challenge is to accept new members into the group, support their movement through these stages, and embrace their new energy and creativity into the mission of the coalition. But there are other challenges to forming a successful coalition of people such as group think, running a meeting, and building trust.

Group Think

Although we all want things to move along smoothly to achieve our objectives, there is always the danger of what is called "group think."[15] This is when those in the group agree too quickly to all decisions, see everyone outside their group as evil and their ideas unworthy of consideration, individuals stop themselves from objecting because of their fear of what "the others" will say, and group members take for granted when no one says anything against a proposal that it is a vote for the proposal.[16] Usually a warning about group think is enough for a group as diverse as a RAC to avoid it. At the same time, as the level of disagreement diminishes with the increase of camaraderie and success (the performing stage), everyone, especially the leaders, should be aware of the possibility of this occurring.

Group Meetings: Making a Get-together into a Meeting

Our past experiences with meetings, for the most part, determine our expectations of how a meeting is organized and run. The variety of stakeholders participating in a RAC meeting almost guarantees that there will be some who expect everything to happen in a lock-step, top-down fashion, and others who will expect everyone's voice to be heard, with the agenda being constructed from moment to moment during the meeting. Somewhere between this seemingly dictatorial meeting and a neighborhood get-together lies the best approach to a RAC gathering. The manner of leadership and the structure of the first meeting are central to the working of the group and its subsequent meetings. We will look at leadership in the next chapter.

Some acknowledged process is necessary to move a gathering of interested people from a crowd to a coherent, purposeful coalition of stakeholders. Central to such a process is *ordered sequence and clear purpose.* Those who initiate the gathering should know exactly what they intend to achieve at each gathering and a general idea of what is to occur in subsequent ones. The reason for having a sense of what is to come is that situations may be taken advantage of as they arise to advance the agenda even though it may not be the primary reason for this particular gathering. For example, the purpose of the first gathering may be twofold: to obtain all contact information (e.g., name, address, phone, etc.) from the attendees, and to exchange views about the meaning and purpose of religious diversity in the schools. You know that a mission/vision statement has to be dealt with, perhaps at the next meeting. However, if it seems at this meeting that the group is getting along well, you have gotten the contact information, and there is strong agreement as to the reasons for dealing with religious diversity, then move it along to creating a mission statement.

Every meeting should *begin and end on time.* Always. The agenda should have been distributed beforehand. When it is re-announced at the beginning of the meeting, members should be offered an opportunity to clarify what is stated. At the same time, too much "clarification" may result in never getting to the task at hand. Clarification usually occurs as members work their way through the task. For example, if the task is to present a calendar of diverse religious holidays to a school district, people may need clarification as to how many religions will be chosen, what norm will be used to choose them, and where you obtained the information. It may be that the answer to these questions was part of the meeting's purpose, but some may not realize this. Following is an outline of a suggested process for each meeting.

The Process of Meeting for a Group of Any Size

Pre-meeting preparations:

1. Posting a meeting date agreed upon by most if not all members.
2. Providing directions to the locale if it is unknown to some.
3. Stating clearly the purpose of the meeting.
4. Providing sufficient information for attendees to make intelligent decisions.
5. Asking for clarifications regarding the purpose of the meeting, and telling them where to send these clarifications.

The Meeting:

At the assigned time welcome all.

1. Have new members introduce themselves to the group.
2. State the purpose of the meeting, modified, if necessary, because of the previously mentioned feedback. (There should be no mention as to how anyone foresees this purpose being achieved.)
3. Supply the information already distributed, plus any other information provided by the members.
4. Gather ideas. Brainstorm (just the ideas, no evaluation of the ideas).
5. Evaluate alternatives.
6. List the advantages and disadvantages of each idea.
7. Whenever discussion is occurring:
    a. Draw out group
    b. Accept feelings; DO NOT CRITICIZE
    c. Use active listening
    d. Wait out pauses
    e. Ask questions
    f. Keep discussion moving
    g. Restate and summarize
8. Watch and comment on group process.
9. Post main viewpoints.
10. Choose a solution:
    a. Review alternatives
    b. Prioritize alternatives
    c. Try for consensus
    d. Agree to disagree
11. If all else fails:
    a. Vote
    b. Postpone decision
    c. Delegate decision to leader

12. Assign who is going to do what and by when.
13. Afterward, review what happened and how to make it better with the entire group (immediately afterward) or a selected few (immediately or later).

The question of whom and how many should be present at a meeting is a significant one. The larger a meeting gets, participants have less a say in what is happening. Organization is everything; personal opinion, while important, must also be organized in some way. I would suggest that RAC meetings always be small. It's better to have many small meetings (25 people or less) than one large meeting. Large meetings can be held once a year or as a way to make a final decision already reviewed and agreed upon by the small groups.

A Process of Building Trust in a Group

Trust is essential to community building and good politics. The only way to trust is by trusting. Support and loyalty to the community and its members are the results of trust within the community. Honesty and reliability are central virtues to both an organization and its members, built upon trust. People must do what they say they are going to do. People must treat each other fairly. These virtues are especially important among a group that not only advocates diversity, but embodies it.

Conflict becomes a means of creative development rather than destruction when trust is present. It does not happen in a day or a moment, but through repetition in which one's reliability is recognized and honesty acknowledged.

Feelings of distrust often arise among those of diverse cultural backgrounds because of a diversity of interpersonal expectations, verbal and nonverbal signals, and first language. There are several ways of "testing your feelings": Ask someone you do trust how she "reads" the individual, check the "facts" that indicate to you dishonesty and unreliability, and, of course, ask the person you have these feelings toward about what you think is true.

MACRO CONFRONTATION

Just as conflict within a group happens in expected stages, so does the inevitable opposition that arises that threatens progress in advocacy and community building. Three cultural attitudes and one physical constant provide the macro confrontation to the mission of the group. They are religious ignorance, professionalism, mechanics, and media.

Religious ignorance in this context refers to individuals' lack of knowledge regarding their own religion and the religions of others.[17] What is significant is that many people do not know, do not want to know, and think they can discuss their own and others' religions without knowing anything about them. "It's all opinion, anyway" is a phrase I have heard over and over again. When individuals lack knowledge regarding religion and say nothing, there is no immediate problem. When individuals bring their lack of knowledge into the public forum, many times intense confrontations occur over matters that are of deep personal concern to the individual but of little relevance to the topic at hand. Two examples of this are when someone demands that all the material found in Dan Brown's *The Da Vinci Code* be included in the course on Christianity, or someone else demands that Jews stop secretly circumcising unsuspecting Hispanic male babies. Our culture is filled with the remnants of such individual fantasies about religion found on the Internet and elsewhere. When truth is determined by how many people are talking about it and what celebrity believes it, religious discussion easily becomes an exchange of imaginary fiction dressed as fact. It is a delicate matter to tell some people in public that they are wrong. Seldom is it necessary. After their short expression of opinion, perhaps the chair may say that she will look into the matter, or it will be dealt with later. Longer expressions of opinion must be shortened by asking the person to summarize his statement, saying you will look into the matter, or ruling her out of order (an action only taken as last resort). In private, perhaps, provide evidence not as a judge but as a loving friend offering other perspectives by those knowledgeable in their faith.

Many times clergy's and educators' sense of pride is offended when those outside their profession suggest new approaches for them or provide information they feel is more properly provided by professionals. That is why both educators and clergy must be part of every RAC. *The issue of professionals* many times is not that the professional doesn't like "being told what to do," but rather that the professional is not aware of current trends in their profession that support RAC positions. When a professional is respected and honored and opinion unquestioned by his clients, he will usually have difficulty among those as knowledgeable as he is. Clergy in particular are seen by many as knowledgeable about their own religion and religion in general. Society sees them as experts in religion, and they expect and are expected to have an opinion on it. In advocating religious diversity, their sense of professionalism many times as much, if not more, comes into play rather than their knowledge. The fact of the matter is that few have formal training in diverse religions, and the years of training in their own religion varies a great deal from religion to religion and denomination to denomination. Always treat the clergy with respect and honor. Usually they will also treat others with the same respect. When some tend to dominate the process, they can be reminded to allow others to speak, take a pause in the meeting and speak with her privately, or, if confrontational, engage some of the following practices.

With *the media*, both ignorance and professionalism reinforce each other. Many times they are more interested in getting their story out than in the particular facts of the event. Their story will also be adversarial and confrontational. There may be, for example, only one person objecting to the presence of an interreligious calendar on the school's Web site, but that person will get more coverage than the event itself. At such times it is helpful to remember that news becomes old once it is read or said. Better to leave it and go on than keep repeating it, since repetition gives it more attention than you may wish.

When machines fail, we fail. A familiarity with their *mechanics* allows comfortable communication among those attending. Always know who to contact in case something goes wrong. Just as organizers of an event are obliged to point out the exits in case of fire, when preparing for a meeting of the RAC, some "pointing out" of what to do in case of sound system, lights, or computer failure should be done for the organizers. Forethought is the way to prevent failure of both the mechanics as well as the meeting.

CREATIVE AND DESTRUCTIVE CONFRONTATION

Some people enjoy conflict; others do not. It is helpful to remember that conflict and confrontation may be both creative and destructive. It is creative when it helps us produce better understanding of people and the issues. It provides stimulation, membership involvement, and increased motivation. As individuals defend a cause, they become more committed to it. If one is honored for standing up for an issue, she becomes empowered to do it again. Just as animals gather together to resist attack, so do human communities. Many times good things come from conflict.

Of course confrontation and conflict may also be destructive and cause bad feelings among those who are conflicted. When conflict is allowed to go on for a long time and becomes intensely personal, it can destroy a community. That is one reason why many worry about what attack politics is doing to national unity. If one side is always cast in negative terms, common courtesies and hospitality refrained from, and no idea held up as worthy of honor, that same side will not only be continually in confrontation with yours, but it will also seek to unite with others to defeat you. When all individual and social interaction is win-lose, you are guaranteed to be on a losing side eventually. Many times bad things come out of conflict.

Within the context of the ten principled attitudes mentioned previously, what follows are two recipes for confrontation. First, we should mention that private meetings are organized and run by private rules. Robert's Rules of Order may or may not be necessary; however, it is important for the group to decide on some general operating principles and decision-making criteria during the first stage of development. If it is a group of 25, the process usually moves along at the pace and direction indicated by the leader(s). If it is a public meeting, the general rules of public discourse and order govern the meeting. In what follows, I am taking for granted that what occurs is a possibly serious disruption that threatens to destroy the purpose of the meeting.

If the chair is aware of what is happening around her, she can tell by a person's nonverbal signals that something is about to happen. Sometimes the person may move uneasily in his seat, mumble, extend his hand to gain attention, lower his head in an aggressive manner, or clench his fists. As chair you may recognize the individual, thus initiating the confrontation. If you do not, you risk a more aggressive outburst of disagreement to the proceedings.

In requesting that he speak, make and keep eye contact as he states his view. Once he is finished, ask if anyone else has anything to say about the stated topic. If you are fortunate, others will ask the person to clarify his stance, and gradually things will evolve to a significant contribution to the discussion. If you are the one disagreeing with the seemingly majority position, remember to express your disagreement, express it sensibly and with sensitivity to all concerned, disagree with the idea, not the person, and react to responses to your disagreement with a spirit of inquiry and not defensiveness.

Key to disagreement, either in one instance or over a prolonged period of time, is to not take disagreement, and its consequent conflict, personally. The best way to do this is to treat the overall issue as a problem to be solved and the disagreements as possible solutions that need data to support their acceptance. Important, too, is to try to have everyone look beyond the immediate issue (problem) to find common ground that all agree on. The ebb and flow is of: "As I see it this is what we agree on . . . is that correct?" and "This is our disagreement. Right? Does anyone see how we can move beyond this? Do we need to move beyond this to achieve our objectives?" These repeated statements usually move the immediate discussion or prolonged disagreement along toward a successful conclusion. Sometimes only one meeting is needed to come to a common mode of action. Other times many meetings and several very small ones bring the problem to a solution.

When someone disagrees loudly in word or action, and refuses to take direction from others, the meeting is at another level. The chair should calmly, while looking at the individual and with nonverbal gestures appealing for moderation, rephrase the objection and ask the person if that is what he means. Humor may be tried to calm the atmosphere. If the person objects to any rephrasing and attempt at humor, the chair might ask him what does he expect to be done? If the purpose of the confrontation is to prevent the participants from discussing the agenda or fulfilling the objectives of the meeting, then taking a short break may be appropriate— during which time the individual should be approached and informed that this behavior is not acceptable at a meeting such as this. If he intends to continue with such behavior, it would be best if he leave. If he does not leave and continues with the behavior, and you have no means to forcibly eject him, adjourn without saying when and where the next meeting will be held. To change the negative atmosphere of a meeting, change the subject that is creating the atmosphere. If you can get the majority of those present to deal with the negativity, it will usually isolate the person. At the same time, if there is organized confrontation by several attendees, the only way to deal with the disruption is to pause and eject the protestors.

OUR SACRED GROUND: A COMMUNAL NECESSITY IN TIMES OF DEEP CHANGE

When one religious people after another destroyed Jerusalem, they did so with ardor and determination—an ardent belief in their cause and the determination to overwhelm the inhabitants with brute force. They poured in from outside the city to destroy all that was within. Destruction resulted in reconstruction—rebuilding that which we know from history was also destroyed.

Our contemporary Jerusalems reside on common ground with a diversity of ways of living and the religions that express and reinforce that life. To attempt to destroy one is to destroy all. All can be destroyed by convincing each that they have nothing in common and must depend on themselves alone or upon those who think and act as they do. If this happens, contemporary culture and all it sustains collapses to be overcome by outsiders. No one in our global community can exist alone while sustaining the life to which we have become accustomed.

We began this chapter by claiming we were in a time of deep change. Three reactions to that change—flight, fight, boredom—highlight the seemingly necessary isolation from those who differ from us. The ego-coping mechanisms that help us deal with change easily become defense mechanisms, shields built to prevent the threatening difference of others from impinging on an unchanging self.

The attitudes and mechanisms we suggested for meetings addressing advocacy for diversity of religions in our schools were offered not as further alienating devices but as means of finding that common ground. Without some common sacred untouchable ground, we can easily lose our way in the change that surrounds us. We must discover this over and over again in our meetings and ways of life. Foundational to that common ground are our children upon whom the future depends. Foundational, too, is our Constitution and the values it has come to embody throughout our history: freedom, the rule of law, concern for the common weal, and physical and psychological security. Without striving to discover these similarities while acknowledging our differences, we only continue the cycle reflected in the old Jerusalem and wait to be destroyed.

CHAPTER 6

The Leaders: Responsibility for Common Life

The difference between crowds and teams is purpose, direction, and longevity. How do we act together with purpose over an extended period of time? How do we energize and enable each of us in a group to have care and concern for the others for days, months, and perhaps years? How is community built and conflict creatively channeled? Although we tend to think in terms of technique, manipulation, and impersonal structures,[1] humans have a surprising quality that moves them in various directions beyond analysis and manipulation.[2] That certain something is found among individuals who take responsibility for and empower us with a sense of purpose and direction beyond external manipulation and control. These individuals, whom we call leaders, enable all of us to make something happen together over and over again, working together for a common good. To recognize the diversity of religions in our schools and to learn about this diversity, we need leaders for our coalitions and for our schools. This chapter will aid in explaining the ways leadership is viewed in our culture, provide a cultural toolbox for discovering the type of school you are examining, and delineate what leaders must do to help the school remain healthy throughout the institutional life cycle.

As stakeholders in our children's education and our nation's future, it is extremely helpful to have a sense of how our educators are trained for leadership in the schools. What follows provides you with some of the same ideas used in those classes to enable you to evaluate leaders in the schools and in any organizations with which you are associated. Naturally, most of the leadership material reflects the thoughts and experiences of our Western culture over the millennia as seen through current views of leadership.

Ideas and history are not somehow "out there" in classroom texts, PowerPoint presentations, and workshops for school administrators. A sense of leadership and followership is part of every human because it is part of life—we are always either following or leading. We follow when directed to do so by laws, police, spouses, peers, coaches, bosses, and parents. We lead when taking the first step off the curb to get to the other side of the street, telling our children what to do, asking our spouse to go this way rather than that, and showing appreciation for a job well done.

Because leadership and followership are part of you, when you read what follows your "gut reaction" will instantaneously approve or disapprove what you read. You may feel good about what you read, slightly uncomfortable, or be ready to throw the book across the room. The fact is that our models of leadership and followership are part of the socialization process; thus our socialized "gut" will be conditioned by our personal and generational history.[3] I would ask that you be conscious of those feelings. If part of your advocacy demands a selection of a leader, there should be a conscious agreement as to what kind of a leader is necessary to help guide the institution in a new direction.

LEADERSHIP TRAITS REVEALED BY RESEARCH

People are always doing research on leadership. An article from a business professor summarized this research by claiming the following as common leadership characteristics of business leaders in the United States:[4]

- *Leaders are typically intelligent.* Do not confuse intelligence with knowledge. Intelligence is a reasoning capacity, whereas knowledge addresses a reservoir of information.
- *Leaders are typically respected.* The success of charismatic leadership has demonstrated that followers often bestow a worshipful characteristic on certain leaders.
- *Leaders are typically self-confident.* They believe in themselves, which translates into followers believing in the leader.
- *Leaders are typically dependable.* The follower knows that a leader's commitment is sacred. An axiom to this characteristic may be a leader's persistence.
- Leaders typically have a *high sociability* quotient. Even evil leaders have been perceived as likeable early in their period of influence and development, for example, Hitler and Jim Jones.
- Leaders typically are *excellent communicators.* The sophistication of communication options of the twentieth and twenty-first centuries demands that the leader be able to function in a variety of technologies.

A bit of trivia may be of interest here. A study of U.S. executives perceived as leaders found that more than 44 percent are firstborn; 61 percent are between 5'10" and 6'1"; more than 80 percent are right-handed; and less than 2 percent are single.

LEADERSHIP MYTHS

Demonstrated research is many times coincidental to what motivates us to follow someone. Our socialization process has stories and images of heroes that go beyond the dry data provided by research. I would suggest five myths are prevalent in U.S. culture:

- *Revolutionary leader.* With skills honed to perfection in some unknown place, this individual comes out of nowhere to make what is necessary happen, and then leaves when the "job" is done.
- *Celebrity leader.* Honored by the media and millions of people, many see this honor as indicating that we should do what the person says and imitate her lifestyle.
- *Charismatic leader.* People follow this person because what she says, does, and requests us to say and do feel right.
- *Ordained leader.* God has blessed this person with leadership qualities and therefore should be followed.
- *Manager leader.* Using proven skills and knowledge, this person knows not only how to empower people to do something over a prolonged period, but also know how they can do it well.

LEADERSHIP: A VERY SHORT HISTORY

Statistical research and cultural analysis still does not explain why we follow some people and not others. There are many theories about what that "certain something" is in someone that stimulates us to work together and expend our energies for a common task. The arguments continue as to whether leadership is an innate or learned ability. Beyond the theories history has taught us, the effective difference between successful leadership is properly using coercive (physical or psychological) or elicitive* (moral, internal) force.

Some historical personalities used coercive force, for example, the whip or the fear of the whip. Other leaders got things done by using elicitive force, being out front and drawing out people's desire to follow them. (It's difficult to whip someone when in front of them.) People followed and reached beyond their individual self without coercion, without fear, to achieve more than if forced to do so. When forced, things got done, but many people died, there was minimal engagement in the work they did, and that work generally was not done well. Obviously one of these ways is better than the other for achieving the common good. But also, just as obvious, one of these ways is

---

*Coercive has the sense of an external force making us do something while the word *elicitive*, based upon the word *elicit*, recognizes that some leaders energize us to perform to our highest level.

easier for the leader than the other and, as long as enough people were available to be used, sustained itself for a longer period of time.

For a long time, one prevalent theory in the West, especially connected to hierarchical leadership, was to see God as appointing and being present in the leaders. The leaders in medieval Europe, for example, were seen as instruments of God. This resulted in kings, bishops, and popes being followed because they were instruments of God's will in society.[5] This belief, when fully engaged, enabled leaders to have that certain something that motivated people to do things because they wanted to, not because they were forced.

Over the last 400 years, different views of leadership and inner motivation evolved as God began to be understood in a variety of ways. At the moment there is neither a perfect theory nor method for getting people involved in working together for the common good—though there are several theories that developed in the twentieth century that are still with us and influence ways we think about leadership.

LEADERSHIP THEORIES: A TWENTIETH-CENTURY HISTORY

As our culture evolved from the rule of humans to the rule of law, from deductive philosophy to inductive science, and from wholistic approaches to life to mechanistic approaches, we searched for that certain something of leadership by using the scientific method. The first results of that search are theories known as *classical,* or *scientific, management.* The paradigm here is the machine with its parts, arranged in a cause-and-effect manner, to produce a certain product or achieve a certain purpose. To do this, authority was centralized with everyone knowing their place, and there was a place for each person and that person's skill. People (managers) told people what to do (e.g., design the car, get the materials to build the car, put the wheel on the car, sell the car, etc.) and were supported in what they were doing (staff)—all on orders from above (the leader/central authority). Clear planning, record keeping, and policies dictated by decisive leadership resulted in everyone working for the common good, on a good product, and in making money. If a leader was able to provide an individual with money, this was a sufficient stimulus for them to follow the directions of the leader/manager. Few skills beyond basic math and reading were necessary to be a worker in this culture. One's feelings for the task did not matter. Just doing the job was enough to get things done. Everyone doing their job resulted in a good organization. An educational institution, according to this theory, was much like a factory with its central authority providing lesson plans to teachers. These lesson plans were like blueprints, which, if followed exactly, would provide a product to be used by the consumer. The teacher needed only basic skills to follow the lesson plan. If he used these skills, with proper direction and staff support, he would success-fully create the product: educated children. Whether it was the one-room schoolhouse or the local school several blocks down from one's house, the desks were lined up in a row, the students folded their hands in front of them, and the teacher kept them in line by physical punishment and rote, repetitive learning. Normal schools and teachers' colleges were established in many places by the beginning of the twentieth century to provide these teachers with the basic skills to do their job. Most children went to school until about grade six. The more determined, or many times wealthier, stu-dents graduated from high school. The more fortunate and wealthy ones went on to college. All were able to find their niche as long as the indus-trial economy was growing.

This system worked very well until about 1950. By then, things were becoming very complicated. Technology became more sophisticated, it took longer to train people, a variety of skills were becoming necessary to do one's job, and things were changing very fast. The development of profes-sions was one of the more influential modifiers of the leadership process. When you became a "professional," that meant that, without anyone telling you exactly what to do every moment of your work day, you had the neces-sary skills and information to perform your task/profession whatever that might have been—teacher, doctor, nurse, lawyer, engineer, and so forth. It also meant that you could perform your task without direct supervision or management—a central idea in the previous model of management/leader-ship. Consequently, a new theory of organizational management evolved known as the *Human Relations* theory. This theory saw an organization more as an organism than a machine and emphasized employee autonomy, trust, openness, delegation of authority, and personal relationships. Now leaders were interested in the feelings of their coworkers and how they affected the organization. They were seeking that "certain something" that would result in an excellent organization. In this milieu, that "certain something" was the member's feelings about themselves and the others in the organization. Money was not seen as a prime motivator in this way of thinking; human interaction was more important.

If you take these two responses, the scientific and the humanistic, as two extremes in an attempt to make people work together for the common good, you might expect a middle way. And there is.

They are two extremes because the scientific works well in some situa-tions, while the humanistic approach works well in others. People also may prefer the impersonality of the scientific bureaucratic workplace with its very clear norms of achievement and ability to change quickly to the need for constant sensitivity to everyone's feelings, painfully slow processes of change, and, at times, the fuzzy norms of success of the humanistic one.

Toward the end of the twentieth century, what might be called *institu-tional theories* of organization and a derivative of that, *cultural theories*, evolved. These theories hold that bureaucracy is best for routine operations, while in nonroutine operations emphasis should be on the interpersonal. Both look at the organization as a whole, while recognizing the complexity of that organizational whole. Each part, as well as the whole, should have an organization that matches its task. The rise of teams is a result of this movement—as is a suggested distinction between managers and leaders. A manager is one who is familiar with the "how to's" of particular situations in an organization; a leader is one always concerned with the entire organization/common good while engaging the managers to fulfill their assigned tasks. An educational institution, according to these models, is composed of both routine and nonroutine tasks. Teachers are viewed as professionals. Vice principals and sometimes teachers are seen as managers, and the principal as the leader of a school.

The institutional approach believes that you can't change organizations through good human relations or through good leadership. Rather, you must change the structures (e.g., rewards, information, expectations, etc.) to change the institution. Conflict is good, and with the proper structure conflicts can be managed for creative growth.

The cultural approach also looks at the whole, but in a more systemic fashion. The "certain something" mentioned before is now found in an inner dynamic that can be identified and enhanced, if beneficial, and changed if detrimental to the overall organization.

These general theories are implemented in a variety of ways as demonstrated in the Five Organizational Models table that follows (see Table 6.1). This table may be helpful in discovering the dominant mode of organization in your local schools. Together with the cultural toolbox, it will help in understanding your school's leadership, organization, and culture. The table is arranged in historical order reading from left to right, with the final right-hand column being the most recent theories.

USING VALUES TO UNDERSTAND CULTURE AND PROVIDE A SENSE OF DIRECTION FOR ADVOCACY

A school is all the stakeholders. It is a very complex organism. The stakeholders have multiple purposes for their involvement. They represent a vast range of ages, experiences, expertise, knowledge, and personalities. How can we come to understand this organism in order to advocate for educational change? The organizational models we have just presented provide many ways of coming to know and change it. I would suggest we use the most recent approach for discerning an organization's life and direction—understanding its culture. This culture is best understood by looking at how people's actions (words, rituals, norms, and organizations) reveal their values, what they think important. Here (see Table 6.2) is an example of a questionnaire that may help you understand a school's

Table 6.1
Five Organizational Models

	Classical		Human Relations		Cultural
Leader is	Boss	Professional	Authentic	Colleague	Whomever is needed
Followers are	Workers/Productive units	Peer professionals	Human beings	Colleagues	Diverse individuals and groups
Basis for decision	Direction from central authority	"Science"	Directions from within	Discussion Agreement	Symbols and value. "What we do."
Forms of control	Rules, laws, rewards, punishments	Facts	Actions aligned with self-concept	Interpersonal group commitments	Culture Tradition
Source of power	Superior	Truth	What I think and feel	What "we" think and feel	Community
Desired end	Compliance	Agreement within scientific parameters	Self-actualization	Consensus	Success of the community
To be avoided	Deviation from authoritative direction, taking risks	Illogical and contrary to proven facts	Not being true to oneself	Failure to reach consensus	Destruction of the team
Position relative to others	Hierarchical	Whatever works	Individual	Peer	Peer
Human relationships	Structured	Pragmatic	Individually oriented	Group orientated	Group
Basis for growth	Following the established order	Actions based on probabilities of outcome	Acting on awareness of self	Peer group membership	Success of the community
Common good achieved	When the leaders say we are successful	When assessment instruments measure that the organizational goals are met	When everyone has a sense of well-being	When an absence of internal strain and a sense of community are present	When all the stakeholders are satisfied

culture. School administrators have found it helpful in examining their institutions. The full questionnaire is found in Appendix B. I begin by explaining its categories and then answer some of the questions to give you an idea of how to do it. Afterward, I explain in depth all the categories so you can modify the questionnaire to fit your needs.

A TOOLBOX FOR CULTURAL ASSESSMENT

In what follows you will *discover symbols*. (Note: Italicized words are those found in the Toolbox.) Symbols are everywhere. But we ask you to pay special attention to words, rituals, normative behavior, and organization. *Words* people say and how they say them, write them, sing, or shout them tell us a great deal about what they value. So, too, do their repeated patterns of action that make up their day, their *rituals*, and what they consider right and wrong as they interact with one another, their environment, and the things they handle. These normative patterns of behavior, *norms*, go beyond what one is punished for, but include the intangibles of guilt. All we look at is what they do. How a school is built and organized is extremely important because it determines how students go from classroom to classroom, whom they interact with along the way, and what opportunities they have to interact with their environment. *Organization* reveals who is important, how feelings are handled, and ideas honored. Words, rituals, norms, and organization are symbols. Symbols are *located* (found) everywhere. Classrooms, playgrounds, buses, halls, and offices are suggestions of where you may find them. The discovery of where they *originated* helps us understand why they occur. It's difficult to discover the origin of symbols in an organization. Sometimes organizations retain symbols long past their original meaning. Words in school songs have many times lost their original meanings. Once we have some of the symbols of the organization, we have the challenging task of interpreting them for ourselves and the various members of the organization. What *value* is being expressed by these symbols? I offer a few values from among many suggested by opinion polls. Some schools and communities have these values out in the open and easy to see. One school district, for example, had its fourth graders make large banners expressing their school's values. The best banners were then enlarged and hung from lampposts in the town park. Filling out the Cultural Toolbox will enable you to discover if the public statement of the school's values are found in the actual educational institution. It would help a stakeholder discover if these banner-symbols, for example, tell us whether the school's symbols encourage the development of the whole person as discovered in its *foundational attitudes*. These attitudes are listed.[6]

The questionnaire-toolbox is best done by walking around a school and talking with those present. Slowly write your impressions in the *locate* columns on the chart. For example, write the word *administrator* or letter A to show where you found this symbol (e.g., mission statement). Suggestions for places to look and people to listen to are provided in each column.

Table 6.2
A Cultural Assessment Chart of Our School

Discover	Locate	Understand	Locate	Understand
Symbols	Found in: Classroom, Playground, Bus, Halls, Offices, Other.	Expresses the value of:[i] We (the school community), Learning, Respect for things, people, and environment. Religious diversity, Other.	Originated among Students, Staff, Teachers, Administrators, Other.	Demonstrates the foundational attitude of: Meaning, Belonging, Fairness, Purpose / Direction, Well-being, None present.
Words				
• Mission/vision statements	Ot Only in policy manual. Key words: discipline, education, respect.	Ot Obedience	A Principal	P
• Bulletin boards	C & H Pets, ghosts, party	W Fun, community spirit	T	We, belonging to a certain national culture.
• Badges, buttons, displayed objects	C & H Pumpkins, harvest items	Ot Tradition	T	B Belonging to a national culture.
Rituals				
• Seasonal rituals such as Thanksgiving	C: Halloween parties	We	T&S	B
• Student disruptions in the classroom				

(Continued)

Table 6.2 (*Continued*)

Discover	Locate	Understand	Locate	Understand
Normative behavior				
• Within a classroom between teachers and students				
• Dealing with other schools in contests	*Bu & H*	*S & T*	*W Team, joy of winning; failure as unacceptable*	*B & M*
Organization				
• Where the offices are placed.	*Ot All offices are at the sole entrance to the school.*	*Ot Everyone goes through this door.*	*R Security and orderly conduct*	*Purpose*
How and when phone calls and e-mails are answered.				

[1]Other values from the Phi Delta Kappa listing in the *Democrat and Chronicle*, op. cit., are honesty, democracy, racial and cultural diversity, patriotism, caring for others, moral courage, and religious diversity; from a summary of research in T. Sergiovanni, *The Principalship* (Boston: Allyn and Bacon, 1995), p. 71, education, honesty, integrity, beauty, care, justice, truth, courage, and meaningful hard work. Your school district or school may have a list of values associated with its mission statement or other programs.

When you are away from the school, fill in the *understand* columns. For example, write the words *religious diversity* or *Rd* to indicate your understanding of the symbol. Each column is composed of a few examples with spaces for other symbols. It is helpful to have a variety of people complete their own observations throughout the year or month in order to provide more points of view and thus more data. If you wish to use programs for quantitative analysis, you will find them in the footnote.[7] Here is an abbreviated version of the questionnaire, with my observations from going through an imaginary K–6, inner-city school during the last two weeks of October (see Table 6.2). The full questionnaire is in Appendix B.

One person walking through a school once leaves room for substantial error in both discovery and understanding. But this is only an example. What might we conjecture from findings so far? Certainly we might guess that the administration is distant from both students and teachers. Probably we might understand that authority, obedience, winning at all costs, and team spirit (for students and faculty) are values. Religion does not seem to be valued since there is no presence of it in obvious places. However, I did not examine how global studies was being taught.

LOOKING A LITTLE DEEPER INTO CULTURAL ANALYSIS

I use the word *culture* to describe what happens to a group of people over time. Whenever people live and work together, they form patterns associated with their lives and work. Their words, actions, and relationships become repetitious, patterned, in such a way that words have a common meaning, actions are a common way of responding to the adventures of life, and the gathering, directing, and interacting of people take on expected routines. These patterns are expressive and formative of foundational attitudes that are necessary to live our lives. The patterns are tangible. We hear them, see them, touch them, and smell them. They act as sensible avenues to the foundational human attitudes of meaning, belonging, fairness, purpose, and well-being. Without some sense of meaning, belonging, purpose, and well-being, our individual and communal lives wither. These patterns are symbols. They act to bind us together as community. Walk into a school and you hear the chatter of many stakeholders. Is the chatter for the most part happy? Argumentative? Confrontational? The sounds of the words tell us something about these stakeholders.

This communal life must be cultivated. If a community does not care for these external and internal patterns, it dies. Culture must be cared for, argued about, attended to, adapted to the changing environment, and encouraged in order to deepen. As communal life deepens through cultivation, the culture and the community depends on and enables members to adapt to the changes that threaten to destroy their lives. How a school is built and its offices arranged tell us a great deal about the community responsible for it. One group of school administrators purposely designed a school where everyone had to go up and down stairs between classes—they valued exercise. Another group placed the principal's office in the midst of the classrooms. They valued shared authority.

Most of the time we are not conscious of our culture. It is good that we do not attend to it. When an individual begins to have feelings opposite to the positive ones mentioned previously, such as patterns of pain, loss, ignorance, alienation, injustice, and purposelessness, they should begin to examine their culture for possible causes of these feelings. If most of the teachers experience constant fatigue and headaches during the school year, something is wrong with the school culture. If 50 percent of the students are failing, something is wrong. If only 10 percent of the students want to be in this school, something is wrong with the culture. Something has to be done.

The Toolbox in Appendix B provides you with a series of observations and questions, which, if answered, will aid in understanding the system of symbols that constitute a school's culture. Symbols are sensory bridges to a culture, its attitudes, values, beliefs, assumptions, and norms. The examples may be adapted to any community. This book emphasizes bringing into a school the admittance and study of diverse religions. The Toolbox enables you to see what are the school's symbols and values and if religion has any place in the total value pattern.

Symbols are what we sense. Words are spoken, read, sung, and shouted. They express our emotions and our thoughts. What words are present in the school to indicate their values and attitudes? People act. Their ritual acting and speaking as well as their normative (right/wrong; good/bad) acting and speaking all indicate what people think is important. Such a small thing as the distance between teachers and students when they speak indicates, in our Western culture, the nature of a relationship. So does the way various stakeholders gather to cheer a team, acknowledge awards, make decisions, and assemble. Are they expressing top-down authoritarianism, no questioning, and obedience to authority? How do those in the school react to authority? Symbols of words, actions, and organization tell us many things. What I provide in the Toolbox is not exhaustive. Consequently, I have left empty spaces in each category where you might want to add new items.

Where do we look for these symbols? Certainly the halls, classrooms, and offices are normal places we find these symbols, but so are the playground, auditorium, buses, and bathrooms. For example, how are people and things cared for?

What do these symbols express? What is important to individuals and the institution? I have chosen four values out of the many suggested by research that people feel are necessary in our schools.[8] Please note we are not talking about values as moral principles, but we are saying that individuals and communities have certain patterns that inform their living.

We know they are important, valuable, because we can see them. These are what are valuable to them—their values. These patterns of values expressed by what they say and do express both importance and attitudes.

What attitudes are evident? We have talked a great deal about how people need to have a sense of meaning (understood as certitude truth, and consistency of personal and social environment), belonging (as a sense of "we-ness" and fellow feeling), fairness, purpose, and physical well-being. A school that lacks these attitudes will result, as mentioned before, in people feeling ignorant, alienated, treated unfairly, without direction in life, and sick in one way or another. What attitudes are initiated and/or supported by the symbols present in the school?

What's missing is also important. Some educators talk about a "null curriculum" indicating what is not taught indicates the values of the school as much as what is taught. In the context of this book, what does it mean when a school has no references to religion at all or only to one religion? What is that telling us about this *public* school? The use of the Toolbox in Appendix B will help discover whether a null curriculum or a null value set regarding religion is present.

LEADERSHIP, CHANGE, AND THE LIFE CYCLE OF SCHOOLS

Schools, like people, are born, live, and die. Every moment we are busy being born or dying—growing or not. There is no staying still without a past and future, without change. At the same time, over those moments that constitute life remains "me," who I am, my identity. The same is true of schools. A truly successful school community is seen when 60-year-old graduates visit the school and still feel it is theirs even though both they and the school have changed. What provides this feeling of identity? The symbol patterns of words, actions, and community in a school culture act like body structure and personality patterns in an individual—they provide the basis of institutional identity. Each generation experiences all the patterns, but may emphasize different ones. For example, four people met Charlie when he was 21 years old, and they each experienced the whole person. Now, at 62, Charlie is identified by one person by his facial features, another by his laugh, another by his keen mind, and another by his limp. So among all the school symbol patterns, the everyday rituals of greeting and dismissal may be memorable and provide identity for some. For others, the way certain teacher's words and methods of instruction helped them learn something may be memorable. Various symbols are present within a school throughout its existence. Some of those present provide special points of contact and identity to various stakeholders. What happens when different symbols and/or different sets of symbols are introduced into the school culture? Such introductions may be in general methods of teaching such as suggested in Chapters 3 and 7, or in teaching math and reading, or in introducing the presence of diverse religions. Such introductions will result in appropriate developmental growth for all the stakeholders if both leaders and community work toward absorbing these differences into the school's culture.

Both the stakeholder community and the leaders of the school are essential for dealing with change. In its own way, a community gets the leaders it deserves or allows to exist. Both leaders and followers are responsible for what happens. To understand what happens, we will first give a general overview of how change occurs and what school leaders must do in dealing with change. We will then offer descriptions of a school at its birth, its midlife, and its dying, its necessary response to change, and leadership's role in facilitating the necessary changes to enable its continued life.

LEADERSHIP AND CULTURAL CHANGE

School culture is always changing, whether it is the surface change of clothing styles and music or the deeper ones associated with new technologies, scientific ideas, social norms, the nature of family, and education itself. The necessity for the recognition of and the learning about diverse religions is only one of these changes. Change may happen because of business interests when a stakeholder wishes to get a contract for serving lunches to the school. It may happen when key personnel change such as a principal who has led the school for the last 20 years or a school secretary who has been at her post for 30 years. Routine, too, may be a deep change when behaviors that were not routine become routinized as people begin to act like machines toward one another rather than as humans with feelings. Change may be good or bad for the school. It may be neutral with a need to be oriented toward the institution's benefit. To recognize and direct change, one must be able to describe, understand, and deal with its culture. Culture-modifying change occurs when the key symbols of word, action, and organization begin to shift. These symbols act as road signs for communal life. When they change, the direction of that life changes, along with all the emotions and conflicts that accompany it.

Indicators of cultural modification abound, if one allows oneself to be aware of their presence. They are there as the old symbol patterns of word, action, and organization begin to shift and cause increased anxiety and disorientation; people say the same words, teach, and act toward each other as they did before, but now it seems that these words and actions have different meanings and stimulate varied responses. This anxiety and disorientation is reflected in the increase of conflicting small groups among students, staff, teachers, administrators, and other stakeholders. Every school has a variety of cliques, teams, and groups that think differently about the school and what it is doing. When these groups grow in number, deepen in antagonism toward each other, and increase in membership, change is occurring. A leader and, if still present, the dominant culture must deal with these conflicting groups to stimulate healthy change.

A new set of symbols may be evolving or the dominant symbols in the school may be shifting. Examples abound. The school may have emphasized learning and now it is emphasizing sports. A shift in these two rituals will certainly instigate change. If the underlying purpose of the school is changing from, for example, socialization of students to academic achievement, things may look normal but expectations are changing.[9] The word *teacher* may be understood by some stakeholders as one who stands in front of the students and makes them learn certain subject matter on which they will be tested; others see the teacher as someone who facilitates the creation of knowledge in students by providing them with the proper tools for learning. Or think about what happens when a school that has been silent about religion now begins talking about it. When things like this begin to happen, change in institutional identity is occurring.

This changing of a culture may be allowed to go on until it destroys the school, or it may be consciously dealt with by bringing it forward to discover the changes and provide a plan for dealing with them. When and how a community begins to deal successfully with a changing situation is a matter of professional competence, good leadership, and acting at the opportune moment. The moment is more an intuitive grasp of the situation. But such good fortune can be aided by proper focus on the crisis nature of the change and the necessity for dealing with it. It is common to find people dealing with change by denying its precise nature and/or import. The leadership cadre must repeatedly make a case that change is occurring, is going to occur, why it is occurring, and how it will be dealt with. Only with a sense of crisis can these types of change occur. If there is high motivation for change, it will occur, but stakeholders must recognize that this is good change and are willing to make that change. Never take for granted that all stakeholders see what the change is that is occurring, that it is a change for the good, and that the institution must have in place means and information to deal with that change. Here, as a series of questions, is a checklist of some of what is necessary for a school leadership to deal with change.

- Does the leadership provide psychological safety?
- Does it provide all the stakeholders with the appropriate information and skill sets for dealing with the change?
- Are they able to absorb the anxiety expressed in such ways as outbursts of anger?
- Are they proactive rather than reactive in addressing the necessary issues associated with change?

- Have they designed compensatory mechanisms such as:
  - short meetings?
  - job security?
  - good references for those who retire or are replaced?
- Do they keep commitments and promises?
- Are they capable of analyzing the present defensive nature of the culture?
- Do they reflect back to key people how the value system is operating?
- Are they helping the institution come to cognitive redefinition of itself by:
  - providing appropriate rituals for clarifying values?
  - clarifying institutional identity?
  - providing the necessary trust for those afraid to commit themselves to the new?

Obviously the stakeholder leaders are central to all change, but especially those associated with religious diversity issues. This checklist may be used at any stage of institutional development, but there are necessary modifications to it that are dependent upon where the institution is in its lifecycle.

INSTITUTIONAL BIRTH: THE LEADER AS MIDWIFE

We have many different types of public schools. Each of them obtains its unique identity in birth as its political and educational leaders and respective stakeholders bring to life a new educational institution. They are the birth parents of a new school. Cultural patterns gradually evolve during their time of leadership. It is also true that changes that occur during these times many not be as challenging to identity formation as later in institutional life since the school is slowly and consciously shaping its identity. Later "identity" will not only be more hardened, but defended by a body of stakeholders who have gathered over time. Policy takes time to evolve from politics, and the politics involved at the beginning is usually filled with enthusiasm and creativity. The smell of fresh paint coincides with the feeling of fresh ideas, relationships, students, and that great reservoir of hope that accompanies any birth. The symbol system, usually dependent upon the surrounding culture and the professions present among the stakeholders, is slowly gaining permanency. A successful leader at this stage is one who keeps the hope alive and whose vision is able to instill everyone with a willingness to risk the mistakes of beginning a new institution whether that institution is in the *gemeinschaft* (community, loyalty) or *gesellschaft* (society, contract) mode. This institutional formation, however, is one of the most significant identity markers for the entire life cycle, as is the institution's relationship to the religions of its stakeholders and peoples of the world.

Acknowledgement of the necessity to recognize and learn about cultural religious differences will be witnessed by accepting religious leaders as important stakeholders in the students' education, respecting religious dress, holidays, and ways of life not only in the ordinary educational paraphernalia found in the halls and classrooms, but also in the policy manuals and hiring positions. When our new schools have as part of their beginning such acknowledgement, the diverse ideas and ways of life represented by these religions become part of its identity. Indeed, the local school becomes global.

INSTITUTIONAL MID-LIFE: FROM MANAGER OF CHANGE TO RENEWER OF IDENTITY

With time, cultural patterns develop. Ways of teaching and institutional goals are in place. Even the types of crisis and dealing with them become part of the school culture. The leaders, in imitation of the culture, are recognized. Many times the leaders are from within, acting more as managers than leaders. Leadership skills are not as important as management skills in mid-life institutions. Socialized into the school culture, they not only recognize it but are quite capable of invigorating it with the vitality necessary to support its clear identity.

Institutional mid-life crises become evident when stakeholders slowly begin to express feelings that something is out of place: "The school is not what it used to be." "Something is missing." It is not that the school is not what it was or that something is missing, but rather change is pouring into the school such that the words, actions, and organizations that provided its *esprit de corps* no longer do so. The characteristics mentioned previously intensify, especially with the increase of small groups vying for leadership in the school, many times offering to bring it back to its former status. Now a different type of leader is necessary, especially as principal—someone who is a "hybrid," knowledgeable about the former culture but outsider enough to bring some necessary objectivity to what is occurring. That person should make especially sure that she diagnoses the situation herself. She should not automatically accept the impressions of those doing the hiring. She will have to get a sense of the culture while making the changes to develop that culture. Habits, or patterns, can sometimes cause us to forget their purpose or make us lazy as to how to deal with a problem. That means that a renewed commitment by all to the school as it is, and as it will be, is necessary. Sometimes the process of writing or rewriting a mission statement provides the means of working through communal difficulties. The process makes public and demands rational support for those viewpoints that are sometimes hidden among the groups that have surfaced in response to the changes.

Staff, faculty, and administrative personnel who favor the necessary changes must be given time to develop the skills and knowledge to instill these changes. There will be conflict. There always is. But those whose sole purpose is initiating negative energy toward change must be dealt with. One way is to show and support the professional benefits of developing toward the needed changes. Of course another way is to help them find employment elsewhere.

Many leaders at this stage find that the change may be healthfully stimulated in six ways:

1. Engaging the stakeholders in planning that stimulates their discussions and insights in regard to the changes.
2. Engaging the stakeholders in planning that encourages them to think beyond this present institution, perhaps to the students of the future, the nation, or some higher cause.
3. Offering new technologies that will be of benefit to key stakeholders.
4. Exposing dominant cultural myths as unsubstantiated and hurtful to the institution. With sensitivity and control, provide the public a look at some possible dirty linen.
5. Making those changes requiring new skill sets and information acquisition incrementally to allow necessary training of key personnel.
6. Making physical changes in the institution such as painting, increased lighting, plants, and space availability.

Proper delegation is a central challenge to leaders seeking change during mid-life crises. No one person can do everything. The ability to recognize good leaders and managers enable the leader to expand his influence, sustain a pool of stimulating new ideas, and provide replacements for everyone in the institutional leadership team, including himself.

INSTITUTIONAL DEATH: LEADERSHIP FOR BURIAL—OR RESURRECTION

Can public schools fail? Why not? Failure is supposed to be part of our style of competition and capitalism; some win, some lose—that means failure. When a product or service lacks consumers, it is finished. It has failed. Close the doors.

A school may also fail because it no longer serves the community. The issue is whether or not the death is recognized. The community may keep pumping in money without ever resuscitating the corpse, much like a family or medical personnel may keep pumping in blood when the person is dead in denial of the plain facts. A school is dead when it becomes an end in itself—the students don't matter, the mission doesn't matter. Nothing except the institution and the paid personnel matter. When this happens, the institution keeps going but the educational institution is finished.

A school is finished, too, when it no longer adapts to its surrounding social environment. Adaptive change is necessary throughout an individual's life cycle: the baby learns to chew solids, the teen to deal with sexual urges, the adult with the responsibilities associated with success and failure, and the older person with the challenge of dealing with limited physical energies and a shorter future. Adapt or die is the human challenge. Adaptation to new technologies are an obvious challenge to contemporary educational institutions—as are shifting value patterns, changes in the types of students present in a school, funding, and increased new discoveries about student pedagogy. When a school faces these challenges by looking backward with nostalgia, those stakeholders who do so may feel good in making their observations, but are turned in the wrong direction to deal with a dying or dead institution. When a person or institution no longer looks forward to the future with hope and creativity, he has abandoned healthy living.

When an institution can no longer adapt and has lost its ability to carry out its mission, it is dead. There is some hope for resurrection, but the pain of resurrection may be such that both community and school may not be willing to find and support a leader who will admit the death, get rid of the what and who of decay, and start anew. A dead school can be resurrected only with massive change in personnel, especially leaders, and in the paradigms central to the present dead culture. New symbol patterns of word, action, and organization must replace the old.

The leadership challenge is a resurrection of identity that can only occur through revolution. The new leadership, brought in from outside the organization, can do this in many ways. Here are some that have been effective.

- Employ outside consultants to make the points about the crisis.
- Confront the institution with the possibility of its actual death.
- Use coercive persuasion when necessary.
- Communicate dedication and commitment to the stakeholders beyond your and their self-interests.
- Review all assumptions of the institution as they surface during the change period. Abandon and/or redefine those that hinder the change. This is done with patience and new symbol patterns.
- Be clear and supportive of the new values that must replace the old. Never leave a value vacuum.
- Never go it alone. Involve all stakeholders who support the change in the redefinition and value change.
- Recognize loyal opposition while dealing with destructive opposition, especially those who exercise unlawful or personal attacks.
- Counter negative responses to your recipe for change. These responses are generally found in anger, abuse of individuals, procedures, and property. Obstruction will occur in whatever way possible to the

proposed changes. The "do's and don'ts" that follow will help you cope with these challenges.

DO'S AND DON'TS OF EDUCATIONAL LEADERSHIP IN TIME OF CHANGE[10]

Do's

- Take time to reflect on where you are going and how to get there.
- Start with a plan, but be ready to change it.
- Look first to new rather than old methodologies in times of extreme stress.[11]
- Act in the light of knowledge, politics, and intuition. Knowledge alone will never provide you with direction.
- Expect criticism and resistance.
- Feel good about what you are doing.
- Remember:
  - Changing symbols changes cultures.
  - People need time to change.
  - People argue and fight.
  - People need people.
  - My vision + your vision = two sets of eyes to see the future.
  - Small things slow change more than big ones. For example, some are uncomfortable with technology, some are shy, and some have tried new pedagogies and been burnt by students and/or administrations.
  - Change takes time.

Don'ts

- Don't wait for someone else to do it.
- Don't think small; think of the whole institution and its environment.
- Don't idolize your own view.
- Don't expect the majority to support change.
- Don't wait to start the change.
- Don't give up the first time someone complains, no matter how much money she or he represents.
- Don't do it alone.

LEADER'S RESPONSIBILITY FOR A COMMON LIFE

At the very minimum, a leader looks out for the common good. If a leader does not accept the responsibility of empowering everyone to achieve their best for the good of all, then she is not a leader. Although everyone in a school should be concerned about the entire school, it is only natural that they will focus first on their immediate responsibility such as teaching the students in grade six, cleaning the hall, driving the bus, or answering the phones. The primary responsibility of the principal or the superintendent of schools is the entire school. But as we ask the teacher not to forget the other teachers, the student the other students, the staff the other staff, and all of them one another, everyone, especially the leaders, must realize that they are responsible for all. And the "all" ultimately is the entire community (not just those who attend and work at the school).

A healthy school has leaders who are or become part of the community. Leaders of advocacy coalitions should also be part of that community. Both schools and advocacy coalitions will fulfill their destinies only by realizing that they have a common mission—one that supports the entire community's common need to live well now and in the future. In our contemporary world, that must include all the religious groups in the community, as well as the world for we are linked technologically, economically, and culturally. Our future is together. Our educational system and its leaders must accept this responsibility.

CHAPTER 7

Teaching about Religion:
Learning about Sacred Grounds

I have taught about religion for 38 years. I stand between two worlds because I have also taught theology for 40 years.[1] Few people seem to understand the difference. They label both of them, along with catechetics, as teaching religion. But to understand the differences is to understand what occurs in our public schools and why all of these are important functions in society.

RELIGIOUS STUDIES AND THEOLOGY

When I first began to teach religious studies, which is a contemporary term for teaching about religion, the profession was in its infancy. Classes in comparative religion had been going on since the late nineteenth century, but religious studies, as it came to be known, sought to understand religions and teach about religion in an objective manner—much like history, psychology, anthropology, and sociology sought to understand a person or community. A center for dealing with teaching about religion in the public schools was still a few years off. The Public Education Religious Studies Center (PERSC) at Wright State University in Dayton, Ohio, was established in 1972.[2] If I was going to make the transition from teaching theology to teaching about religion, I had to change my approach.

A person who teaches theology thinks and teaches within a religious tradition. My religious tradition, for example, is 2,000 years old. Others are much older. Socialized into my religion, I took for granted that what we said, did, and thought were important to ourselves and others. The socialization resulted in providing an aura of sacredness to that way of life and many things within it. Theology is done within the context of such sacredness, socialization, and acceptance of the authorities within that tradition. I am a Catholic theologian, so that means I take for granted that the authority of the Bible, the bishops, the pope, and the actions of God among us must be taken into consideration in my theological thinking and teaching. For example, I, and my religious tradition, think that Jesus is important. Part of that importance is expressed in this tradition by saying that Jesus is both human and God. I can't, as a Catholic theologian, say I'm not going to consider this fact in my thinking and teaching. At the same time, I can try to figure out what it means to be human, to be God, and to bring these two realities together in one individual who is Jesus. Theology is done within a religious community and it accepts as important those realities and authorities that have shaped its character. So in thinking about Jesus, that means that I would have to take into consideration what others in my tradition have said about Jesus, his humanity, and his divinity. At the same time, as a theologian, I accept that Jesus is really God and really human. Much like an American cannot think about what it means to be an American without the constituent elements of his American tradition, American history, Constitution, and rule of law, so too a theologian cannot think or teach without the constituent elements of her tradition.

When I teach as a professor of religious studies, my profession is my tradition. I accept the authorities that are present in the various disciplines represented in this profession. When I teach about Jesus in religious studies, my personal belief and the authorities associated with it do not matter— just as a person's political party should not matter when doing research in political science. The facts, as determined by the various academic disciplines, are the only authority and all that matters. Do I still believe? Sure I do. Are there students in the classroom with the same belief? Sure there are. Do you need to believe in Jesus to study about Jesus? Absolutely not— no more than I have to believe in Buddha, Mohammad, Moses, or Confucius to study religions in which they play an important part. When I teach about religion, I admit that everyone's religion is sacred to them the same as mine is to me. My job in teaching about religion is to help enable everyone present to understand a religious way of life and the sacred symbols that express and reinforce the sacredness present through them.

TRADITIONAL PEDAGOGIES FOR TEACHING RELIGION BEFORE WE BEGAN TO TEACH ABOUT RELIGIONS

Memorization of an entire text or parts thereof has been the historical means of formally teaching and being taught one's sacred religious books. Students memorized the Quran, the Torah, the Bible, or selections from these texts. Christians in the West memorized their catechisms. Catechisms for teaching the young are a recent (sixteenth-century) phenomenon.

In the twenty-first century, memorization is still the dominant way most Abrahamic religions formally pass down their religion from one generation to the next. It is less so in Europe, the Americas, and some parts of Asia, but still, it is the most common way. Until the creation of such formal religious instruction as contained in catechisms, children learned their religion within their family and among their peers. They learned how to act, speak, feel, and think regarding the religious realities in their life. With the advent of modern educational techniques, religious education, regardless of age, changed wherever these techniques were accepted. Gradually, a move away from rote education began, and it continues to evolve.[3]

Formal teaching about another's religion is a recent phenomenon originating in the colonizing done by the Western nations. It has a twofold emphasis: (a) missions and conversion, and (b) liberal knowledge, comparing different cultures and therefore their religions. The latter movement, which resulted in the study of the so-called world religions, and recent immigration from the colonies into the Western nations, resulted in the necessity for the various peoples within one nation to learn about the other peoples and their religions. This teaching has increased in the United States since the 1963 Supreme Court decision *Abington v. Schempp* that, while ruling prayer and devotional exercises as unconstitutional in public schools, advocated teaching about religion. The pedagogies available for doing this paralleled whatever educational theories were current at the time.

DISCIPLINES THAT TEACH ABOUT RELIGION

My initial steps in thinking about and doing religious studies were very tentative, reflecting to some extent on how religion was being taught in the past and the present. Other teachers were accustomed to teaching about religion in the social sciences and liberal arts. Subgroups within these professions were forming to bring together those interested in, for example, the psychology of religion, or the sociology of religion, or the Bible as literature.

Talking to those with similar interests in other disciplines and reading what they authored helped me, and others, begin to understand what we must do to teach religious studies. We became convinced we must take an interdisciplinary approach to understanding and teaching about religion rather than restrict ourselves to only one disciplinary perspective. That meant we had to think not only about how to teach in an interdisciplinary manner, but also how to research in an interdisciplinary, wholistic, manner. Professional associations, such as the American Academy of Religion, were slowly developing a sense of professionalism in this regard. Beneath it all, to those who began by teaching theology, were three challenges: (a) What religions will I teach about? (b) How do I, in a neutral manner, teach things I think are true and, more importantly, some I think are false?

and (c) How do I teach in an interdisciplinary manner? What are the necessary attitudes for teaching religious studies?

WHAT TO TEACH

In previous chapters, we wrestled with the definitions of religion. That was also a way of arguing about what religions to teach. If, for example, Buddhism, Hinduism, Taoism, and Confucianism are philosophies, they do not belong in a religious studies classroom. To ask the question about what to teach demonstrates the bias of both questioner and respondent. To ask the question presupposes that religion exists, and that the question can be answered, that is, the questioner has a definition of religion and can recognize religions when he finds them. The initial search for an answer was, and still is, from a Western perspective, although we are seeing an increased interest in Chinese religions such as Taoism, Confucianism, and Pure Land Buddhism. In the early days of religious studies, the question was answered with the phrase "world religions" understood as Judaism, Christianity, and Islam, which were usually labeled monotheistic religions, and Hinduism, Buddhism, Taoism, and Shinto, which were usually labeled monistic religions. We began to study these religions using four categories: belief, ritual, morals, and polity or organization. This emphasis was on belief understood as written documents of stated beliefs. These texts provided an easy and accustomed instrument for learning. *Belief*, after all, was a word used in Christian religions, especially Protestant Christianity, which saw belief and text as the core of religious life. Those early divisions between monotheistic and monistic also reflected the same Christian emphasis upon belief, but this time in God. *Ritual*, while accepted as a necessary part of the description of a religion, was usually quickly passed over to spend most of the time studying belief. Notice how easily teachers and students focus on what they think important, belief and text, while setting aside something that may be more important to the religion, ritual, or community. Taking all of this into consideration, I learned the world religions and taught them in various ways trying to gain the interest of students who were slowly gaining a more global view of their world, and who also preferred getting an objective view of these religions.

TEACHING OBJECTIVELY, IN A NEUTRAL MANNER

Although the students wanted an objective view and religious studies proclaimed that it was giving it, the entire exercise of objectivity was flying in the face of the intensification of pandering to individual tastes and concerns. Objectivity and neutrality suggested somehow we could take the subjectivity of "me" and "you" out of teaching and learning. Recently, I found a good summary of what we had to do in the book *Finding Common*

Ground published by the First Amendment Center. These guidelines were agreed upon by 17 religious and educational organizations. I have rephrased them to focus on the teacher.[4]

- The teacher's approach to religion is *academic*, not *devotional*.
- The teacher strives for student *awareness* of religions, but does not press for student *acceptance* of any religion.
- The teacher sponsors study *about* religion, not the *practice* of religion.
- The teacher may *expose* students to a diversity of religious views, but may not *impose* any particular view.
- The teacher *educates* about all religions; she does not *promote* or *denigrate* religion.
- The teacher *informs* students about various beliefs; he does not seek to *conform* students to any particular belief.

This is an excellent summary of what we tried to do. A great deal has been done to achieve such neutrality in our teaching. We had as our model the sciences and a professional culture that emphasized *gesellschaft* (contract-based) communities where people treated each other in an unfeeling way. The third and last task was more challenging.

TEACHING IN AN INTERDISCIPLINARY MANNER

Each of the major categories initially accepted for describing a religion lent itself to one of the major disciplines: belief to philosophy, texts to literature, ritual to anthropology, morality to philosophy and/or psychology, and community/polity to sociology and political science. An interdisciplinary approach used in religious studies demanded crossing the boundaries of these disciplines and developing new methods of research and teaching. Such an approach was usually looked down upon by the dominant disciplines in the education system. They reflected the modern reductionist approach to learning and the building block approach to education. This approach reduced knowledge to pieces of data discovered by the scientific method, and placed them in a causal sequence dependent upon one "foundational" piece. The world around us was divided by various academic disciplines, each in charge of a large packet of data with its coinciding foundational pieces. Each discipline concentrated on its packet of data garnered from reality. Thus our modern hard and soft sciences evolved in such a way that reality was reduced to a foundational bit of information from which everything else developed. To attempt to cross the boundaries and look at Humpty Dumpty as a whole, not as pieces, was judged both impossible and denigrating to our search for knowledge; but that did not deter many in religious studies. The methods of research and teaching that gradually were formulated led the way for other interdisciplinary studies such as gerontology and gender studies. As this began to occur, the world of research and teaching was changing. The necessity of interdisciplinary research was discovered in the hard sciences as well as the social sciences. The modes of constructivist knowledge and the admittance of varied types of intelligence were advocated as necessary presuppositions for the development of new ways of learning from K–12.

We have not yet fully answered the interdisciplinary question. Some attempts have been made, but we still have a long way to go. This does not mean we stop teaching about religions, for doing so is one of the most invigorating and creative opportunities a teacher is offered.

WHAT A TEACHER *NEEDS* TO TEACH ABOUT RELIGION

The challenges were invigorating and offered a creative opportunity to think and teach about religion in new ways. They were such because I liked what I was doing and had the support of various administrations as I attempted to do it. *Liking what you do* is always a necessary prerequisite for a teacher and especially in one who teaches religious studies. I have worked with and observed teachers who either do not like or do not know how to teach material in a neutral, or objective, manner. If someone is constantly tense while in the classroom, feeling a deep dissatisfaction in portraying material in a noncontroversial manner, not able to control outbursts of disdain toward a religious way of life different than her own, and not in contact with others who teach these topics, she should consider abandoning the profession. She is doing a disservice to her profession, religion, peers, and students. Disdain, as well as enthusiasm, for what you teach is contagious.

Enthusiasm, however, is only part of what makes a good teacher. *Knowledge and skills are also necessary.* Each religion produces a great deal of information about itself from a partisan perspective. There is nothing wrong with that—it should. The challenge for us in the early days of the profession was to take these partisan accounts of religions and convert them into nonpartisan or neutral descriptions. Some religions take offense when a nonpartisan account of their religion is offered. Essential, they feel, to any description of their religion is the necessary claim that it is the only religion, or, in some cases, that if you do not adhere to this religion you will go to hell. This refusal by some religions in those early days was evidenced in their demand that when their religion was discussed, such a discussion and description must be done by those certified by them—their catechists and/or theologians. Such a demand was not unusual. Most countries had public school systems that contained religious schools as part of that system. Higher education many times, in those countries, found stand-alone colleges and universities with a specific religious orientation supported by public funds. The same presupposition, that one can learn about religion only from those who adhere to that religion, is manifest in those countries that retain one school system and mandate that only one religion be taught in that school system. In those places, they believe there is only one true religion. All others are false. Falsehood should not be found in a modern school. Thus no other religion should be discussed. If it was discussed, it was to show their errors. Our challenge in religious studies was to describe each religion without claiming any one religion as the one holding all truth. When you do not take sides in describing religions, many religious authorities are uneasy about these descriptions.

Such content descriptions were also provided by the social sciences. They were good sources for the information that was to be taught about the religions. But this content, while not religiously partisan, was methodologically narrow because it represented only one field of inquiry. To describe religion only from a psychological, social, historical, anthropological, or literary perspective did not offer an accurate portrait of the whole religion. It seemingly reduced religion to only one of these disciplinary perspectives such that someone seemed religious only because of their socialization process, only because of their psychological makeup, or only because of their economic condition. While such reductionism is part of the modern method of study, it does tend to lead some to see this reduced explanation as the only, if not best, way to understand religion in general, and religious people in particular. Religious studies sees the religions as an independent variable not, as in the sciences, a dependent one. Early on, what came to be known as a phenomenological approach to religious studies, dominated the scene because it attempted to provide a wholistic approach to understanding each religion without the categories of social science, its reductionistic methods, or the demands of comparative religion. It took each religion as it was, described it from as many perspectives as possible, and offered it in as neutral a way as possible.

Today such neutral perspectives are found in many of the texts and Web sites dedicated to helping one learn about the religions of our country and the world. These can be found in Appendix A, Sources. But the older religious protagonists in opposition to religious studies had a point—we can never remain neutral before the major questions of existence: life, death, what future to choose, and what can we hope for? The modern point of view, represented by many of the Supreme Court decisions found in Chapter 2, and the early development of religious studies claimed the existence of the "objective," a stance beyond all feeling and bias. The contemporary "postmodern" point of view claims no such stance exists. We are always in some linguistic community, physical, psychological, and cultural from which we think and teach. Our search in the second half of the twentieth century for neutral texts and sites produced excellent materials for learning and teaching. At the same time, these have their bias. Everyone does. To become good teachers we must recognize these biases; true objectivity is recognizing our and others' biases—and thinking and acting in the light of these biases for the good of all.

Reflection is essential to every teacher, but especially to one who teaches religious studies.[5] *Reflection* enables us to test reality, to seek out our presuppositions, and discover the contexts of our thought and teaching. Such reflection has been introduced under the rubric of reflective practice among educators. Donald Schon first used the term in 1983.[6] Kettle and Sellars suggested that such reflection is best as part of teacher collaboration with each other.[7] Reflective practice, of course, finds its base in John Dewey's work in the first half of the twentieth century.[8] What is important, I think, is to recognize that, with Dewey, reflection is another way of thinking. And, with postmodernists, that reflective thinking enables us, with time, to understand our biases toward the religions we teach. This type of reflection has five dimensions to its continual use: careful listening, concentrated reflection, continual search for information, conversation about the topic, and exchange of ideas and methods when appropriate.

Careful listening, which we outlined in Chapter 2, enables us to hear in a neutral way the nuance of sacred language present among religious practitioners, those who describe this practice, and those who offer these descriptions. It is not unusual, for example, that cultural expectations surface among both teacher and students. In the United States it means there will be an expectation that all religions possess a personal God. Teachers will find themselves struggling with descriptions of Hinduism, Buddhism, Shintoism, and Confucianism to provide some comparison or example similar to a Western "God." It is difficult to say no to cultural expectations whether of God or of spirit. The struggle to portray in hunter-gatherer religions their view of life's inner workings without using our contemporary view of spirit is always a tension—as it is to spend more time studying religious belief than ritual or community. Listening to the language of all concerned is both an intellectual tool for learning and a pedagogical one for teaching.

Concentrated reflection means that a religious studies teacher needs to take time at the end of the day to think about the content, methods, and experiences of the day. This may mean developing a habit of making quick jottings of what is occurring during the day, or going back over what was planned to think about how it turned out, and writing down on those plans what happened. Concentrated reflection means, however, that the teacher goes beyond the jottings and journal writing to think about the presuppositions of what has occurred. For only in examining those presuppositions can one become aware of one's biases.

Conversation with others is essential to test the reality of what and how one teaches. We see things through our eyes. But only when we are able to put together the multiple views of all those who saw what is said and done can we begin to know what was said and done. In the sociology of religion, for example, it only gradually dawned on many researchers that they were using a biased method of authentic religiosity by asking if people worshipped weekly in their religion. Only in some Christian religions is weekly Sunday worship considered a sign of being an authentically religious person. It was only with the different perspectives of sociologists from other religious backgrounds that they were able to see this type of research category as biased. An important "other" that must be included in any conversation is a knowledgeable representative of the religion or religions being studied. One bias of a neutral study of religion is neutrality itself, since essential to any religion is the conviction that this religion is sacred, important, and pivotal to one's existence. Such conviction can only be found in one of its adherents. To bring them into the conversation both in one's study and one's teaching of a religion is essential to learning about that religion.

Continual learning is absolutely necessary for every teacher of religious studies. The pressure of preparing lessons, talking with students, parents, and administrators, grading, doing administrative paperwork, and attending meetings cannot leave a teacher empty of the desire to learn about her topic. New methods do not absolve one from learning new information. It is essential to professional reflection.

Change is the result of this professional reflection. Slowly, or sometimes suddenly, one realizes the bias that demands the selection of certain content, or suggests this pedagogical emphasis rather than that one. And the realization leads to change. To change is to be alive, to be enthused, and to enjoy what one is doing. If one is to change, the *support of one's peers and administrators* is necessary.

DOING IT TOGETHER IS NECESSARY TO TEACH ABOUT RELIGION: WHO DO I NEED TO SUPPORT ME?

We need as many people as possible to support us. In the late 1960s, when I first began to change from using the lecture method all of the time, I was one of the few interested in changing. I knew that change had to take place, but I had difficulty discovering why it had to take place and what to do. If what I did was to be more than a subjective whim, where was the research that could help me make substantive decisions?

My concern about changing pedagogies, however, led me to discover a few others at my university who were interested in new methods in teaching. Serendipitously, I also became part of a Danforth grant to test in-service training and the action-reflection method in an ecumenical setting. Over the years, I have found what happened back then essential to pedagogical change—gathering with those of like mind in my home institution and getting together with those willing to test new pedagogies outside my own institution. We need those with the same issues in our own institution because we can support one another when the majority of the faculty, students, and administration have another definition of what makes a good teacher. When I first began to use film in my high school classes as a means of bringing religious questions into the classroom, I encountered our school principal in the hall. "When did you get a degree in projection technology?" he asked. "Maybe we should get one of the electricians to take over your class!" he threatened. I needed others both at home and nationally to acknowledge the validity of what I was doing in order to deal with such questions and threats.

We need people outside our institution to provide us with a sense of accomplishment and visions for pedagogical futures. I have always found that involvement in new educational endeavors enables me to have a sense of control over the changing attitudes of students, faculty, and administration. The shrill complaint of an older teacher during the years we were testing the action-reflection method is still a challenging presence today: "How can I teach them if they do not have the right background?"

One group of students wanted to learn about a number of biblical themes as a result of their work among the poor. We were talking with a renowned scripture scholar. When I inquired as to whether she would help them understand the relationship between the Bible and life, she responded, "How can I teach them if they do not have the prerequisites?" It is a response I have heard more and more as classrooms become more pluralistic. The first time I heard it, I felt threatened. Today I feel curious and challenged—curious as to why teaching has to be a linear, causal system of building blocks (prerequisites) that does not allow full knowledge unless one can play with all the blocks; and challenged to find other ways of teaching-learning that do not depend upon this system of prerequisites. The complaint today is many times a cry for a return to the former uniformity with its consequent insensitivity to the teaching-learning event.

We need support because when we begin to change pedagogies away from direct instruction (see Chapter 4) we are beginning to change the culture of an institution. Intuitively the entire culture responds to such threats. As we gather together the various pedagogies that differ from those used in direct instruction such as in-class peer tutoring, the use of role plays and dyads, as well as collaborative learning,[9] we are actually beginning a new school. A conscious realization of the processes necessary to change pedagogies is essential for us to take complete charge of the transformation.

WHERE TO LOOK FOR SUPPORT

We must look for support everywhere. There are three groups who may support us in our endeavor to change pedagogies: the administration, the departmental chair, and faculty outside our department.

Most contemporary administrators have discovered the student. Without going into the reasons for such discovery, we can take for granted that today administrators will, at least verbally, commit themselves to updating and/or changing teaching pedagogies. How deep a commitment this is can usually be discerned by in-service programs, tenure decisions, pay raises, and professional development grants.

More and more schools have an individual or team whose sole task is to stimulate pedagogical innovation. For those members of a department who advocate changing pedagogies in the face of a majority of faculty who do not, these outside experts or advocates are essential to personal pedagogical change. They at least provide us with validity for proposed changes.

What provides us with the most support is to attract teachers to change by teaching about religion with innovative pedagogies. Some parts of my research indicate that teachers who are most likely to change are those who are middle-aged, tenured, confident in past teaching methods, and secure in their discipline.[10] In addition, those who successfully change always have enthusiasm for teaching and for contact with students. At the same time, we must remember that most faculty and students will resist change.

CHANGING TOGETHER

It usually takes three years to know whether faculty will support and/or teach about religion using appropriate pedagogies. When our campus team for new pedagogies offered a workshop on student management teams, one of our department members began to use some of the ideas. She was so enthusiastic about its use that after one semester she began to encourage those of us who advocated changing pedagogies to join her. To be honest, this particular individual sometimes would try things that were not tested and, to my mind, ill-conceived. Consequently, I listened, but was slow to imitate. I was worried that there was not sufficient data regarding its effectiveness and that it might be a passing fad and a waste of my time. A few members of the faculty outside of our department also began using management teams, so she did not need support from her departmental peers. After one year, I saw that others outside the department were using management teams, that she was successfully able to use teams in all of her classes, and that the students were responding favorably to their use, so I started to use them in my classes.

As I reflected upon this process of acceptance, I realized that I was typical of what happens as peer faculty advocate for pedagogical change. Reflection upon the process may help you in your own changes.[11]

1. *Awareness:* I am not concerned about it.
2. *Informational:* I would like to know more about it.
3. *Personal:* How will using it affect me?

4. *Management:* I seem to be spending all my time getting the material ready.
5. *Consequence:* How is my use affecting the students?
6. *Collaboration:* How is what I am doing like or unlike what other teachers are doing?
7. *Refocusing:* I have some ideas about something that would work even better.

I was also aware, from previous experience, that the fact that other faculty were using student managers was an important stimulus to my final acceptance of the method. It took three years for me to finally begin to use student managers. As I later found out, this is about average for a teacher to change her style of teaching. Sometimes pedagogical change is urged upon the faculty by chief administrators without consideration of the previously mentioned process of acceptance. Many faculty are, deservedly, hesitant to take on a certain new way of teaching merely on the urgings of a chief administrator, especially if that administrator had never taught religious studies.

At the same time, research shows that the adoption of new methods usually occurs for the following reasons: (a) administrators offer significant rewards and prestige associated with the acceptance of new pedagogies; (b) friends and colleagues are getting involved; (c) a new pedagogy promises a direct "payoff" in making one's student evaluations better; and (d) a new method provides better interaction among everyone in the class.[12]

STAYING TOGETHER: LEADERSHIP

Good leaders are necessary for pedagogical change. Trying to change things in a school takes time and perseverance. It took three years for my friend to convince me that student management teams were worthwhile. Years later, the majority of our department is still convinced that lecture must be the methodology of choice. Change away from the sole use of the lecture method, in my lifetime, is still not complete. Thirty-eight years is a long time, but some change has occurred; 38 years of perseverance is paying off as religious studies departments, professional organizations, and public and private schools are changing their approach to teaching about religion.

Two other essential aspects of leadership in pedagogical change are *networking and availability of handouts*. We must seize the opportunity to play the role of pedagogical leader during conversations at lunch, in the hallways, and at committee meetings. For many faculty, their only conversation about teaching is complaining about how dumb the students are. I have found that many times this is a facade behind which faculty hide. Many are genuinely interested in talking about teaching, but are hesitant to do so. Once faculty begin to talk about teaching, there must be available examples of what can be done. Two types of handouts are helpful in this regard: well-researched arguments advocating a particular pedagogy, and teaching checklists or recipes that provide security for faculty as they change their ways of teaching. We are finding that most faculty appreciate not only the paper handouts associated with PowerPoint® usage, but also CDs containing the images used in any of the workshop presentations. Most of us teach as we were taught. To change one's teaching methods is fraught with fear and anxiety. Anything that can lessen that fear and anxiety will heighten the teaching-learning event.

EVALUATIONS

If we see the necessity of changing how we teach about religion, we must develop new methods of assessment to be used to improve our classes, to obtain merit pay, and to know if the teaching-learning event is actually happening. Evaluations reveal the commonsense reality that all new pedagogies are not effective. Some fail the evaluative tests we are slowly developing, and some reveal they can be used to dominate the classroom as easily as the lecture method. Because one abandons the sole use of the lecture method does not mean that one has abandoned the coercive and manipulative power inherent in the role of teacher. Just think about what the tests associated with the No Child Left Behind Act of 2001 have done to the power of the teacher. A case study becomes an exercise in manipulation as a teacher refuses to hear all the experiences arising from the study or allows the voice of only one group of students to be heard. This is especially true in a modern American culture that encourages stories of victimhood. Sometimes the voice of the oppressor is seldom allowed to be heard except through the mouth of the oppressed. If only one voice is heard, be it the teacher's or a particular group of people's, then that pedagogy does not support the pluralism and diversity present in our classrooms.[13]

Sometimes pedagogical change is actually the advance of one cultural movement. Many methods and programs, therefore, are expressive of larger movements. The people "we do it together with" are like-minded advocates of a certain ideology. Movements are usually clear about who/what they dislike ("them") and are convinced that "we" have the truth. The differences between facts, fads, fashions, and movements are many times in the eye of the beholder. "Educational innovations are highly perishable goods."[14]

And finally, new pedagogies are sometimes destructive of our educational community. They must be recognized as such and abandoned when not reflective of the diversity present in our classes, oppressive of the various voices there, and/or destructive of community.

Personal evaluation of one's teaching is ongoing. The various types of professional reflection, plus collaboration with others, generally keep one honest in such evaluations. The reality of institutional evaluation of one's teaching moves the practical, personal need of assessment into the politics of institutional policy, leadership styles, and expectations resultant from diverse views of the purpose of education. If the teacher has been collaborative and respectful of the chain of command in the development of his teaching styles, he will know what to expect when what he was doing becomes exposed to the larger audience of principal, peer review, coaching, or whatever other evaluative processes are used by the school. These processes are so diverse and so imbued with different presuppositions that it would take another book to review them. A few points should be made about them.[15]

A first and necessary distinction is introduced by the question: Why are you or your institution seeking evaluation? Knowledge of why you seek assessment determines the assessment methods. As we all know, if someone wants to cut wood and they use a hammer, they have picked the wrong instrument to achieve their intended objective.

If you are trying to discover how to improve your classroom teaching, you are doing *formative assessment*. Formative assessment is diagnostic. Its sole purpose is to improve what you are doing in the classroom. *Summative assessment* is done to rank the outcomes of your teaching-learning process with others for reward or punishment. From summative assessments come your salary, your promotion, and other "rewards" for your service in the teaching profession.

Some authors suggest that it is best to keep these two types of assessment separate from each other. If that is possible, we should do it. Both types of assessment answer the same question: Are you a good teacher? The purpose of the answer in both instances is to improve teaching. The principal reason for the competition (summative assessment) among teachers is to make them better teachers, not to give them more money or prestige. It may be true, however, that the instruments we use to answer the question of whether we are a good teacher may not always "fit" our intentions. For example, quantitative answers help to make summative assessment more easily than qualitative answers. Qualitative answers are better responses to formative assessment questions.

Quantitative assessment focuses on the collection of large numbers of numerical data. Its models are based on the scientific tradition of experimental and quasi-experimental research methods. It seeks clear and distinct results from research. It analyzes and generalizes these results for use. It is a good research tool when the results are valid and reliable. Its weakness is the triviality of findings and the lack of application to the actual classroom. Many times the questions asked are not examined for the particular bias of the researcher. Their "generalizability" and numerical nature make them easy to use for comparing teachers "objectively" among themselves, and for presentations about the state of teaching to the various stakeholders.

Qualitative assessment focuses on describing the event(s) within its/their natural settings. It seeks to understand the underlying presuppositions of what is happening to enable one to work better with this group over a prolonged period of time. Problem-centered and pragmatic, it many times is based on ethnographic methods found within anthropology. Its weakness is its limited scope, particularity, and subjectivity. Because it many times is nonnumerical in nature, it seems more subjective than a quantitative report. Its narrative form usually takes more time to read than the charts and formulas of quantitative reports, thus it does not receive the same attention by the many stakeholders when they seek summary results of evaluative procedures.

Some other things to keep in mind as we face institutional assessment are the following:

- One "assessment" is never enough. One instrument of assessment (e.g., example, a survey) needs other instruments. Formative assessment needs encouragement from administration and colleagues in the form of rewards such as time off to improve one's teaching methods or money to go to a conference (summative assessment). The goals of the classroom must fit into the goals of the school and, in turn, into the goals of the district. One assessment is never enough.
- Expressed dissatisfaction may not be an expressed complaint.
- Stephen Brookfield's advice should always be recognized in our continual struggle to become a better teacher: "Don't misinterpret poor evaluations," "Be wary of the myth of the perfect teacher," "Don't confuse academic success with teaching skills," "Accept the normality of failure," and "Be realistic about your limits."[16]

WHEN "DOING IT TOGETHER" CREATES A NEW COMMUNITY

Michel Desjardins[17] once described those who teach religious studies as being on the edge of the teaching profession and the cultures within which they live. Some of us may experience this marginality, but "doing it together" begins to build another community of shared concern. "Doing it together" means that we share our teaching experience, teaching scholarship, and teaching concerns with those in our institution. That means both that we support one another in what we are doing in our departments, as well as work together to create a new pedagogical culture in the school. It sometimes means that we actually team teach with those from other departments, or enter their classrooms as we mutually build learning communities or critique one another. Moving across departmental and professional boundaries is fearful for many of us who have been socialized into our profession through the degree-granting process. Our sense of professionalism makes us hesitant to enter, in any way, into the classroom of another. Yet, if we are to encourage others, and participate and share with others, this has to be done. Our ability to be empowered and to empower others to cross those boundaries, will create new pluralistic communities of learning and teaching that directly affect what happens in our classrooms.

IN THE CLASSROOM

Doing things together includes doing, thinking, and talking with our students no matter what age, gender, religion, economic status, or type of intellect. In our training we learn how to deal with such diversity of student and student behavior. In our professional development we gain depth in the knowledge and skills to empower those with whom we learn and share our knowledge. In this chapter I have reviewed some of what is required in both knowledge and skills. More resources for both of these are found in the appendix. What we need to reflect on here are the necessary attitudes a teacher needs when teaching about religion. Some of these are common to all teachers; others are not. I would suggest the following attitudes as essential to anyone who teaches about religion either as a stand-alone subject in religious studies or as more discipline based such as history, global studies, music, literature, and social studies—neutrality toward religion, but not toward the student; curiosity about religions in their cultural context, reflection, and appreciation for the sacred and diversity.

A *neutral attitude* toward religion means that every religion and religious person, including those who deny the value of any current religions, is treated with equal appreciation and time. Equality of treatment is always a judgment call because it will reflect local conditions as well as present global interests. Of course, it will also depend upon the teacher's knowledge and time allotted within the entire curriculum for whatever religion or religious topic is presented. It also means that a teacher's knowledge and skills should be used to provide equality when a student's knowledge is lacking. Many times, for example, Christian students do not know that the religion they practice is Christian. Neutrality does not mean that one allows a student to remain in ignorance that historically Lutherans, Presbyterians, and Baptists are called Christians. Neutrality also means that if a student offers an opinion about some religious topic and does not realize that it is also held by many famous thinkers, the teacher tells her about her "famous" opinion. A teacher might inform a student, for example, who tentatively claims that Christians may acknowledge the legitimacy of gay marriage, that many Christian theologians would support him in his claim, while not necessarily agreeing with his argument. A neutral attitude attempts to provide an equal window through which each religion is seen.[18]

Equality needs knowledge. Knowledge builds on focused *curiosity*. A generally curious attitude is helpful in learning about religions. More helpful for a teacher, however, is to focus the curiosity upon the religions found in her classroom or in the local area. Thematic curiosity is also helpful. I have found that students are interested in how people worship and pray in addition to their attitudes on sexual and gender matters. These are going to come up in class. If the teacher has them using the community as a learning tool, it will come up as they visit and discuss things with people of various religions. It is good to satisfy one's curious appetite every now and then, but true intellectual nourishment comes with a focused curiosity.

Religious curiosity finds its roots in ignorance and mystery. Like the night sky suggests at once the limit of a dark surface and the possibility of transcendence in the traces of light upon or beyond it, so religious curiosity sees the immediacy of human symbols and the possibility of the infinite they indicate. Foundational to all religions is the mantra, "We don't know," repeated *ad infinitum*. Yet, as with every mantra, the regularity of its saying provides security for life, now lived in acknowledgement of both mystery and ignorance.

A teacher will often find himself saying, "I am not sure." "I'll find out." "Where do you think I should look?" to his students. We can never know all about all the religions of the world. We enjoy the moments of discovery and the instances of experience. We attempt to stimulate in our students the same curiosity based in a confidence that we can live well with the ignorance and the awareness of mystery that arises from it.

We have already talked about the necessity of *professional reflection*. It is only as this is practiced daily will it become attitudinal, part of one's character.

I have emphasized the sacred nature of religion. Such emphasis results in the teacher's treatment of religious objects, people, times, dress, ideas, rituals, and moral imperatives as holy to them. The *attitude of reverence*, which is associated with the holy, is, hopefully, found in other aspects of life, but it is essential in how he treats what other people treat as holy. One does not make fun of the holy, nor treat it without care. Sometimes silence is the only context for what is holy. This may be difficult when teaching about objects that the students may find amusing. Unease before the unfamiliar many times is dealt with in our culture by crude, self-centered remarks. Many of the images of Eastern deities, for example, with their portrayal of elephant heads and naked maidens, certainly find naive students twittering in response to seeing or touching them. Sacred music may easily be unfamiliar to many of them and cause uttered derogatory remarks. Part of a student's religious education is learning to respond to the sacred with silence, with care, with permission for touch, for dealing with that which people find beyond understanding and projecting a source of power. If the teacher has an attitude of reverence for the sacred, teaching these things is much easier.

KNOW YOUR STUDENTS

Knowing one's students is central to any teacher's identity and function as a teacher. The needs of the students are in the forefront of any religious studies program. In a religious studies classroom this student-centered learning easily translates into Carl Rogers's "unconditional positive regard" seen here as accepting the student without any negative judgments as to their basic worth and religious motivation.[19]

Such acceptance does not mean that we encounter them without preconceptions. "Unconditional positive regard" does not mean that we abandon the training we underwent to teach. Everything we described about religious identity is important for teaching about religion. Decisions about which religions to include and how much to discuss about religion are determined by the grade level of the students, these psychosocial aspects, and the academic requirements of the course being taught. Advisory boards such as the one noted in Chapter 1 are helpful for filling out the details of what and how to teach about the religions of the United States and the world. The following is a general outline of what is taught at each level. Sources for curricula and appropriate pedagogies are found in the resources section of this book.

Elementary Students

Elementary students are introduced to the basic ideas and practices of the world's major religions by focusing on the generally agreed-upon meanings of each religious way of life—the core beliefs and symbols, as well as important figures and events. Stories drawn from various religions may be included among the wide variety of stories read by students. This generally occurs during the study of family, community, various cultures, the nation, and other themes and topics that may involve some discussion of religion. Hands-on pedagogies enable students to actually see and feel religious objects.

Secondary Students

On the secondary level, social studies, literature, and the arts offer opportunities for the inclusion of study about religions—their ideas and practices. An especially helpful method may be found in the integrated curriculum approach found in many middle schools.[20] The academic needs of each course determine which religions are studied. In a U.S. history curriculum, for example, the study of some religious communities may be given more time than others, but only because of their predominant influence on the development of the American nation, past and present. In world history, a variety of religions are studied in each region of the world in order to understand the civilizations and cultures that have shaped history and society. The overall curriculum should include all of the major voices, and some of the minor ones, in an effort to provide the best possible education. When presenting such snapshots of a religion, the teacher must attempt to indicate that these are vital religions that are constantly developing and alive today in ways different than the snapshot presented in class.

Fair and balanced study about religion on the secondary level includes critical thinking about historical events involving religious traditions. Religious beliefs have been at the heart of some of the best and some of the worst developments in human history. The full historical record (and various interpretations of it) should be available for analysis and discussion. The challenge in such historical critiques is to provide a balanced and sensitive discussion of how religions change throughout time. Using primary sources whenever possible allows students to work directly with the historical record. Teachers will need scholarly supplemental resources that enable them to cover the required material within the allotted time, while simultaneously enriching the discussion with study of religion. Hopefully in the upper grades opportunities are provided for students to gain a more complete view of religions by offering religious studies classes.

We all know there is a great diversity of students in our classrooms. Students typically know very little about religion in general and about their religion in particular. In some smaller towns and certain urban areas, many students know a great deal about the religion they were socialized into, but little about that particular religion's history, classifications, and present-day disagreements. They do have more religious knowledge than most students. That means that most students are insecure and uncertain with the language and presuppositions used when talking about religion. This is not unusual. The same can be said, but sometimes not admitted, of all the other disciplines. Everyone should admit that while curiosity comes naturally to most of us, learning is much more of a challenge to all of us. Learning begins by our mutual admittance that "we do not know." This is especially true in religious matters where many think one's opinion loudly stated trumps knowledge.

Some students, as a result of their home environment and maturation, are familiar, however, with the language and meaning of objectivity and neutrality. While perhaps lacking the content and experiences associated with religion in general and one religion in particular, they are prepared to enter into an examination of the religions of the world.

The result is that we find four types of students in our classes: (a) those who are very certain about religion and are very verbal about their knowledge; (b) those who see all religion and religious knowledge as relative, usually meaning "useless"; (c) those who are seeking to meet some religious or other need through taking a class; and (d) those from a mixed religious background who have experienced diverse religions and seek to know more about the ones they have experienced.

With good fortune, the right mix of students, and proper pedagogy, the views of all of these students gradually come to light. Here are some brief suggestions of how to deal with the variety of religious viewpoints as expressed among these types of students.

The views themselves should be treated:

- by acknowledging them.
- by acknowledging them as their speaker intends.
- by helping everyone understand them.
- by providing a space and time for interaction between those who hold these views/lead these ways of life.
- by establishing an atmosphere of respectful dialogue, for example, by beginning with, "In my opinion . . ." or "Today, I think . . ."
- by establishing the hospitality of listening: delay immediate judgment.
- by recognizing voices representative of current or past religious views or ways of life as truly authoritative because of those they represent. For example, "This view is Lutheran/Muslim. Here is where you can find out more about it." Support them as legitimate positions that people of good heart and mind could hold, with a substantial following, despite their minority status in this class or institution.
- by taking the opportunity to explain the strengths of the "other's" point of view and set it in a sociohistorical context to demonstrate how people would hold such a view.
- by providing the respect shown through critical questioning and not pandering or speaking in a condescending manner.
- by modeling our response upon how we expect the students to respond.
- by respecting a student's right to privacy, especially when expressing an opinion contrary to the majority.
- by allowing diversity to emerge.
- by establishing a process with the students when something is permissible and when something is not permissible.
- by taking into consideration that many professionals want to "fix things" right away. Many times we, and our students, need space to develop a response, for example, one can allow participants to hold responses until the next week.
- by reaffirming that the norm is dialogue, not diatribe.
- by empathizing rather than tolerating. (Tolerance = "We'll accept you, but we're better attitude." Empathy = appreciation, seeking common ground with the other(s), imaginatively entering into the "world" of the other.)

LOOKING BACKWARD/LOOKING FORWARD: TEACHING ABOUT RELIGIONS

We have come a long way since I began teaching religious studies. The First Amendment Center and the Council on Islamic Education demonstrate how far we have come in a study that offered these conclusions: (a) Teaching about religion is mandated in some form in both the primary and secondary schools by most of the states; (b) Teaching about religion occurs in the social sciences, for example, in descriptions of communities, U.S. and world history, geography, and civics; (c) There is a national consensus as to how to teach about religion in a constitutionally appropriate manner; and (d) There is a growing consensus among professional organizations as to what should be covered in a comprehensive plan for teaching about religions. These may be found especially in the seven major national social studies standards developed by the National Council for History Education, the National Council for the Social Studies, and the National Council on Economic education.[21] Curricula for religious studies may be found in many places. The American Academy of Religion's Web site is especially noteworthy because it offers not only different curricula, but also extensive reflections on many topics such as teaching about the Bible in public schools.[22] Religious studies itself is taught in the majority of our public and private colleges and universities. Indeed, we have come a long way.

FUTURE NEEDS

- We need to solidify these gains in the face of budget cuts and national exams or there is a great danger of losing them.
- We need to develop and support better research as to content and methods for teaching, especially the use of critical thinking about the religions in the upper grades, college, and university—to move beyond description to analysis.
- We need to develop advisory committees that are representative of the community to support public institutions willing to encourage learning about diverse religions.
- We need to create hospitable climates for religious expression in our schools that encourage empathy for diverse religious ways of life.
- We need to provide professional development funds for religious studies.
- We need to support library budgets that provide information on various religious ways of life, especially in an autobiographical manner.
- We need to seek, discover, and encourage the twin necessities for a creative future—that which unites us to work together; that which provides individual choices for when some of those futures fail.

CHAPTER 8

Religious Bullies: My Way or No Way

When two people look in a mirror they see difference. When a panel of five people responds to a question from the audience they hear their differences. When you squeeze into a crowded bus you feel and smell differences. Walk into a perfume store and you realize there is someone who is attracted to each of these smells. Growing up is growing to acknowledge difference.

At the same time as you look in the mirror, hear the panel's responses, squeeze onto the bus, and smell the varied perfumes, you may also realize what you have in common with others such as language, human physiology, and laughter. Growing up is growing to acknowledge similarities.

Some people never grow up. The challenge of growing up is to strike a harmonious balance between difference and sameness, individual and community, me and you. This is a never-ending challenge, but it is especially true of those at the beginning of the socialization process where the pull between sameness and individuation is just being felt. What happens there marks many for life.

This chapter is concerned with a type of person who never matures enough to recognize significant similarities and differences among people, who has the ability to demean or dominate difference into personal insignificance and to enable those around her to do the same, while protecting herself. Through repeated physical, social, and psychological intimidation, this person uses her power to harm those who differ from her, especially in those who possess less power. Many times the word used to describe this person is *bully*. The one harmed, the victim, is the "bullied." And those who support the bully, for whatever reason, are called the enablers, bystanders, supporters, or gang. The religious bully is a bully because he uses religion as a means of intimidation. Depending on the circumstances, he may bully those not of his religion, those of no religion, or even those who are religious.

This chapter is necessary because advocates for recognizing and learning about diverse religions deal with many people, some of whom differ from them with deep conviction and oppose them with vigor. Most in opposition do so not by attempting to harm the advocates, their families, and friends. Respecting their person, they deeply disagree with what their opposition advocates. Some, however, have no empathy for the advocates, repeatedly attempt to harm them, and seek to dominate the school community not through the power of argument but the power of intimidation. It is these people we highlight here and seek to understand and work with.

To think about bullies we must begin in the schools where most of us first experience them. We will spend some time talking about current research on bullying in order to both provide an understanding of their mindset as well as suggest a marker for how well diversity of religion is accepted in the school. A bully will find any weak spot as leverage for his bullying. If there is no religious bullying occurring, that could mean that religious difference is not recognized as one of those weak spots. Then too, the school experience is not always one that occurs among the students, it also happens between teachers, staff, administrators, and parents. We will briefly reflect on this interaction.

THE BULLY, THE BULLIED, AND THEIR ENABLERS

Research on bullying concentrates on children K–12. It could be that other terms are used to describe similar adult behavior such as *harassment, persecution, hate crimes, domestic violence,* and *genocide.* Recently, however, we do find phrases such as *political bullying, sexual bullying, physical bullying, emotional bullying,* and *verbal bullying* being used. It seems that every author has her own interpretation of exactly what bullying is.[1] Most would agree that bullying consists of the following behavior pattern: (a) the purpose of what is done is to harm someone; (b) it is done repeatedly; (c) it is an expression of power either actual or perceived; and from the standpoint of a neutral observer, (d) it is unprovoked. Even though most commentators agree that any definition of bullying includes these four descriptors, some hesitate to support the repeated nature of the actions because just the fear of one action being repeated fulfills the bully's desire to intimidate. A few do not include the imbalance of power as a descriptor for bullying because they feel that any unprovoked attack is bullying.[2]

It seems to me that the controversies over the definition of bullying suggest we are only at the beginning of understanding that bullying investigative categories for research need a great deal of refinement. Simply put, if we do not have a clear idea of what we are searching for, we do not know when we have found it. Those authors who reject the repeated nature or imbalance of power in the bully's action do so because the children do not include them when talking about bullying. Such rejection may reflect the uncertainty of language as discussed in Chapter 5 and may lead one to wonder how those just learning the language should determine the meaning of that language for everyone. It is possible that the children do not yet know how to describe this power imbalance despite their experience of it. Language is both a communal heritage and a means of individual expression. To take only an individual's or group's meaning and say we all must accept it is the height of solipsism. For the purposes of this book, we will accept the previous four descriptors as a description of a bully.

Multiple disagreements as to definition remind us that a great deal of bullying is in the eye of the beholder. I am not saying it does not exist, but that many in the actual situation describe it differently than the bully. A bully might say, "I was only joking," and then declare, "He hurt me." At the same time, the enablers say, "He deserved it." or "We didn't mean it." Key questions for the reader, therefore, are what do you consider bullying to be? Have you ever been bullied or been an enabler of bullying? Have you, or do you, act in a bullying manner? An awareness of your answers to these questions provides a personal lens for understanding what follows, as does an understanding of religious bullying in light of the previous descriptive elements.[3]

A *religious bully is* an individual or group whose actions have as their main purpose: to harm someone physically, emotionally, or socially; that is done repeatedly; that is an expression of power either actual or perceived; and, from the standpoint of a neutral observer, is unprovoked and uses a person's religious difference as a source of attack. Everything we say about bullying in general may be said about religious bullying in particular.

How Does It Feel To Bully Someone?

It feels good to totally control someone so they fear you, obey you, and pay attention to you. When those around you are afraid to oppose you, it means you're important—because you are. You are the only one who counts: what you need, what you feel, what you say and do. Those you bully deserve it. In their own way, they ask for it. As a bully, I'm only doing what they ask for.[4] Such expressions are common among those who bully. Jo C. Dillon emphasizes three skills that a bully must develop to become mature: (a) accepting differences; (b) expressing empathy and understanding of others; and (c) apologizing.[5]

These feelings, or lack thereof, are expressed both through words and actions: physically (e.g., threats of physical harm, taking money, hitting the person, stealing, pushing, or threatening gestures); emotionally (e.g., name calling, harassing phone calls, or offensive gestures and graffiti); and socially (e.g., gossip, threats to those who associate with the person, getting everyone to ignore the person, or enticing the person into embarrassing situations). Certain of these expressions are found more among males (physical threats and gestures) than females (actions and social), though these gender differences were more distinctive in the 1990s than in the first decade of the third millennium.[6] This bullying attitude finds expression in whatever way will satisfy its ends. Thus individuals will be picked on because of their size, sexual orientation, religion, dress, language, and intellectual acumen. Because of the bully's lack of social skills, she will always feel a need to bully unless something or someone intervenes to help her change. But a bully always needs someone to bully to meet her needs. One cannot exist without the other.

The Bullied

The bully is not alone in attitude, with underdeveloped social skills, and negative feelings. Neither is his victim. In some cases, those who are bullied develop into a bully themselves. For our purposes, though, we are talking about those who, without cause, are repeatedly picked on, demeaned physically, socially, or psychologically, and isolated from others. They seem to send out signs that indicate they would be good victims.[7] Olweus lists the major signs as: physically unattractive caused by things like bad hygiene, grooming, stature (tall or short), clumsiness, and lack of strength; psychologically insecure, anxious, and afraid of getting hurt; and socially inept and isolated. These characteristics are demonstrated by the bullied's inability to be assertive in their peer group and their ability to relate to adults.[8] They feel fearful, embarrassed, and hopeless in the face of the bully. They lack the confidence and skills necessary to deal with the bully. Consequently, they remain silent day after day, week after week. Three skills would help them break their silence and deal with their problem: learn to make friends, to ask for help, and to stop the negative thoughts that numb their ability to hope.[9] Easier said than done, these skills are not learned in a day or through a quick read of a how-to book. It is a real challenge for a victim to struggle through his depression and pain to take possession of his life, but it can and has been done. Many famous people describe how they were bullied in school and struggled to be who they are today. There are also bullied people made famous for killing large numbers of their schoolmates in Littleton, Colorado; Santee, California; Pearl, Mississippi, and countless other places.

The Enablers

The bullied need to develop friends who can help them gain the confidence they need to face both bully and life. Both the bullied and bullies need people. The enablers are those who support the bully in what she is doing. A home team playing in front of their own fans is energized by their support. Anyone who has ever stood in front of a group of people and sensed their response through laughter, anger, or interested questions has sensed her importance. These fans and audiences enable the performers to do what they do. It is the same for the bully. She needs her audience, and her fans to enable her to do what she does.

Not all enablers are the same. M. McGrath[10] provides three helpful distinctions: (a) those who join in the bullying but do not start it; (b) those who encourage the bullying by their cheers and laughter; and (c) those who remain silent but watch. There may be some present who try to stop the attack. Why do these young people allow the terrorism to continue? Probably for the same reasons a lot of adults do not get involved—they don't want to. "It's not my problem." "Let the victim handle it." "The loser had it coming to her." "I like the guy who is doing it." "It's better to be with the bully than against him." "Let someone else deal with it."[11]

It's estimated that 75–80 percent of school-age students are aware of, directly involved in, or witness bullying and do nothing about it.[12] No matter what the number, everyone is aware that bullying does occur. For those actively involved as enablers, their attitude parallels their type of involvement. Most of the enablers are caught up in fear, guilt, and ignorance resulting from their involvement—fear that the same thing will happen to them or that if they tell anyone, both the bully and his friends will pick on them instead of the previous victim; and guilt from doing nothing in the face of obvious pain of someone who does not deserve it. These feelings many times come because of ignorance, not knowing what to do to create an atmosphere of respect and tolerance in the place of disrespect, intolerance, and indifference. This ignorance can be overcome and the necessary skills learned. Students have to learn how to resist negative peer pressure, how to show concern for someone who has been hurt, and how to report the incident. These are difficult, but necessary, life-enhancing skills for both the student and her peers. They enable them to empower the positive values inherent in communal living rather than the negative ones that burden their involvement in the bullying.

WHAT WE CAN AND SHOULD DO ABOUT BULLYING

Bullying is a serious offense that sometimes borders on crime. Lists of the violent revenge of the bullied fill many of the books dealing with bullying. Some of the statistics, if believed, suggest that all of our schools are dens of victims ruled over by bullies. The National School Safety Center calls bullying the most enduring and underrated problem in American schools.[13] At the same time, they say that the statistics also indicate a significant reduction of bullying as students progress into high school. In response to such stories and statistics, I would suggest four things: (a) whole-school workshops on bullying, (b) finding out precisely what is going on in the school and/or school district, (c) implementing effective and enforceable bullying policies, and (d) becoming sensitive to the various contexts of bullying.

Workshops

"Bullying is a systemic problem that requires systemic solutions."[14]
A religions advocacy coalition is accustomed to looking at the entire system.
In this instance it is best to go to the experts. It is not enough to talk only
to the teachers, only to the administrator and staff, only to the parents, or
only to the children. Nor is it enough to spend only one day "taking care"
of the issue of bullying. A systemic problem means that there must be
changes in the entire system and among all the stakeholders in that system.
How do you know that you have a systemic problem? Certainly when the
vast majority of people in the school or school district say there is none. It's
a simple fact of life—bullies exist. They are wherever students are taught.
To say they are not present and ignore the problem means that some students, and maybe even teachers, are being bullied. Something has to be
done.

In Appendix A: Resources, I have listed and evaluated some Web sites,
books, and possible suggestions of where to go to enlist help. It is important
to realize that many times help is within your school or school district. In
any case, the first people to talk to are the administrators who are in charge
of the schools. It is no use going outside the school or district to enlist help
if no one in the district favors such help. The RAC will need to bring the
necessary information that will help sway those in charge to do something.

Discover Precisely What Is Happening

A school district should not have to wait for multiple shootings or
teachers quitting because of student harassment. What could have caused
teachers to begin carrying guns to class in the Harrold Independent School
District in North West Texas?[15] On the other hand, an administrator in
another Western school district tells the story of a local parent being up in
arms because her son was being bullied. Students were calling him names
like "Pot Head" and "Wiz." Teachers, vice principals, and the superintendent were not able to satisfy her demands for action. This administrator
was asked to talk to her. He made an appointment with her and her son.
They arrived at the appointed time. Her nine-year-old son wore a shirt
with Harry Potter stitched on it, round-rimmed glasses, and a haircut just
like the Harry Potter of the movies. . . . and the mother wondered what
caused the students to call him "Pot Head"? To know exactly what is going
on is essential.

Teachers, staff, administrators, and parents should know what is happening at school. This is easy to say, but difficult to accomplish. Knowing
what is happening in a school is like trying to know what is happening to
a cat, a mouse, and a bat that come into a dark barn. A school district
with its multiple personalities, young middle and high schoolers with their

rampant hormones, parents with intense interest and no interest, school boards with future political plans—all and so much more are in movement. Added to this normal difficulty, present in any attempt to manage people, is the silence that surrounds bullying. It is like trying to catch that cat, mouse, and bat in the dark. To attempt to freeze them for analysis, understand them, and provide a safe environment for all concerned is, to put it mildly, a challenge—a challenge, however, that can be met.

Burke, Dillon, and Pratt provide us with some excellent information gathering techniques, some of which I will provide and briefly comment on.[16] They suggest that the best sources of data regarding bullying include surveys, informal observation conversations with everyone in the school, injury reports, and office referral data. Where did it seem most of the difficulties were occurring: parking lot, halls, classrooms, gym, cafeteria, buses, and locker rooms? What were the top five offenses? Who are the top twelve offenders? Who monitors these areas? How frequently?

In light of this information, policies must be made and action must be taken. Here is where the workshops fit in because sometimes people just don't know what to do. The social skills I described as necessary for the bully, the bullied, and the enablers should be reviewed. We all realize that any skill takes time to develop. We all realize, too, that each school already has so many objectives and goals that it seems impossible, time wise, to add any more. With a little creativity the necessary additions can be made to provide a sense of safety to everyone. Part of that sense of safety is awareness in what happens in a bullying situation. Short skits are helpful in not only calling attention to what happens, but they show what skills are necessary to overcome this threat. Positive behavior should be constantly reinforced by everyone—praise for kindness and good deeds, for working together, and for respecting differences all contribute to the overall atmosphere of safety, togetherness, and anti-bullying.

Implement Effective Policies

If rules are broken, consequences must occur. Everyone should know what those consequences are, and they must be implemented whenever a rule is broken. Teachers cannot delay in such action. All threatening or negative comments and behaviors must be taken seriously. If someone is caught in such actions, they must be detained—always.

If a school or classroom has an atmosphere of "anything goes," it will take awhile before such detention is taken seriously. And, of course, the detention must be a punishment, not a reward. For a student who does not like school to be taken out of school is no punishment. I remember one young student in elementary school who enjoyed detention because he had an opportunity to either play chess with the principal or watch the nurses work. Changing habits and values inherent in an organization always take time and always happen in spurts. Those responsible for creating change in the organization are many times challenged, ignored, or isolated. This is educational change, and everything we said in Chapter 5 about such change can be repeated here. But the change must occur because people's well-being is at stake—even at times their lives.

Become Sensitive to Differing Contexts: Bullying as Symbol

To focus only on K–12, as most bullying literature does, neglects the social context of bullying and what it symbolizes to the society within which it exists. An ability to understand bullying in our public schools enables us to understand other types of bullying in society and vice versa. Each of us may be a bully depending on the context.

Remember how a symbol has many meanings, and while remaining essentially the same, is seen differently by people depending on the context—that is the kind of symbol bullying is. Is hurting people sometimes good? Is stealing sometimes good? Is demeaning sometimes good? Is lying sometimes good? Is killing innocent people sometimes good? We might argue whether it is always ethically good or not, but certainly some people will answer "yes" and some "no" to all of these questions.

There are two famous experiments and one historical example that show how normal people are turned into bullies: the Milgram experiment (1961),[17] the Stanford Experiment,[18] and the Nazi prison camps.[19] All of these examples demonstrate how ordinary people can be turned into bullies. Milgram showed how undergraduate students would inflict pain at the direction of a seeming scientific professional; Zimbardo, in the Stanford Experiment showed how undergraduates eagerly accepted their roles as prisoners (the bullied), guards (the bullies), and enablers (experiment director); and Jay Lifton in historical detail wrote about how the best of German doctors sterilized, experimented on, and killed for the good of the state. All of these studies and historical research lead one to believe that people simply doing their job and without any particular hostility to anyone in particular can easily become agents as a bully or an enabler. Even when the effects of what they are doing clearly are seen to be incompatible with fundamental standards of morality, most people will continue with their actions when told to continue. Though none of these were directly dealing with bullies in schools, it is not hard to see how in some contexts anyone can become a bully, an enabler, or a victim. Why can this happen to any of us? Because, as Carol Tavris and Elliot Aronson claim in their book *Mistakes Were Made (but not by me)*,[20] we learn the art of self-justification quite early in life and have difficulty breaking the habit. This habit enables us, just like a bully, to never admit we do anything wrong and, therefore, seldom apologize.

It is because bullies cannot admit they are wrong that the skills of apologizing, empathy, and acceptance of differences are necessary for a healthy community. These skills cannot be developed and we cannot admit our mistakes as long as we continually need to justify ourselves. Some justification is good; it helps us keep a good self-image. The need for a good self-image, however, can also be an ego-coping mechanism that becomes a defense mechanism—a shield we refuse to take down in the face of evidence to the contrary. Say, for example, I feel very angry because someone dented my car in the parking lot. I come home, still angry, and the dog is lying on the steps. I kick the dog. The dog goes yelping away. My wife comes out to find out what happened: "The dumb dog was in my way!" Of course it wasn't. I felt I had to let my anger out; the dog was there, and I kicked it. Aggression begets self-justification, even if I am wrong.[21]

Bullies pick on their victims purportedly because they are different than them and their enablers. Difference and similarity, them and us, are foundational categories for self-development. "Us" is family, peer group, team, and devotees of a certain kind of music. It is so easy for "us," for example, to become all the brown-eyed people and "them" to become all the blue-eyed people. "We" are better, should go to the water fountain before them, have more recreation time than they, and get out of school earlier. Why? Because "we" are better than "them."[22] Brown eyes can be easily replaced by sexual orientation, stature, religion, accent, skin color, or athletic or intellectual ability. Conflicting information about "them" is discounted because it makes us feel uneasy. We might be wrong. Our feeling is telling us something—the information is wrong! As in the previous example, self-justification does amazing things to our psyche. "We" continue to act aggressively toward "them." "We" continue to justify our actions. After all, "that's who I am." The cycle continues. In these contexts are "we" a bully?

"We" usually develops as certain words and actions take on meanings unique to the group. In its own way each group has its mini-socialization process, which, in order to be considered a member of the group, you must do and say certain things in a certain way. Religious communities, as we have seen, also have their words and actions that help shape who they are. If you are not an acknowledged member of their religion, your ability to say and do what they say and do indicates to them you are, in some way, one of "us."[23] The recent (2008) political campaign was an exercise of each religious group seeking for assurance that the candidate was one of them. In a telling two-hour interview session with the presidential candidates, Pastor Rick Warren of the Saddle Back Church in California and author of the famous *Purpose Driven Life* interviewed the candidates. He asked them whether they were *saved*, a word with special meaning to evangelicals, and the candidates each in almost identical language repeated back to him that indeed they were saved through Jesus's cross and that their sins were forgiven. They had given their life to Him. These are special words used to indicate a unique event in some people's lives. Interestingly, they both replied as any evangelical Christian would. The vast majority of Christians, while believing the fundamentals of the statement, never phrase it this way.[24] Were these candidates evangelical Christians? Why did Pastor Warren feel that he had to ask them that question? What would he, and the congregation gathered there, have done if one of them answered that he was a devout Buddhist? I am sure the pastor could justify why he asked the question. I am almost equally sure that many in the United States might agree with his justification. But I can't help remembering an equally powerful scene from the movie *And There Will Be Blood* (2007), where the central figure of the story is commanded to accept Jesus and be baptized, thus joining the local religious community. In doing so, he would be able to buy the oil land and become richer than he already was. The pastor demanded that he repeat his confession of Jesus, using words similar to the presidential candidates, repeating it more and more loudly, each time hitting him and demanding that he speak louder. Only when the man was beaten both physically and emotionally, lying on the floor, would the pastor accept his confession—to all a repentant sinner, now saved because he said the words. Obviously this pastor, in the context of the movie, was a bully. Pastor Warren, in the context of the 2008 U.S. presidential campaign, was not considered such. But it is not only Pastor Warren, but leaders of the Jewish and Catholic Christian religions as well, who demanded the candidates repeat certain set phrases or lose their support. Were those candidates who refused to utter the proper phrases less human because they were not one of "us"? Were those who refused to vote for a candidate because he was unable to repeat exactly the words they wanted to hear, justified in their vote? Context makes a difference in your answer.

One thing the Stanford and Milgram experiments taught us is that when we begin to dehumanize the other, we are on our way to bullying the other. A key, and necessary, ingredient in any war is to dehumanize the enemy. The role of propaganda is to do just that. Killing another human is easier if we are convinced they are not really human, that is, not like us. These religious leaders were not trying to kill anyone. But it would help their own political agenda if their followers saw the one interviewed as one of them, or not.

Is it possible to dehumanize bullies? I am NOT saying we should excuse them. I am NOT saying they are irresponsible. I am NOT saying there should be no laws. I am NOT saying every school should not have an active, enforceable policy regarding bullying. I am asking, however, if we quickly condemn the young person (K–12) but not those present in the rest of society, are we are missing the broader context of bullying? In my experience and research in undergraduate and graduate schools, for example, teachers were often religious bullies as they condemned those who were religious.[25] Or, in other instances, where students, attending a religious college, were allowed to kneel outside a student's door praying that the student inside change his religious orientation. Contexts are important. Bullying, by many other names, exists.[26]

ON THE EDGE OF CONTEXT; ON THE
EDGE OF SOCIETY

Bullies exist on the edge of the educational process. These are what some describe as the toxic zones or the unclaimed areas of the educational process such as the restrooms, halls, playground, and buses. Within institutions that claim to prepare students for life, we can see how life is lived in these toxic zones and what the student's education does toward making that life better in the unclaimed areas on the edge of the school.

The same can be said of the various societal contexts in which we live. We become so enmeshed in the "we" and its justification that we cannot see our true selves. Tavris and Aronson tell the story of their visit to the Museum of Tolerance in Los Angeles. The entrance to the museum is filled with interactive exhibits all designed to convince you that everyone is prejudiced. At the end of this entrance area and leading into the museum proper, are two doors: one marked *Prejudiced* and the other marked *Unprejudiced*. The unprejudiced door is locked. You can, obviously, only get out if you go through the prejudiced door. But not everyone wishes to do so. They recount that on the day they were visiting they saw four Hasidic Jews pounding on the Unprejudiced door trying to get into the rest of the museum.[27] Many times all of us are like those four people. Through self-justification we refuse to admit the many ways we set the stage for bullies to act upon. Even more, the "we" that develops prevents us from seeing what is really happening.

On the edge of the various communities where we live, work, and play are those who can tell us who we are. Just as the bullies lurking in the unclaimed zones of the educational process tell us what our educational process is doing, so those who live on the edge of our communities can tell us, by their reactions, what we are doing and what our values really are. Over time I have come to realize that, in researching any community, examining those on the edges will tell me a great deal about the community. So I talk to those just hired or who have recently joined the group. I question those who may service the group in some way either as providers of food and drink, landscaping, or salespeople. By talking to these people on the edge of the community, I can become aware of the unspoken structures and values of the community. Bullies can do that for an educational institution. Look at them and what they are saying and doing. You will find among them many community values.

RELIGIONS ON THE EDGE: ADVOCATE FOR
THEM TO BECOME PART OF "US"

When we meet and come to understand the religious other, we come to understand something about ourself and our spiritual and religious nature.

What are our common religious ideals and differences? The American style of Christianity dominates the airwaves and literature in such a way that the "us" of American life may seem to suggest that it is part of being an American. That is not true, of course, but it certainly places all other versions of Christianity and other religions on the edge of the national American religious consciousness. That means that bringing other religions into national and personal awareness may be able to help us in our growth to becoming a consciously pluralistic democracy if we begin to understand and be sensitive to their way of living.

A good example of how understanding other religions helps us grow as individuals and as a pluralistic society is found in a course in world religions designed by the Modesto City school district in California. It originated among teachers who sensed that their students did not understand the necessity of religious freedom and what the various religions meant to their adherents. They went about designing and gaining support from the entire community for a world religions course for all ninth graders. They began teaching this course in 2000. Out of the many evaluative claims of the course, the one most notable here is the discovery that it "played a significant role in converting public schools from a battlefield in the culture wars into common ground." Or, one not mentioned in the course evaluations, the fact that after September 11, 2001, there was not one incident of bullying or harassment of Muslim students on any of their campuses.[28]

Bullies were probably on the school grounds. They always are. But in this instance people were not bullied because of their religion. The advocacy and implementation of recognizing and learning about various religions, hopefully, will achieve the same results in other schools. This means, of course, that we must begin to open the door marked *Prejudiced*, walk through it, and begin to see the nature of our American religious life differently than before. It also means that those who attempt to place all religions on the edge of American society walk through the door and accept religion in general as an admitted part of American life.

RELIGIOUS BULLYING

One reason that both those who advocate for no religion in our schools and those who advocate for only one religion in the schools do so is because they believe those "others" force or bully people into believing the way they do.

They may have a point. In the past when religious people won wars they demanded that the conquered become members of their religion or die. A few offered the choice of added taxation rather than death. It was taken for granted that if you were not of their religion you were not to be trusted. Most of this happened before the concept of religious freedom became a human right, or that such a thing as human rights even existed. Nevertheless, many look to those times as examples of religious oppression and, thus, bullying. Some also look at one of the models of God embraced by Abrahamic religions as a God-bully—someone who threatens with eternal pain those whom he does not favor, or who break his rules, or because he wishes to demonstrate his power. When the God-bully is imitated by his followers, there is destruction of the pagans, heretics, nonbelievers, and idol worshipers. Read the original words to the "Battle Hymn of the Republic" to get a taste of how and why God's followers go to war. Such examples tell us something we already know—that religion does not prevent someone from becoming a bully. A religious person, like everyone else, must pass through the door of prejudice.

At the same time, all religions demand that their adherents face up to any attempt at self-justification. There are explicit ethical norms that must be adhered to, and all the excuses in the world do not justify breaking them. An authentic religious person must be sensitive to self-justification in any form. The Hebrew prophets were good at being brutally honest to kings, the rich, and the powerful in that regard. They usually paid the price of ostracism or death for their honesty, but they are a reminder that every religion has its prophets, writings, and beliefs that demand its followers be honest with themselves when trying to justify their actions of repeated unprovoked brutality or ostracism in word or deed, indirectly or directly, and physically or psychologically toward those different from them.[29] An authentic religious context for bullying, therefore, does not permit bullying.

LISTENING TO THE RELIGIOUS BULLY

"My way or no way!" shouts the bully in words and actions. The victim shrinks in fear, many times harboring revenge. The bullying of the past roars into the present with the attempted genocides in the Balkans, Georgia, the Middle East, and Africa. Today the sounds of gunshots in our schools shout out the results of the bullying of the present. We hear the victim's response to the bully: "Then, No Way." And the world as we know it begins to crumble. The enablers? Hearing, but not listening, they continue as before, feeling guilty but doing nothing.

To listen, one must do more than hear. To hear without response is to be deaf to what is said. It is not listening. The *Bullying Behavior Chart* provided by the U.S. Education Department[30] shows three levels of bullying behavior: those not against the law such as pushing, teasing, and gossiping; those that may be against the law, as assaulting, harassing, defacing property; and those that probably are against the law such as extorting money, destroying someone's locker or clothing, and public humiliation. To listen is to respond appropriately at each of these levels.

One response is through our surrogates, the law and the police who enforce it. The law provides the minimum of behavioral expectations.

Many skirt around the law's social intent by deconstructing each word and letter of the law. The consequences, of course, are more laws and increased anarchy; when power and inequality alone determine societal order, only the most powerful and wealthy rule. The law and belief in its fairness at least hold anarchy at arm's length. Those who do so for us are the police. When bullies, anywhere in society, speak the words and actions of anarchy, there should be laws to stop them and police to enforce the law. Such behavior, through our surrogates, demonstrates we have listened.

Another response to bullying is to advocate for anti-bullying policies and changes in school culture. Any school system that allows its students to freely and viciously abuse one another is not listening to the bullies in its midst. It is an enabler. It has lost its identity as an educational institution. With the loss of identity, it is dead because it has not listened. Someone must tell institutions, educational and otherwise, that bullying must stop.

Bullies are violent. In the first three decades of my life, I worked on several farms where animals were regularly slaughtered for meat. It never bothered me; but it has taken me quite a while to become accustomed to human slaughter for entertainment. "Oh, it's only a story," they say. "It's the news," they say. "Oh, we don't want to offend you," they say. Or, as the schoolyard bully says, "I didn't mean it." I am an enabler now in the face of the surrounding violence. I am not listening to the bully in our midst.

Bullies exclude those who they say are different. I always remember how a neighbor of mine said his son's coach cornered him one morning and demanded he pray with him. I also remember reading how a school's football team always met for fellowship prayer the day before a game. Were students excluded from sports because of religion? Probably. Some of us still remember how people of certain ethnic origin were not accepted as fully human because of their skin color or the sound of their last name.[31] I went to a school that, by happenstance, was all Irish. I was a second-generation immigrant and obviously not one of them—therefore a target for bullying. Are those days gone? Of course not. We have and will continue to pass laws to deal with the "uncivilized" and noncultured, that is, not of our civil society and of our culture. We still have not grown up as a culture because we are not able to deal with difference.

Bullies are enforcers of uniformity. This is the same as excluding those who are different. Bullies in K–12 are found on the edge of society, in the toxic areas. When some graduate, however, they sometimes graduate to larger arenas where they carefully and repeatedly punish those who are, or attempt to be, different than they are. In doing so they enforce uniformity and decrease the freedoms we may exercise. It is not by law that they enforce uniformity, but by name-calling, hitting, and exclusion of difference in their life and that of others.

I can tell when someone writes on a wall in pencil, pen, marker, screwdriver, ax, or a wood saw. What they use to write determines what I see. It affects my reading. As the philosophical proposition goes, "We cannot use a bad means to achieve a good end." What we use to do something affects what we do. What do the means (instruments) of violence, exclusion, and uniformity tell us about ourselves and our society? Are we listening?

What should we listen for in the midst of so much bullying? After discussing so many things in this book, I would suggest three necessary things that we must hear to make advocacy achieve its objective: fellow feeling, future living, and laughter.

The fellow feeling of similarity and difference must be discovered anew. So many things emphasize difference and uniqueness: niche marketing, mission statements, branding, and pedagogies that focus on the individual are examples. This emphasis grew out of the communalism and nationalism necessary to win World War II. But there have been many generations since then. Researchers have placed labels on generations to distinguish one from the other such as the "me" generation or "generation x." Each generation was told that government, the expression of the common good, was useless. Each individual in each generation was protected in order to have a good self-image. The presuppositions of mid-twentieth-century culture are seldom heard in the twenty-first century. Without these presuppositions we are without a necessary balance to individualism while we walk into a dangerous future.

Too many times the sound of others is heard as uniformity, conformity, and suppression of difference. We need two ears to survive what is coming: one to listen to difference and one to listen to similarities. With two ears we can hear the sound of a team, an orchestra, a laboratory, a corporation, or a university while remaining ourself. When we listen with both ears, we hear and feel the energizing exhilaration of the togetherness necessary to face the future.

Such energy leads to creative future living. Grab a small child and hold him tight so he can't move and he will cry and struggle to move and be free. We must hear the future and struggle to be free of those things in our past and present that prevent us from moving on. How much prejudice, self-justification, power seeking, and objectifying of the other binds us from listening to the future's call? Hopefully this book has helped you answer this question for yourself and our schools.

And some times, hopefully many times, we just laugh—never in disdain for what we hear, sometimes at the irony of what we and others do, and always in joy. Advocacy must be a joy. If not, we end up looking for scapegoats for failure and the loss of past hopes of success. Joy opens us to the future and seeks to share it with other human beings—for laughing alone is okay but having others laugh with us is paradise.

In the end, it's all about being safe, respecting difference, affirming community, and growing in knowledge, justice, togetherness, well-being, and joy. What more can we advocate for our children? For ourselves? The bullies say "no way" to our future. We must truly listen to them—and respond.

CHAPTER 9

Conclusion: The Stakeholders' Challenge—Putting Humpty Dumpty Together Again

"How easily things get broken," sings the crazed principal celebrant of Leonard Bernstein's *Mass*.[1] It is so much easier to destroy than to build or to grow. How easy it is to push the various humpty dumpties off the wall. "How easily things get broken."

Our journey of advocacy has witnessed many humpty dumpties tottering on the wall of American culture. The most prominent of them was our educational system with the public schools as a central ingredient. Our schools try to keep their balance and retain their vigor in the face of conflicting purposes, uncertain lines of authority, and low graduation rates. Stakeholders seem at odds with each other and with the school concerning their children's welfare. Our children, enmeshed in an ever-changing world, engage their school surroundings seeking, many times, to satisfy unknown personal and social needs. Sometimes they appear to be a bundle of needs waiting to be satisfied in an atmosphere incapable of providing a maturing influence. Networked into these needs is that amorphous desire for the sacred initiated at birth and nurtured early on by the responses of the parenting individuals in a child's life. This desire is not left unformulated by the vast majority of Americans. For at least 80 percent of Americans, the sense and expression of the sacred is socialized within culturally recognized religious institutions. This fact, evident outside the public schools, was not, until recently, recognized within them. Slowly teaching about these various religious ways of life is becoming part of public school curricula. But the teaching occurs as the humpty dumpty of American religion lies broken in our midst.

The vast majority of the religions treated in our public schools originated millennia ago outside the United States. Each of them began as a new, minority religion in a culture that already had a long-established religion. Within time each spread from its place of origin and became an established religion in the same or other cultures. All come into the United States with a centuries-long history and as part of an ancient culture of which they were an essential part. When a religion is essential to a culture, it has helped shape its stories, beliefs, rules, calendar, values, and language. Those ancient religions coming into the United States enter a culture that treats its religion differently merely because the U.S. culture is different than the one where they lived at home. In addition, the United States has developed an understanding of religion derived in part from its founders and in part from its unique historical development. For most of its history, it had a certain understanding of religion. This understanding created a unique American religious environment.

This is an environment that understands religion as belief in one God who provided humanity with a book that contains all the truth and knowledge to make this life and the next one better. This life will be better through belief in this God, following God's commands, and experiencing what God has done for us. Religion, from this perspective, has a God, a book, truth capable of being understood by everyone, emotionally satisfying rituals, easily recognized commandments for living, and a preacher capable of making you feel religious, and does all this so you will enter a supernatural world better than this natural one. As part of the American ethos, it professes a religious free market wherein its adherents must be permitted to "sell" their religion to those who do not have it.

This is the religion that was first accepted as "American." It is broken. We are at the historical juncture where the courts and legislatures have said that the public schools should not be the instrument of socialization into that American religion. I have argued, the courts have suggested, and a global education demands that in the place of this religion, students in our public schools must learn about all religions. The schools must evidence freedom for all religions within the confines of the U.S. Constitution. In both the teaching and the recognition of these religions, our schools will then reflect the present fact that the vast majority of students in the United States are not of this American religion but of other American religions, including other forms of Christianity. To learn about these religions both foreign and domestic is to become sensitive to the ways others live their lives. Knowledge about and empathy for other religions enables the students to recognize how others believe, obey, celebrate, and come together around what they sense as sacred in their own and others' lives. It enables them to understand that all religions in America share common American values that may easily distinguish them from their coreligionists in other lands. The values of equality, freedom, separation of church and state, and respect for those who are different provide a common ground for new religious development among all religions.

But to do such learning, to gain such empathy, one must acknowledge that the humpty dumpty myth of one country, one religion, and one uniform culture is broken and its banner torn apart. Any reality that may have supported this myth disappeared a hundred years ago. We have lived the liminality of the changes since then. What to do with the pieces? Who has a stake in looking and doing something? I have suggested that the stakeholders in putting humpty together again are all those who look to America's future with confidence in its diversity and assured of a common vision for that future that insures prosperity and hope.

PICKING UP THE PIECES

Let us continue this review of what we have read for a little while longer by looking at some of the pieces we have seen strewn amongst U.S. culture.

The first necessary piece of any human undertaking is to bring together those who seek to perfect the world in which they live. Each of us who wishes to make things better is a stakeholder in the new world being born. We stakeholders recognize that the uniformity of the past led to its death, and that the diversity of the present will lead to a creative future. We recognize, too, that religion plays a central role in how we think and act, and in what we hold as sacred.[2] We are stakeholders in the diverse religions of our common culture.

A common culture gave birth to a common public school. This school now acts as an interlocutor between the culture(s) of the past and present with the future. Part of that future will be the diverse religions that power nations and peoples toward models of change.

Our laws place those diverse religions on an equal footing in the nation and in our schools. To protect equally, as the laws do, is not necessarily to direct equally and to discover our common values. Politics must do that. Politics is the art of bringing people together to act for the common good. Its role is to provide direction and discovery. That is why the politics that occur at every level of life—family, school, religious institutions, sports, business, and leisure—must build upon present laws to create a healthy future. Politics is what puts humpty dumpty's pieces together. For politics to achieve its goal of bringing things together, it needs a sense of community, good leaders, and an ability to make conflicts creative rather than destructive.

In the future, this sense of togetherness must somehow be a mix of what provided it up until now. What we described as *gemeinschaft* and *gesellschaft* must give way to a new form of community and togetherness that is a mixture of equality and freedom (*gesellschaft*) enlivened by the loyalty and trust of the other (*gemeinschaft*). This mixture enables us to have both diversity and community, difference and unity. Politics built upon responsibility, common values, and compromise among various ideologies will do this if we are fortunate enough to have good leaders.

Good leaders do not exist without good followers. Our American stories are filled with a diversity of ideal leaders. Leaders come in all shapes, sizes, colors, and dispositions. How they lead (ancient, classical, human relations, and cultural) fits their leadership style and their followers' needs—for the leader's role ultimately is to enable people to work and live together over a prolonged period of time for their own and others' good. Whether one leads the stakeholders present in a religions advocacy coalition, town school board, state parent-teacher association, or nation's congress, their role is to bring together unique individuals, through politics, to make life better. In our schools that better life means that we use whatever appropriate means to make the socialization process of our children such to prepare them for the new future being born. That future admits who we are and who we will become. Religious diversity is part of that future.

The role of teachers reflects the role of the educational system as an interlocutor between cultures. As with leadership, we have seen diverse images of a good teacher. At times these images conflicted with each other. Each of these images reflected past ideas of education, leadership, truth, and what is necessary for someone to survive and prosper in that past. While the experience of liminality reveals to us that the past is no longer with us, these images of teacher and leadership are present with us since the past resides very much in each generation that was born and grew up in it. Our children were not born then. They are born now. The contemporary teacher must have many of the skills of those who went before them, but primarily they must be able to assist the student in working the problems of the present to enable him to cope with those of the future. The teacher, particularly of religious studies, must be able to comfortably bring students together to learn about one another and their world. Knowledgeable, reflection, capable of providing ideas and feelings in an objective manner, the teacher of religious studies enables a student to sense the sacredness of her own life while becoming knowledgeable of the sacredness of others—especially as they believe, celebrate, judge right and wrong, and come together in ways that are different, yet the same, as theirs.

Thus the pieces, not of egg or flag, but of: peoples, communities, leaders, laws, politics, and religions. Broken from the way they were held together in the past, they must be put together again for our common future. Our tools are the ability to listen, to discern the values of those we live and work with, to select leaders appropriate to our needs, to understand our culture, to manage conflict, and to know our past. With the pieces and tools in hand, how do we put humpty together again?

PUTTING THE PIECES TOGETHER

We can never put the pieces together again. What is past is past. Whether the United States was ever the unified country portrayed by the myth of one country, one flag, one religion, and one culture is historically debatable. That the United States is currently diverse is certain. It also seems certain that at present diversity of religions, ideas, economic status, education, ethnicity, and geography have become divisions.[3] Each person bundled with others in one niche or another is pandered to for the benefit of the one bundling them and to satisfy a need of the individual. Many pieces of humpty dumpty or the flag lay strewn over the countryside.

Maybe the tales begin with an improper focus: humpty's and the flag's pieces. Instead, we should be concerned about the king's men and the parents who tear and run. It is people, not pieces, that are important. It is people who are responsible for and will live in the future they must make. It is people who must come together, not pieces glued in the case of the egg, or sewn, in the case of the flag. The questions are: "How do the people come together in their diversities?" "Why do people find similarities in the midst of their differences?" Religion is the best test case because it is so encompassing in scope and so much a part of life in its dealing with the sacred. It is the best test case, too, because of its interconnectedness with all of life. Religion is part of culture; and culture is part of religion. To learn about one is to learn about the other.[4]

Why do we have to rediscover our common values, talents, and ideas? Because we need others to survive. We cannot survive alone as an individual, as a region of the country, as one with or without money, or as a spiritual or religious person. There is no mountaintop for a person to sit alone. We are all connected. We all have the means of connecting with others. These we must discover where we are at the present moment.

No one separated from your moment and place can describe in detail what you should do, think, value, and believe. Only you and those who accept the common task can do that. This book has provided you with the ideas and methods that may help you. Only you together with others can succeed *where* and *when* you are.

HURT, NOT BROKEN; HEALED NOT REPAIRED

Mister Rogers of *Mister Rogers' Neighborhood* fame, as always, provided us with valuable wisdom. He said that children often worry when toys or stuffed animals are broken that the same things could happen to them— that their arms or legs might fall off or that their insides could come out.[5] They needed to know that people and toys are different. Our bodies can grow and heal.

When we heal physically, mentally, or spiritually, we are different than before we were hurt. To heal well we need nourishing care. Such care creates a wholistic atmosphere that provides us with the necessary physical, mental, and spiritual means to grow to health—an ability to function well in our world. A society heals only when it envisions a beneficial future for all. Essential to any human future is children. To attempt to visualize or create a future without taking into consideration those who will be born into, develop, and finally live it, is totally absurd.

If we are hurt because of our divisions, we and our children must be healed of these divisions. The place to begin this healing is in our public schools. An essential means to bring about this healing is to accept the diversity of religions in our nation and world, and learn and have empathy for these religious people. Perhaps the lessons our children learn, they can teach to those who may still want to make diversity into radical divisiveness.

APPENDIX A

Resources

By the time you read this book, there will be more laws, research, and world events than when it was written. What was written was done with the purpose of providing a foundation for the interpretation of those laws, research, and world events. It should hold for quite some time.

What is included here enables you to know what is happening now and reflect more deeply on what is offered in the body of the book. Consequently, Internet sites dominate what follows since they reflect change more quickly than print media. The resources are offered thematically in alphabetical order.

Your unique needs will lead you to seek other sources than those provided. If you need any help in finding and evaluating resources, go to http://www.library.cornell.edu/olinuris/ref/research/webeval.html. Short descriptions of books and articles may be found at http://www.worldcat.org/. This site also shows the nearest library that has these materials.

COMMUNITY

- The Saguaro Seminar: Civic Engagement in America at: http://www.hks.harvard.edu/saguaro/index.htm. This provides an excellent link to what is happening today and ways to deal with it.
- Community and Conflict: theories of change, conflict management, and organizational theories and their implementation at: http://www.onepine.info/mgrp.htm.

DIVERSITY

Religious Diversity

- How to act when attending diverse religious ceremonies. Arthur J. Magida, *How to Be a Perfect Stranger: A Guide to Etiquette in Other People's Religious Ceremonies* (Woodstock, VT: Jewish Lights Publishing, 1999), 2 vols.
- How to gather ordinary people to discuss their religions at: www.commontables.org.

Ethnic Diversity usually contains within it religious diversity.

- For federal government statistics and references dealing with U.S. diversity, see: http://amlife.america.gov/amlife/diversity/index.html.
- It should also be noted that by the middle of this century, the founding ethnic groups will be in a minority. The schools, especially in the cities, are experiencing this in the early decades of the twenty-first century. See http://usinfo.americancorner.org.tw/amlife/education.html.

Generational Diversity much like ethnic diversity results in significant interpretations of foundational values within each religion. R. Zemke, C. Raines, and B. Filipczak, *Generations at Work* (New York: AMACOM, American Management Association, 2000).

EDUCATION

Views of community within an educational setting.

- *Breaking Ranks II: Strategies for Leading High School Reform* (Reston, VA: National Association of Secondary School Principals, 2004).
- Thomas Sergiovanni, *Strengthening the Heartbeat: Leading and Learning Together in Schools* (San Francisco, CA: Jossey-Bass, 2005).
- Lucinda Pease-Alvarez, *Subtractive Schooling: U.S.-Mexican Youth and the Politics of Caring* (Albany, NY: State University of New York Press, 1999).

PURPOSE OF EDUCATION

- For all the current diversity of purposes offered for public education see http://www.pbs.org/kcet/publicschool/get_involved/guide_p2.html.
- For the complexity of the decision-making process see http://www.pbs.org/kcet/publicschool/get_involved/guide_p3.html.

STAKEHOLDERS IN PUBLIC EDUCATION

- National School Board at: http://www.nsba.org/default.aspx.
- National Education Association (NEA) at: www.nea.org. The NEA is America's oldest and largest volunteer-based organization dedicated to advancing the cause of public education.
- U.S. Department of Education at: www.ed.gov. It offers detailed information on educational policy and programs, as well as up-to-date research and statistics on education.

- National Parent Teacher Association (PTA) at: www.pta.org. The PTA is the largest volunteer child advocacy organization in the United States. Information about PTA resolution dealing with teaching about religion in the schools is at: http://www.pta.org/2008.htm.
- Educational Commission of the States (ECS) at: www.ecs.org. ECS is a national nonprofit organization that was created in 1965 to improve public education by facilitating the exchange of information, ideas, and experiences among state policymakers and education leaders.
- American Federation of Teachers (AFT) at: www.aft.org. AFT is a labor union that represents more than 1 million teachers, school staff, health care professionals, and state and municipal employees.
- Association for Supervision and Curriculum Development (ASCD) at: www.ascd.org. ASCD is a nonprofit, nonpartisan organization that represents more than 175,000 educators from 119 countries and nearly 60 affiliates.

LAW

- Federal Law: The Library of Congress THOMAS site is the source for federal legislative information. THOMAS provides several options for finding bills and resolutions at: http://thomas.loc.gov/.
- State Law: For state laws it is best to go to the state's legislative homepage and most will have a link to research options where a person can search for state laws and rules.

A helpful book for the social context of all laws and their interpretation is:

- Lawrence M. Friedman, *The Republic of Choice: Law, Authority, and Culture* (Cambridge, MA: Harvard University Press, 1990).

Books dealing with law and teaching about religion in the schools:

- Joan DelFattore, *The Fourth R: Conflicts over Religion in America's Public Schools* (New Haven, CT: Yale University Press, 2004).
- Kent Greenawalt's *Does God Belong in Public Schools?* (Princeton, NJ: Princeton University Press, 2005) provides an explanation of why some things may and may not be done.

Religion and the interpretative history of laws:

- See www.religiousfreedom.com/articles/caino.htm for Bruce J. Casino, *Defining Religion in American Law* (May 15, 1999).
- http://www.aclu.org/religion
- http://www.law.cornell.edu/uscode/html/uscode20/usc_sec_20_00004071— 000-.html

Laws and materials dealing with First Amendment issues, religion in particular are:

- The Southern Poverty Law Center at: http://www.tolerance.org/ teach/?source=redirect&url=teachingtolerance.
- Freedom Forum, a nonpartisan foundation at: http://www.freedom forum.org/.
- First Amendment Center's Web site, features comprehensive research coverage of First Amendment issues and topics, at: http://www. firstamendmentcenter.org/.
- Both Jewish and Muslim sites are helpful in looking at the legal interpretations. See Jewish perspective at: http://www.adl.org/main_ Religious_Freedom/default.htm.
- The Muslim perspective at: http://www.soundvision.com/Info/education/ pubschool/pub.free.asp.

SCHOOLS, RELIGION, EMPLOYEES

- Freedom of religion in the workplace from the U.S. government at: www.dol.gov/dol/topic/discrimination/ethnicdis.html.
- www.eeoc.gov/types/religion.html. http://www.america.gov/st/washfile-English/2007/November/20071128173019xlrennef0.1781427.html
- Civil Rights Division of the U.S. government is helpful for its many references at: http://www.america.gov/st/washfile-english/2007/November/ 20071128173019xlrennef0.1781427.html.
- Employment law information network at: http://www.elinfonet.com/ fedarticles/18/6.

RELIGION

Its Definition

- T. Jeremy Gunn, "The Complexity of Religion and the Definition of 'Religion' in International Law," at: http://www.law.harvard.edu/ students/orgs/hrj/iss16/gunn.shtml.
- See Harold R. Isaacs, *Idols of the Tribe: Group Identity and Political Change* (Cambridge, MA: Harvard University Press, 1975), ch. 8.
- See www.religiousfreedom.com/articles/caino.htm for Bruce J. Casino, *Defining Religion in American Law* (May 15, 1999).

Religion as Identified with "The Holy" or "The Sacred"

- Rudolf Otto, *The Idea of the Holy: An Inquiry into the Non-rational Factor in the Idea of the Divine and Its Relation to the Rational* (New York: Oxford University Press, 1950), 2nd of 12 eds.

- Mircea Eliade, *The Sacred and the Profane: The Nature of Religion.* Translated by Willard R. Trask (New York: Harcourt, Brace & World, 1957).
- Detailed arguments for linking the sacred and an individual's identity are made by Hans J. Mol, *Identity and the Sacred* (New York: The Free Press, 1976); Thomas Luckmann, *The Invisible Religion; The Problem of Religion in Modern Society* (New York: Macmillan, 1957).

Religious Diversity

Membership in a religion follows the same definitional consequences as religion. Some consider membership only when one freely joins the religion as an adult; others, when one lives in a certain country; and still others, when one is born into a family with a declared religious orientation. Membership numbers are only hints at an organization's health and growth. One site that consciously demonstrates the relationship between definition and membership is http://www.religioustolerance.org. One may also find here descriptions of the various world religions.

Religious Diversity: Membership

- Frank Mead, Samuel Hill, and Craig Atwood, *Handbook of Denominations in the United States,* 12th ed. (Nashville, TN: Abingdon Press, 2005). Descriptions of the belief, worship, ethical imperatives, and organizational forms of the various religions in the United States.
- Eileen W. Lindner, *Yearbook of American and Canadian Churches 2008* (Nashville, TN: Abingdon Press, 2008). Provides essential organizational information of religious organizations. Online access provides constantly updated information.

It is best to look at several sites for membership numbers and descriptions of the religion since each will view the same data differently. Especially helpful are the following:

- For basic information about specific religions, recent surveys, and opinion polls, see http://pewforum.org/about/ and http://religions.pewforum.org/reports.
- http://www.beliefnet.com/ This site is devotional in orientation yet provides quick comparisons on subject matter across diverse religions, for example, end of the world.
- http://csrs.nd.edu/ A site for the social studies and scientific study of religion.
- http://www.adherents.com/ The religions of the world are enumerated here, as well as descriptions of various religions. Some referral sites are not as objective as first indicated.

- http://www.thearda.com/index.asp The Association of Religion Data Archives (ARDA) supports this site. Data included in the ARDA are submitted by the foremost religion scholars and research centers in the world. Religious membership by zip code is found here. Research ability may be limited by one's professional competence.
- A site that provides detailed profiles of more than two hundred marginal religious groups and movements is http://web.archive.org/web/20060907005952/http://etext.lib.virginia.edu/relmove/.

TEACHING

Diverse Views of Teaching Religion and Teaching about Religion

- Charles C. Haynes, Oliver Thomas, and John Ferguson, eds. *Finding Common Ground: A Guide to Religious Liberty in Public Schools* (Nashville, TN: First Amendment Center, 2001); also found at the following Web site: http://www.freedomforum.org/templates/document.asp?documentID=4020.

Lesson Plans, Workshops, Seminars, and Journals for K–12

- The American Academy of Religion (AAR) at: http://www.aarweb.org/Public_Affairs/Religion_in_the_Schools/default.asp http://www.aarweb.org/Public_Affairs/Religion_in_the_Schools/Lesson_Plans/art.asp.
- The First Amendment Center, which is a program within the Freedom Forum, at: http://www.freedomforum.org/templates/document.asp?documentID=4020.
- The University of Northern Iowa provides excerpts of its journal *Religion and Education* online at: http://www.uni.edu/coe/jrae/.
- Two places provide workshops that prepare and help teachers to teach about religion. These are at the Project on Religion and Public Education at California State University at Chico at http://www.csuchico.edu/rs/rperc/proj.html, as well as Harvard Divinity School's Program in Religion and Secondary Education at http://www.hds.harvard.edu/prse/about.html.

Examples of How to Teach about Religion

- For the Modesto, California, public schools: http://www.firstamendmentcenter.org/PDF/FirstForum_ModestoWorldReligions.pdf.
- Bryan F. Le Beau. "Science and Religion: A Historical Perspective on the Conflict over Teaching Evolution in the Schools." *Radical History Review* 99 (Fall 2007), pp. 187–201.
- Music and religion: Mary Theresa Reed, "Religion and Law." In *Illinois Music Educator* 68:1 (Fall 2007), pp. 65–66.

- Remember that many times diversity in general search may help find or at least present opportunities for applying what works in other diversity situations to religion. For example, Ricardo L. Garcia, *Teaching for Diversity*, 2nd ed. (Bloomington, IN: Phi Delta Kappa International, 2005).
- These lesson plans include references and recommendations regarding many valuable curriculum resources. Some of the books and videos (e.g., Paula J. Carlson and Peter S. Hawkins et al., *Listening for God: Contemporary Literature and the Life of Faith vol. 4* [Minneapolis: Augsburg Fortress, 2003]) and Web sites (e.g., http://www.buddhanet. net and http://home.earthlink.net/~mysticalrose/jesusart.html) are primarily faith-based or religious rather than purely academic in their approach. These materials contain text and especially graphics that can be very useful in the classroom, but teachers in *public* schools must be mindful of the First Amendment guidelines for teaching about religion and should be sure to select and use curriculum materials in ways that are consistent with these guidelines.

RELIGIOUS BULLIES DIVERSE VIEW OF WHEN BULLYING IS ALLOWED (SCHOOL, BUSINESS, GOVERNMENT, ETC.)

- The federal government's education department has many valuable sites. See http://www.ed.gov/admins/lead/safety/training/bullying/bullying.html.
- Jose Bolton and Stan Graeve, eds. *No Room for Bullies: Teaching Respect, Stopping Abuse, and Rewarding Kindness.* (Boys Town, NB: Boys Town Press, 2005.)
- Mary Jo Grath, *School Bullying: Tools for Avoiding Harm and Liability* (Thousand Oaks, CA: Corwin Press, 2007).

APPENDIX B

Cultural Toolbox: A Cultural Assessment Chart of Our School

Purpose: To determine the patterns inherent in a school's culture by:

- **Discovering** where the **symbols** (**words, rituals, normative behavior,** and **organization**) are located;
- **Understanding the values** (as listed) inherent to the symbols;
- **Understanding the foundational attitudes** (as listed) present in these symbols.

Method: Complete the chart by discovering the symbols, and locating, and understanding them. This is best done by *talking* to as many stakeholders in the school as possible, and then:

- *Complete* both **locate** columns. Place the appropriate bold print letter (e.g., **C** = Classroom, **P** = playground, **Ot** = other, **S** = students, **St** = staff) or word in the appropriate row.
- *Complete* the understand columns using the appropriate bold print letters (e.g., **L** = learning, **R** = respect, **M** = meaning, **B** = belonging) or write the complete word in the row.
- If necessary, answer the additional questions at the end of the chart.

After finishing the Tool Box, you will gather with others to discuss the results of your investigation.

Table App. B.1
Toolbox for Cultural Assessment

Discover	Locate	Locate	Understand	Understand
Symbols	**Found in:** Classroom, Playground, Bus, Halls, Offices, Other.	**Originated** among Students, Staff, Teachers, Administrators, Other.	**Expresses** the **value** of:[1] We (the school community), Learning, Respect for things, people, and environment. Religious diversity, Other.	**Demonstrates** the foundational **attitude** of: Meaning, Belonging, Fairness, Purpose / Direction, **Well**-being, None present.
Words				
• Mission/vision statements				
• Newsletters • Policy books				
• Bulletin boards				
• Badges, buttons, displayed objects				
Rituals				
• Opening and closing day rituals for students, staffs, administrators				
• Seasonal rituals such as Thanksgiving				
• Daily beginning and end of school day rituals				
• Student disruptions in the classroom				

Table App. B.1 (Continued)

Discover	Locate	Locate	Understand	Understand
Normative behavior				
• Within a class-room between teachers and students				
• Speaking among peers				
• Dealing with other schools in contests				
• Students, teach-ers, and/or administrators in making requests of staff				
Organization				
• Where the offi-ces are placed				
• How and where people sit in the lunchroom				
• How and when phone calls and e-mails are answered				
• School assemblies				

Three other sets of questions are also helpful for assessing a school's culture.

- At the end of the year, ask the students, teachers, and staff what their feelings are about the direction of their school.

  ○ Are you happy to get out of here? Would you prefer another school or occupation? Are you afraid of returning?
  ○ Do you think a great deal of change must come to improve the school? Do you have some ideas for change? Are you looking forward to trying some of these?
  ○ Are you bored with it all? One year done. Rest and start again?
  ○ Are you satisfied with the year? Are you looking forward to the challenge of a new year where you can continue to improve on what you have done?

- Ask responsible stakeholders about the history of the school in light of the categories outlined herein and/or their responses to the following:

  ○ How long has the school existed?
  ○ Why was it built, and who were the first inhabitants?
  ○ Who has had a major influence on the school's direction?
  ○ What were its core values?
  ○ What critical incidents occurred in the past? How were they dealt with?

- Ask those who provide services to the school what they think of the students, teachers, administration, and education it provides.

NOTES

INTRODUCTION

1. See Jared Diamond's book for examples of how people will discount obvious impending threats to their culture because of ideological reasons: *Collapse: How Societies Choose to Fail or Succeed* (New York: Viking Books, 2005).

2. Most Christians live in Third World countries. See Philip Jenkins, *The New Faces of Christianity: Believing the Bible in the Global South* (New York: Oxford University Press, 2006). See the charts and additional information that demonstrate this claim at http://www.lausanneworldpulse.com/766/08-2007?pg=all. This material may also be seen at Todd Johnson, Sun Young Chung, "Tracking Global Christianity's Statistical Center of Gravity, AD 33-AD 2100 in *International Review of Mission*, Vol. 93, No. 369, April 2004, 166–181.

CHAPTER 1

1. An excellent breakdown of major categories of Christian membership may be found at: http://www.religioustolerance.org/chr_deno.htm; U.S. religious statistics: http://lermanet.com/cisar/usa/040101.htm; http://www.adherents.com/rel_USA.html.

2. Frank Mead, Samuel Hill, and Craig Atwood, *Handbook of Denominations in the United States*, 12th ed. (Nashville, TN: Abingdon, 2005).

3. See *In God's Name* by John Micklethwait in *The Economist* (November 3, 2007) for a discussion of house churches.

4. Stephen Prothero, *American Jesus: How the Son of God Became a National Icon* (New York: Farrar, Straus, and Giroux, 2003).

5. Paperback edition (New York: HarperCollins, 2008).

6. Ibid., p. 8.

7. Ibid.

8. See *American Jesus: How the Son of God Became a National Icon*, op. cit.

9. See www.commontables.org for a Denver interreligious initiative of ordinary people meeting regularly to talk about their religion.

10. Thomas L. Friedman, *The World Is Flat: A Brief History of the Twenty-first Century*, Updated and expanded edition. (New York: Farrar, Straus, and Giroux, 2006), p. 309.

11. Ibid.

12. For all the current diversity of purposes offered for public education, see: http://www.pbs.org/kcet/publicschool/get_involved/guide_p2.html.

13. For the complexity of the decision-making process, see: http://www.pbs.org/kcet/publicschool/get_involved/guide_p3.html.

14. *Times Digest*. Friday, August 29, 2008, p. 3.

15. http://www.pbs.org/kcet/publicschool/get_involved/guide_p2.html.

16. For federal government statistics and references dealing with U.S. diversity see: http://amlife.america.gov/amlife/diversity/index.html. It should also be noted that by the middle of this century, the founding ethnic groups will be in a minority. The schools, especially in the cities, are experiencing this in the early decades of the twenty-first century. See http://www.america.gov/st/washfile-english/2006/May/20060510161059cmretrop0.5127222.html. A quick comparison with our neighbor to the north, Canada, indicates the deep Christian difference between it and the United States. There are few evangelical churches, even fewer Christian fundamentalist churches. Their "religion" is formal, ritual, closely connected with the state. Their religions reflect this difference with the United States. Most people belong to four Christian religions.

17. For the exact reference, see http://pewresearch.org/pubs/743/united-states-religion. To keep up with all religion changes, see: http://religions.pewforum.org/reports.

18. This is a condensation of suggestions made by David Tracy in his book *The Analogical Imagination: Christian Theology and the Culture of Pluralism* (New York: Crossroad, 1981).

19. What follows comes from a document distributed by the Pittsford Central Schools District. Pittsford Central Schools, 42 West Jefferson Road, Pittsford, NY 14534. The committee's name has changed over the years from the Religious Observance Advisory Council to Religious Expression in the Schools Committee to Religion in the Schools Advisory Committee.

CHAPTER 2

1. For an extended discussion of this evolution, see: Nathan Kollar, "Pivotal Cultural Turning Points: Examples, Processes, and Signposts: The Religious Canary's Role in the Mining of Cultural Signposts," as found in *Humanity at the Turning Point: Rethinking Nature, Culture and Freedom*, Soja Servomas, ed. (Helsinki: Renvall Institute Publications 23, University of Helsinki Press, 2006).

2. The meaning of this term varies among groups of Christians who call themselves nondenominational or interdenominational churches as opposed to denominational churches. It is used here in the meaning given by several dictionaries. See ZebraWords.com.

3. See the classic work of William G. McLoughlin, *Revivals, Awakenings, and Reform: An Essay on Religion and Social Change in America, 1607–1977* (Chicago: University of Chicago Press, 1978).

4. *Everson v. Board of Education*, 330 U.S. 1, 18 (1947).

5. *Engel v. Vitale*, 370 U.S. 421, 422(1962).

6. An excellent review of all the cases and their context may be found in Joan DelFattore, *The Fourth R: Conflicts over Religion in America's Public Schools* (New Haven, CT: Yale University Press, 2004), p. 72. Kent Greenawalt's *Does God Belong in Public Schools?* (Princeton, NJ: Princeton University Press, 2005) provides an explanation of why some things may and may not be done.

7. *Everson v. Board of Education*, 330 U.S. 1, 18 (1947).

8. *Abington Township School District v. Schempp* (consolidated with *Murray v. Curlett*), 374 U.S. 203 (1963).

9. *Schempp v. Abington*, 177 F. Supp. 398 (1958), p. 399, n. 3.

10. *Abington v. Schempp*, op. cit., 374 U.S. at 226.

11. *Waltz v. Tax Commission*, 397 U.S. 664, 670 (1970).

12. *Lemon v. Kurtzman*, 403 U.S. 602, 612–613.

13. On the development of individualism and its enormous impact on law and culture, see Lawrence M. Friedman, *The Republic of Choice: Law, Authority, and Culture* (Cambridge, MA: Harvard University Press, 1990).

14. http://www.law.cornell.edu/uscode/html/uscode20/usc_sec_20_00004071—000-.html is where the act is most easily found.

15. Answers to the quiz: 1)T, 2)T, 3)T, 4) F, 5)F, 6) F, 7) see attorney, 8) T, 9)T, 10)T, 11)T, 12)T, 13)T, 14)F, 15)T, 16)T, 17)T, 18)F, 19) T, 20)T, 21) T.

16. Much of what follows is based upon the *Joint Statement of Current Law on Religion in the Public Schools* (April 12, 1995) provided by the ACLU at: http://www.aclu.org/religion/schools/16146leg19950412.html.

17. For these laws, see www.dol.gov/dol/topic/discrimination/ethnicdis.html and www.eeoc.gov/types/religion.html. One fascinating consequence of reviewing for religious ramifications for both tax and work law is how much broader the definition of religion is when dealing with freedom of religion in the workplace. See www.religiousfreedom.com/articles/caino.htm for Bruce J. Casino, "Defining Religion in American Law" (May 15, 1999).

CHAPTER 3

1. See Rudolf Otto, *The Idea of the Holy: An Inquiry into the Non-Rational Factor in the Idea of the Divine and Its Relation to the Rational* (New York: Oxford University Press, 1950) 2nd of 12 eds. Mircea Eliade, *The Sacred and the Profane: The Nature of Religion*. Translated by Willard R. Trask. (New York: Harcourt, Brace & World, 1957).

2. A more-detailed argument for linking the sacred and an individual's identity is made by Hans J. Mol, *Identity and the Sacred* (New York: The Free Press, 1976). Thomas Luckmann, *The Invisible Religion; The Problem of Religion in Modern Society* (New York: Macmillan, 1957).

3. Much of what follows is dependent upon Nathan Kollar, "Religious Socialization," in *Survey of Social Science: Sociology* (Pasadena, CA: Salem Press, 1994). Frank N. Magill, ed. 5 vols.

4. For a review of the various meanings of "religion," see Harold R. Isaacs, *Idols of the Tribe: Group Identity and Political Change* (Cambridge, MA: Harvard University Press, 1975), ch. 8.

5. There is a long history of this term, its understanding, and its consequences in the United States. See Robert Neelly Bellah and Phillip E. Hammond, *Varieties of Civil Religion* (San Francisco: Harper & Row, 1980); Robert Neelly Bellah and Steven M. Tipton, *The Robert Bellah Reader* (Durham, NC: Duke University Press, 2006); and Craig A Forney, *The Holy Trinity of American Sports: Civil Religion in Football, Baseball, and Basketball* (Macon, GA: Mercer University Press, 2007).

6. While such headlines are typical in Western media, it obviously goes against the worldwide facts of increased membership in institutional religions worldwide. See *In God's Name* by John Micklethwait in *The Economist* (November 3, 2007). A Special Report on Religion and Public Life.

7. See for the following material Erik Erikson and Joan Erikson, *The Life Cycle Completed* (New York: W. W. Norton, 1998).

8. B. Inhelder and J. Piaget, *The Growth of Logical Thinking from Childhood to Adolescence* (New York: Basic Books, 1958); B. Inhelder and J. Piaget, *The Early Growth of Logic in the Child: Classification and Seriation* (London: Routledge, 1964); and J. Piaget, *La psychologie de l'intelligence* (Paris: Armand Colin, 1961, 1967, 1991).

9. Ronald Goldman, *Religious Thinking from Childhood to Adolescence* (New York: Seabury, 1964).

10. Lawrence Kohlberg, *The Philosophy of Moral Development: Moral Stages and the Idea of Justice* (San Francisco: Harper & Row, 1981); Sohan Modgil, Celia Modgil, and Lawrence Kohlberg, *Lawrence Kohlberg, Consensus and Controversy* (Philadelphia: Falmer Press, 1986); and Lawrence Kohlberg and Dawn Schrader, *The Legacy of Lawrence Kohlberg* (San Francisco: Jossey-Bass, 1990).

11. William G. Perry Jr., *Forms of Intellectual and Ethical Development in the College Years: A Scheme.* (New York: Holt, Rinehart, and Winston, 1970); William G. Perry Jr. (1981), "Cognitive and Ethical Growth: The Making of Meaning," in Arthur W. Chickering and Associates, *The Modern American College* (San Francisco: Jossey-Bass, 1981), pp. 76–116. Also see S. Parks, *Big Questions, Worthy Dreams: Mentoring Young Adults in Their Search for Meaning, Purpose and Faith* (San Francisco: Jossey-Bass, 2000); Patrick G. Love, "Comparing Spiritual Development and Cognitive Development," in *Journal of College Student Development* 43:3 (May/June 2002): 357–373.

12. In the Christian way of life, for example, the radically different understandings of how one becomes a Christian are many times unrecognized as the individual Christian matures. See Thomas F. Best, *Baptism Today: Understanding, Practice, Ecumenical Implication* (Collegeville, MN: Liturgical Press, 2008).

13. This closely knit past still influences us in our sense of blood, nationalism, race, and so forth. See Harold R. Isaacs, *Idols of the Tribe: Group Identity and Political Change* (Cambridge, MA: Harvard University Press, 1975).

14. Amartya Sen, *Identity and Violence: The Illusion of Destiny* (New York: W. W. Norton, 2006).

15. Any religion with several years' tradition has had to adjust in such ways in the past. But once the adjustment becomes part of the tradition, the consciousness of the adjustment is lost among those being socialized into the present religious way of life while the adjustment itself continues as part of the religion.

CHAPTER 4

1. See Robert Bellah et al., *Habits of the Heart: Individualism and Commitment in American Life* (Berkeley, CA: University of California Press, 1985). 3 eds.

2. Edward B. Fiske, "A Nation at a Loss," in *New York Times*, April 25, 2008.

3. Ferdinand Tonnies, *Community and Society (Gemeinschaft und Gesellschaft)* 22nd ed. (East Lansing, MI: Michigan State University Press, 1957). Charles Price Loomis, trans.

4. If you are accustomed to an economic interpretation of all human relationships, seeing all in a contractual manner, you have already rejected this division of Tonnies and its presupposition that humans can act in a nonegoistic manner.

5. See Harold R. Isaacs, *Idols of the Tribe: Group Identity and Political Change* (Cambridge, MA: Harvard University Press, 1989).

6. http://www.msnbc.msn.com/id/18090277/.

7. For further statistics for Catholics and others see http://www.catholicregister. org/content/view/239/858/ and http://www.religioustolerance.org/ifm_fact.htm.

8. R. Zemke, C. Raines, and B. Filipczak, *Generations at Work* (New York: AMACOM, American Management Association, 2000).

9. See *Breaking Ranks II: Strategies for Leading High School Reform* (Reston, VA: National Association of Secondary School Principals, 2004); Thomas Sergiovanni, *Building Community in Schools* (San Francisco, CA: Jossey-Bass, 1994); Thomas Sergiovanni, *Strengthening the Heartbeat: Leading and Learning Together in Schools* (San Francisco, CA: Jossey-Bass, 2005); Lucinda Pease-Alvarez, *Subtractive Schooling: U.S.-Mexican Youth and the Politics of Caring* (Albany, NY: State University of New York Press, 1999).

10. This is an adaptation of what she says in Nel Noddings, *The Challenge to Care in Schools* (New York: Teachers College Press, 1992), pp. 72–73.

11. Many ancient religious traditions have a difficulty with religious pluralism because choice is inherent to it. Choice is part of contemporary life. It is part of contemporary religious life whether religious leaders wish to accept it or not. For the rise of the modern types of choice and its implications for life and law, see Lawrence M. Friedman, *The Republic of Choice: Law, Authority and Culture* (Cambridge, MA: Harvard University Press, 1990).

12. An excellent example of how Judaism, Christianity, and Islam had to deal with the Greek philosophical and rational perspective in the early part of the Common Era may be found in F. E. Peters, *The Children of Abraham: Judaism, Christianity, Islam* (Princeton, NJ: Princeton University Press, 2004), Chapter 8, "Thinking and Talking about God."

13. See Nathan Kollar, "Doing It Together: Changing Pedagogies," in *Teaching Theology and Religion* (October 1999); "Assessing Teachers of Religion in U.S. Post Secondary Education," in ERIC database 2005 (ED490587); "Pedagogies of the Oppositional Religious Other: Theory and Practice" in ERIC database 2007 (ED497739).

14. Christian missionaries in Africa and elsewhere had to face the questions of African non-Christians who saw many churches proclaiming a different version of Christ's way of life for his disciples. The modern ecumenical movement of the eighteenth and nineteenth centuries, as well as the establishment of the World Council of Churches, resulted from such experiences.

15. This division and subsequent claim, stated using the church-sect typology, may be found in, among others, Max Weber's (1864–1920) *The Protestant Ethic and the Spirit of Capitalism* (New York: Scribner, 1958), 61 eds.; and Ernst Troeltsch (1865–1923) in his *The Social Teachings of the Christian Church* (New York: Harper and Row, 1960), 21 eds. A brief summary of these views with their critiques may be found at: http://hirr.hartsem.edu/ency/cstheory. htm.

16. There have been several editions since 2005. The most recent is: New York: Farrar, Straus, and Giroux, 2008.

17. The Anti-Defamation League's Web site on religion in the schools in general is excellent for reviewing appropriate laws, and the one on dress provides many references in the footnotes. See http://www.adl.org/religion_ps_ 2004/dress_codes.asp. The Muslim site is also good, but without the legal references. See http://www.soundvision.com/Info/education/pubschool/pub.free.asp. Joan Pedzich provides an excellent annotated bibliography on the law and student dress until 2003. See Joan Pedzich, "Student Dress Codes in Public Schools: A Selective Annotated Bibliography" at: http://aallnet.org/products/ pub_llj_v94n01/2002-03.pdf.

18. See the U.S. government Web site: http://www.america.gov/st/washfile-english/2007/November/20071128173019xlrennef0.1781427.html. Also, the Civil Rights Division of the U.S. government is helpful for its many references: http://www.america.gov/st/washfile-english/2007/November/ 20071128173019xlrennef0.1781427.html. Also see the Employment Law Information Network: http://www.elinfonet.com/fedarticles/18/6.

19. "From the Guru, I have obtained the supremely powerful sword of spiritual wisdom. I have cut down the fortress of duality and doubt, attachment, greed and egotism. The Name of the Lord abides within my mind; I contemplate the Word of the Guru's hymns." (Guru Ram Das, Maru, p. 1087) See http://www.sikhs.org/art12.htm.

CHAPTER 5

1. On November 29, 1947, the United Nations General Assembly passed Resolution 181, which, among other things, called for Jerusalem to be an international city administered by a trusteeship council under the aegis of the

UN. In the course of its history, Jerusalem has been destroyed twice, besieged 23 times, attacked 52 times, and captured and recaptured 44 times.

2. An early example of how technology affects learning is the printing press. For expanded commentary on the consequences of reading on cultural values, see Neil Postman, *The Disappearance of Childhood* (New York: Delacorte Press, 1982); *Amusing Ourselves to Death: Public Discourse in the Age of Show Business* (New York: Viking Press, 1985).

3. For radical turning points with religion as an indicator, see Nathan Kollar, "Pivotal Cultural Turning Points: Examples, Processes, and Signposts: The Religious Canary's Role in the Mining of Cultural Signposts," as found in *Humanity at the Turning Point: Rethinking Nature, Culture and Freedom*, Soja Servomas, ed. (Helsinki: Renvall Institute Publications 23, University of Helsinki Press, 2006).

4. See Malcolm Gladwell, *The Tipping Point: How Little Things Can Make a Big Difference* (Boston: Little, Brown, 2000) for what makes fads and the importance of context.

5. R. Jay Lifton, *Death in life: Survivors of Hiroshima* (New York: Random House, 1967).

6. See "Passages, Margins, Poverty," in Victor Turner's *Dramas, Fields, and Metaphors: Symbolic Action in Human Society* (Ithaca, NY: Cornell University Press, 1974).

7. Many mystics also have this time of in-betweenness when it seems all of the past has been for nothing and the future holds no promise. The God they have been so close to is no more. The words of Jesus on the cross, "My God my God why have your forsaken me," rumble through every moment of their existence. It is called *"Noche obscura del alma,"* "the dark night of the soul." See St. John of the Cross, *The Dark Night of the Soul* (New York: Image Books, 1990). Allison Peers, trans. and ed.

8. For a description of what happens within each of these dialectical events, see N. Kollar, "The Death of National Symbols: Roman Catholicism in Quebec," in *Ethnicity, Nationality, and Religious Experience*. Peter C. Phan, ed. (Lanham, MD: University Press of America, 1995).

9. See *Generations at Work* (New York: AMACOM, American Management Association, 2000).

10. A book that describes how to educate these subcultures, although it is not intended to do so, is Judith Berling, *Understanding Other Religious Worlds: A Guide for Interreligious Education* (Maryknoll, NY: Orbis Books, 2004). She describes the learning theories and views of one's own and other religions that are necessary to live in a pluralistic universe.

11. Much of what follows is adapted from Ernest Becker, *The Denial of Death* (New York: The Free Press, 1973).

12. *The Jewish Ledger* (May 15, 2008), p. 15. He worked for the U.S. State Department for 25 years and founded Seeds of Peace. He is the author of *The Much Too Promised Land: America's Elusive Search for Arab-Israeli Peace* (New York: Bantam/Dell, 2008).

13. James Surowiecki, *The Wisdom of Crowds: Why the Many Are Smarter than the Few and How Collective Wisdom Shapes Business, Economics, Societies, and Nations* (New York: Doubleday, 2004) is a good summary of the literature up until its writing.

14. See B. W. Tuckman, "Developmental Sequence in Small Groups," *Psychological Bulletin* 63 (1965), pp. 384–399.

15. See Irving L. Janis, *Victims of Groupthink* (Boston, MA: Houghton Mifflin Company, 1972); Clark McCauley, "The Nature of Social Influence in Groupthink: Compliance and Internalization." *Journal of Personality and Social Psychology* 57:2 (1989), pp. 250–260; and Diane Vaughan, *The Challenger Launch Decision: Risky Technology, Culture, and Deviance at NASA* (Chicago: University of Chicago Press, 1996).

16. There are other characteristics that may be found in the above referenced sources.

17. See Stephen Prothero, *Religious Literacy: What Every American Needs to Know—and Doesn't* (San Francisco, CA: HarperSanFrancisco, 2007).

CHAPTER 6

1. Much of the "mechanical" descriptions of leadership result in the methodologies that, by their nature, use a machine model of analysis.

2. Some would call this "free will." See John Cowburn, *Free Will, Predestination and Determinism* (Milwaukee, WI: Marquette University Press, 2008) for a defense of free will in the face of many types of contemporary paradigmatic methodological constraints.

3. See Chapter 3.

4. Jim Oldson, "Super Leaders Wear Many Hats," as found in *Loyola* (Summer, 2001), p. 35.

5. A fascinating example of this is the transition in legal arguments, using the Bible, from residing this power in the king to law. See Yvonne Sherwood, "The God of Abraham and Exceptional States, or the Early Modern Rise of the Whig/Liberal Bible," *Journal of the American Academy of Religion* 76:2 (June 2008), pp. 312–342.

6. These are further explained in Chapter 3 in dealing with the socialization process.

7. Sources for qualitative analysis may be found at: A Program for Qualitative Research and Data Analysis: http://www.QualisResearch.com/; some have found the United Kingdom site helpful, Qualidata-ESRC Qualitative Data Archival Resource Centre: http://www.essex.ac.uk/qualidata/.

8. Jack L. Nelson, Stuart B. Palonsky, and Mary Rose McCarthy, *Critical Issues in Education: Dialogues and Dialectics*, 7th ed. (Boston: McGraw-Hill, 2007). Phi Delta Kappa as reported in *Democrat and Chronicle* (October 22, 1993).

9. Research suggests, for example, that native-born U.S. mothers see innate ability rather than working hard as essential in academic achievement, and that the purpose of the school is to help the children become popular, excel in sports, and become well adjusted. Academics are not primary. See N. Caplan,

M. N. Choy, and J. Whitemore, "Indochinese Refugee Families and Academic Achievement," *Scientific American*, February 1992); H. Stevenson, *The Learning Gap* (New York: Summit Books, 1992); A. Sanker, "Where We Stand," *New York Times* (March 22, 1992).

10. Most of the following is based upon Michael Fullan, *The New Meaning of Educational Change*, 2nd ed. (New York: Teachers College Press, 1991), pp. 105–107.

11. This is not a claim that "old" is not the proper choice. It is, instead, acting in light of research that indicates that in time of stress we revert to our old methods as the most comfortable and ego-rewarding. For further research on this theme, contact Alenoush Saroyan, PhD, at the Centre for University Teaching and Learning, McGill University. SAROYAN@EDUCATION. MCGILL.CA

CHAPTER 7

1. One concern that has linked the two is education. This concern is expressed by teaching graduate education for 29 years.

2. For a fascinating look at how intercultural education, religious education (not religious studies), and teaching about religion in the public schools were linked before this, see John L. Elias, "Intercultural Education and Religious Education: 1940–1960," *Religious Education* 103:4 (July–September, 2008), pp. 427–438.

3. See John L. Elias, *A History of Christian Education: Protestant, Catholic, and Orthodox Perspectives* (Malabar, FL: Krieger Publishing, 2002).

4. Charles C. Haynes and Oliver Thomas, *Finding Common Ground: A Guide to Religious Liberty in Public Schools* (Nashville, TN: First Amendment Center, 2001), p. 76.

5. A recent demonstration of the necessity to "test one's reality" is found in Grace Huert and Leslie Flemmer, "Identity, Beliefs, and Community: LDS (Mormon) Pre-service Secondary Teachers' Views About Diversity," in *Intercultural Education* 16:1 (March 2005), pp. 1–14. References to contemporary research dealing with how diversity challenges teacher's self-image are found throughout.

6. Donald Schon, *The Reflective Practitioner: How Professionals Think in Action* (New York: Basic Books, 1983). There have been five editions since this one.

7. "The Development of Student Teachers Practical Theory of Teaching" in *Teaching and Teacher Education* 12(1), pp. 1–24.

8. John Dewey, *How We Think: A Restatement of the Relation of Reflective Thinking to the Educative Process*, rev. ed. (Boston: DC Heath, 1933).

9. Many of these methods may be found in the ERIC database, but their use may easily be seen in Outward Bound (http://www.elschools.org/contactus. html) and the Institute for Learning (http://www.instituteforlearning.org/).

10. See my "Doing It Together: Changing Pedagogies," in *Teaching Theology and Religion* (October 1999).

11. This model is adapted from Thomas J. Sergiovanni, *The Principalship: A Reflective Practice Perspective*, 3rd ed. (Boston: Allyn and Bacon, 1950), p. 282. Another "Stages of Change" model used in treating addiction may be helpful. See http://www.umbc.edu/psyc/habits/content/the_model/index.html.

12. See "Doing It Together," op. cit.

13. For a more inclusive view of victimhood and its various spokespersons, see Miguel A. De La Torre, *Liberating Jonah: Forming an Ethics of Reconciliation*. (Maryknoll, NY: Orbis Books, 2007).

14. Sergiovanni, op. cit., p. 279.

15. Much of what follows is based upon my "Necessary Cynicism About Contemporary Assessment Methods and Motives," *The Council of Societies for the Study of Religion Bulletin* 34 (February 2005).

16. Stephen Brookfield, *The Skillful Teacher: On Technique, Trust, and Responsiveness in the Classroom* (San Francisco, CA: Jossey-Bass, 1990), p. 11.

17. Michel Desjardins, "Like a Cook in a Cafe." *Studies in Religion/Sciences Religieuses* 27:1(1998), pp. 69–78.

18. While being neutral toward a religion is a necessary rubric in teaching about a religion, it is impossible to be neutral in the face of the diversity of contrasting internal positions within a religion that each supporting group sees as the sole description of the religion. All that can be done is present these diverse opinions as part of the diversity present in religions.

19. See Carl Rogers, *Client-centered Therapy: Its Current Practice, Implications and Theory* (London: Constable, 1951). Student-centered learning is a recent movement largely associated with constructivism as a learning theory. This was reviewed in Chapter 3.

20. See, for example, "Spark up American Revolution with Math, Science, and More: An Example of an Integrative Curriculum Unit" in *The Social Studies* July/August (2007), pp. 159–164.

21. These may be found in Susan L. Douglass, "The World in the Classroom—Teaching About Religion—Here Are Guidelines for Incorporating the Study of Religion into the Curriculum," in *Educational Leadership: Journal of the Department of Supervision and Curriculum Development, N.E.A.* 60:2 (2002), pp. 32–36.

22. http://www.aarweb.org/Public_Affairs/Religion_in_the_Schools/default.asp.

CHAPTER 8

1. The federal government's education department has many valuable sites. The one for bullying is especially helpful. It offers, for example, many different definitions of bullying. See http://www.ed.gov/admins/lead/safety/training/bullying/bullying.html.

2. Ibid.

3. All the following descriptors, except for religion, are found in the *Bullying Behavior Chart* at ibid.

4. See Margaret R. Hohut, *The Complete Guide to Understanding, Controlling, and Stopping Bullies and Bullying* (Ocala, FL: Atlantic Publishing, 2007), pp. 106–107.

5. Jo C. Dillon, "The Role of Social Skills," in *No Room for Bullies: Teaching Respect, Stopping Abuse, and Rewarding Kindness*, Jose Bolton and Stan Graeve, eds. (Boys Town, NB: Boys Town Press, 2005), pp. 124–127.

6. A review of how young women are becoming more physically assertive and the consequences of this may be found in Michael Sokolove, *Warrior Girls: Protecting Our Daughters Against the Injury Epidemic in Women's Sports* (New York: Simon & Schuster, 2008).

7. Kohut, op. cit., p. 112.

8. D. Olweus, *Bullying at School* (Malden, MA: Blackwell, 1993); and Kohut, op. cit., pp. 111–113.

9. Dillon, op. cit., pp. 127–130.

10. M. Grath, *School Bullying: Tools for Avoiding Harm and Liability* (Thousand Oaks, CA: Corwin Press, 2007); and Kohut, op. cit., pp. 117–118.

11. B. Coloroso, *The Bully, the Bullied, and the Bystander* (New York: HarperCollins, 2003); and Kohut, op. cit., pp. 116–117.

12. This is an extremely high percentage given the difficulty with definition, research, and the 17 percent of bullying that is claimed during the school year. For this percentage, see op. cit., p. 115.

13. As found in Bryan Grapes, ed., *School Violence* (San Diego, CA: Greenhaven Press, 2000), p. 11.

14. Bolton and Graeve, op. cit., p. 191.

15. As found in the *New York Times Digest*, August 16, 2008, p. 3.

16. Ray Burke, Jo C. Dillon, and Denise Pratt, "Assessing the Bullying Climate," in Bolton and Graeve, op. cit. pp. 61–85.

17. The best reflections on this experiment are those of its designer, Stanley Milgram, *Obedience to Authority; An Experimental View* (New York: HarperCollins, 1974). All further references to that experiment will be from Philip Zimbardo, *The Lucifer Effect: Understanding How Good People Turn Evil* (New York: Random House, 2008). Zimbardo was responsible for the Stanford Experiment.

19. Robert Jay Lifton, *The Nazi Doctors: Medical Killing and the Psychology of Genocide* (New York: Basic Books, 1986).

20. Carol Tavris and Elliot Aronson, *Mistakes Were Made (but not by me): Why We Justify Beliefs, Bad Decisions, and Hurtful Acts* (New York: Harcourt Books, 2007).

21. Ibid., p. 26.

22. An excellent demonstration of this may be found at the following site: http://www.pbs.org/wgbh/pages/frontline/shows/divided/etc/view.html.

23. These signal words and attitudes are studied in depth in Nathan Kollar's "Secular Fundamentalism and Secular Humanism: Value Sets for the Twenty-first Century" in *Studies in Formative Spirituality* XIX (May 1993).

24. See, for example, the Nicene Creed that speaks of Jesus "coming down for our salvation" and "Baptism for the forgiveness of sins."

25. Nathan Kollar, "Pedagogies of the Oppositional Religious Other in Theory and Practice" in *ERIC* database 2007 (ED497739).

26. I realize that many groups against bullying refuse to accept laws that do not have the word *bully* included because, as they say, everyone knows what that words means. In that light, in August 2008, they listed the states that have laws that meet all their criteria. See www.bullypolice.org/grade.html.

27. Tavris and Aronson, op. cit., pp. 40–41.

28. http://www.firstamendmentcenter.org/PDF/FirstForum_ModestoWorld Religions.pdf

29. These are the descriptors of a bully as offered at the beginning of this chapter.

30. http://www.ed.gov/admins/lead/safety/training/bullying/bullying.html.

31. For a short history of who was considered nonwhite, see Sam Roberts, "A Nation of None and All of the Above," in the *New York Times, Week in Review*, August 17, 2008, p. 6.

CHAPTER 9

1. Leonard Bernstein, *Mass: A Theatre Piece for Singers, Players & Dancers* (New York: Amberson Enterprises, 1971).

2. Aside from the discussion in Chapter 3, listed here are some of the authors supportive of this claim: Peter L. Berger and Thomas Luckmann, *The Social Construction of Reality: A Treatise in the Sociology of Knowledge* (Garden City, NY: Doubleday, 1966); Thomas Luckmann, *The Invisible Religion* (New York: Macmillan, 1967); Original title *Das problem der Religion*, 1963, Mircea Eliade, *The Sacred and the Profane: The Nature of Religion* (New York: Harcourt, Brace, 1959); Hans J. Mol, *Identity and the Sacred* (New York: The Free Press, 1976); and J. Milton Yinger, *The Scientific Study of Religion* (New York: Macmillan, 1970).

3. This theme and its explanation may be found in many places. Robert D. Putnam, *Bowling Alone: The Collapse and Revival of American Community* (New York: Simon & Schuster, 2000) and subsequent discussions provide the best data as to the divisions and explanations for their cause. The "Saguaro Seminar: Civic Engagement in America," at http://www.hks.harvard.edu/saguaro/ index.htm, provides an excellent link to what is happening today and ways to deal with it.

4. Some who still sustain both modern methods and opinions in this postmodern age attempt to reduce religion to only feeling, belief, ritual, or rules. In doing so, they not only lose sense of the religious reality, but also of religious people. For a strong argument for moving beyond these modern categories toward recognizing the whole religious person, see Robert Orsi, *Between Heaven and Earth: The Religious Worlds People Make and the Scholars Who Study Them* (Princeton, NJ: Princeton University Press, 2005).

5. For this episode of *Mister Rogers' Neighborhood*, see http://www.aptv.org/ schedule/showinfo.asp?ID=163136.

APPENDIX B

1. Other values from the Phi Delta Kappa listing in the *Democrat and Chronicle*, op. cit., are honesty, democracy, racial and cultural diversity, patriotism, caring for others, moral courage, and religious diversity. A summary of research may be found in T. Sergiovanni, *The Principalship* (Boston: Allyn and Bacon, 1995), p. 71, agreeing to education, honesty, integrity, beauty, care, justice, truth, courage, and meaningful hard work. Your school district or school may have a list of values associated with its mission statement or other programs. In 2008, the Global Network of Religions for Children (GNRC; http://www.gnrc.net/en/) suggested the following as essential for supporting interreligious living: respect, empathy, responsibility, and reconciliation.

INDEX

About the Author

Nathan R. Kollar is Emeritus Professor of Religious Studies at St. John Fisher College, Adjunct Professor in the Graduate School of Education, University of Rochester, and co-founder and chair of the Board of the Center for Interfaith Studies and Dialogue at Nazareth College, Rochester, New York. He is author of *Death and Other Living Things* and *Songs of Suffering* and editor of *Options in Roman Catholicism*. He has also authored dozens of book chapters and articles.